The Feeling Soul

A Roadmap to Healing and Living

The Feeling Soul – A Roadmap to Healing and Living
© 2005 by Mark Linden O'Meara, M.Ed.

Library and Archives Canada Cataloguing in Publication
O'Meara, Mark Linden, 1958-
   The feeling soul : a roadmap to healing and living / Mark Linden
O'Meara.

Includes bibliographical references amd index.
ISBN-10 0-9680459-2-8
ISBN-13   978-0-9680459-2-3

        1. Emotions. 2. Self-actualization (Psychology) 3. Mental
health. I. Title.
BF511.O47 2005   158.1   C2005-903388-6

Published by Soul Care Publishing,
Suite 378-2906 West Broadway, Vancouver, BC, Canada, V6K 2G8

Cover design by Estelle Liang

Printed in Canada

Excerpts from the *Fundamentals of Co-Counseling Manual* reprinted with
permission of Harvey Jackins and Rational Island Publishers, PO Box
2081, Main Office Station, Seattle, Washington, 98111, USA

Lyrics to "*Cry (If you want to)*" reprinted with the permission of Casey
Scott and Signal Songs/Tainjo Thang (ASCAP) All Rights Reserved/
Used by Permission

Excerps from It Could Never Happen to Me by Claudia Black reprinted with permission of M.A.C.Publishing, 1850 High St. Denver
CO. USA.

About the Author

Mark Linden O'Meara is an insightful, compassionate yet dynamic author who inspires others through his journey of openness and healing. He has been featured in print, on radio and TV, and presents at numerous conferences and seminars, warming his audiences with personal stories, anecdotes and wit.

Mark is openly able to relate the challenges he felt from his childhood such as health problems, low self-esteem, a strict religious upbringing, as well as experiencing bullying to the point of changing schools. Having learned to hide his pain away at an early age, he developed numerous health and personal problems associated with emotional repression.

Having made a commitment to himself to heal and get better, Mark began to search for a better way of dealing with life. Through the recollection of painful childhood memories and the use of self-expression, emotional catharsis, and challenging his beliefs about himself and others, Mark learned to release and resolve his emotional pain and began to experience a reconnection with joy and a deepening of his friendships.

Mark is the author of The Feeling Soul, Spiritual Prayers for Spiritual People and Healing The Ghosts of Christmas Past, a powerful and moving story that has appeared in numerous publications. He is also a professor at a local university college in Vancouver.

Dedication

This book is dedicated to all the people who came into my life when I needed them, to provide support, encouragement, to teach me a lesson I needed to learn, or to tell me the name of a book I needed to read. Without them, my healing process wouldn't have been possible, or the creation of this book.

Thanks to all the people who helped me greatly with editing suggestions and proofreading, and especially my friends Phil and Helen, Cecily, Steve, Margo, Margaret, Andrew, Theresa, and my nieces Meghan and Rachel. Thanks to Ross who has provided unconditional encouragement and helped me to see the bigger picture.

Many thanks to my friends in China, especially Estelle who taught me about Buddhism, and to my friends Grace and Trish who helped make such a life changing trip come about.

Special thanks to Stephanie - a true friend, and John Leblanc, for the encouragement to believe that I had a valuable book. Thanks also go to Jose, an angel who gave me a special message to rise up again from adversity. Thanks also for support from my friends Andrew, Chris, and Helani.

I also give special thanks to my parents who gave me life.

Mark O'Meara, July 22, 2005

Table of Contents

Setting the Stage

Introduction

In our quest to heal from troubles many of us have heard that we should "move on and let go." Although the advice seems appropriate, many of us do not know how to let go. In some way we feel stuck, knowing what we want, but unsure how to proceed or what even the true problem might be. Although you may have an intuitive sense of yourself that is untouched by hurt, trauma and fear, you are unsure of how to achieve this sense on a daily basis. You somehow hope that you can rediscover a sense of childlike joy in adult living. Many of you have been hurt and are surviving yet there seems to be something missing in your life.

While a great number of psychology and self help books have focused on one's thinking, few have accurately and articulately described the nature of feelings or emotions and how to safely and successfully heal the pains of adversity, growing up, entering into adulthood and the various losses and challenges that we encounter in life. There are great joys in life, but they are often clouded over with layers of blocked emotion, hindering the free expressive ability that we were born with.

I believe that there are many factors that facilitate or hinder the process of letting go and moving on, but it is a process you can learn, practice and improve upon. The actual process of letting go is something you may not have experienced, and you may therefore need to learn how to achieve this. While much of this book focuses on the nature of letting go, it also focuses on the nature of healing, for by learning about the process of healing, you learn the process of letting go and moving on.

In this book I describe the notions, ideas, techniques and attitudes that facilitate letting go and healing. I firmly believe in the balance of emotions, thoughts and behaviors and their interrelation. Study after study has shown the value in releasing emotions, particularly the benefit of increased clarity of thinking. In applying the principles in this book, you too can learn and experience the benefits of getting in touch with your emotional self and your associated thought processes. Just like learning to drive a car, you can develop the skill of releasing and managing your emotions, attitudes and behaviors that will promote healing and teach you to let go. In doing so, you can become less fearful of your emotions and inner thoughts and learn to let go of them. You can learn to develop healthier emotional attitudes, thoughts and behaviors that will affect your relationships and friendships.

Originally I thought that emotional expression was the key to my healing, but in retrospect I understand that both thoughts and behaviors needed to be challenged, as well as the knowledge of my talents and gifts. I've learned that I have a great sense of humor, an ability to do stand up comedy, a nice singing voice, and that I am well liked by kids. In addition to discovering and expanding your rainbow of emotions and creative talents that exist within yourself, you will be learning to nurture yourself and begin to promote healthy thinking and behavior. Indirectly, this book becomes a tool for better communication, closer relationships, greater joy, and a greater sense of connection with our selves and with others. All of these things are tied together in our ability to express, communicate and resolve our emotions and the associated difficulties. In a sense, this summarizes the process of healing and moving on.

By reading this book, you will find yourself developing an awareness of your emotions, patterns, and what has hurt you. You will then learn about uncovering and expressing emotions through various healing concepts, practices, and rituals, and how to challenge your thinking and integrate your new thinking into your life. In doing so I hope you will gain a sense of renewal and find measurable changes in your life as I have! You will also find additional chapters on healing anger, forgiveness, and getting un-stuck, all of which were very important to my healing process. I am certain that these will be helpful in your healing process too!

My First Level Healing

Prior to learning the concepts in this book, my life was greatly affected by a backlog of emotion. Having learned to hide my pain away at an early age, I developed numerous health and personal problems associated with emotional repression. All of this led me to a troubled state of crisis. I was fatigued, isolated and my thinking was troubled. A friend confided to me that no matter how hard I tried to have a good time, it seemed that something was pulling me down. I was in a great deal of emotional pain, yet could not communicate this to others, nor could I admit it to myself. I kept myself very busy, at many times compulsively, yet even though I realized I needed to slow down, could not. Although emotionally wound up, I was also extremely numb to my feelings. Due to my unresolved grief I gave the impression I wanted to be left alone even though my heart longed for companionship. Most of my obsession with projects and my irrational behavior were the means of avoiding my feelings. It is from this state however, that I moved to a sense of serenity and connectedness with others. This change came about as I learned to deal with my emotions more effectively and challenged the beliefs held within those emotions.

Ironically, the beginnings of this book came about after making a New Year's resolution to experience more joy in my life, yet it was through the facing of my troubles that brought about a greater sense of joy. In the three years following my New Year's resolution, I experienced a tumultuous period of change in my surroundings, social life and self-knowledge. During this period I learned a great deal about the dynamics of releasing, letting go and healing. At first I believed that catharsis was enough. As I observed my own process, I quickly learned that changing one's beliefs and behavior were also necessary and that these aspects, as well as emotional expression, were intricately linked in very subtle ways.

The Deeper Healing

Learning about and healing my childhood troubles brought great improvements in my life, but greater troubles lay ahead for me as I completed my masters degree and self-published my first book. The deepening of my healing came about after the most difficult period I had ever experienced. While I did considerable work on myself and healed a great part of my pain, there came a period during which I experienced a great deal of adversity - health problems, fatigue and burnout and financial burdens.

In the first three years after my master's degree I experienced a great number of financial difficulties and health problems. While helping friends move I was asked to help carry a heavy trunk of books. After lifting up the rear end of the trunk, the other person lost their grip and the trunk slammed to the ground, wrenching my already tensed neck and shoulders forward. The next few days I was stuck in bed with a terrible whiplash headache. This took over 4 years and tens of thousands of dollars to heal the daily headaches and damaged muscle tissue. Furthermore, my masters program took a lot longer than planned, causing further financial difficulties. Already struggling financially, an employer made an error in my workload calculations. My pay was cut by 25% and I had to pay back over $1500 over 3 months. I received this news just three hours after I had started expensive dental work, which ended up being troublesome due to incompetence on the dentist's part. I also ended up with a hernia operation, developed Lyme disease from a tick bite, had a cancer scare and eventually went bankrupt.

Despite having done a great deal of healing work, I realized that I was a mess. I was angry, bitter, resentful, and in great pain. I seemed to have lost most

3

of my hope that things would get better. Instinctively I knew it was a great challenge that I had to overcome. Although I had done a great deal of healing work, I knew that something was missing. A powerful dream provided the answer.

In my dream I was trying to get to the top of a mountain. Driving my car up a hill to get to the park, the clutch began to slip, and I had to let the car slide back down the hill and park it. I then got on a bicycle and took a different route, but found my chain broken. I then carried my bicycle up a path and joined a tour group. Next in my dream I came upon a sign that said "Level eight to 10 dangers exist on this path." Other people were coming down the hill on bicycles and nearly hitting me. Eventually I came to a clearing where a sign pointed to an odd-looking tree stump about 12 feet round. It said, "Level 10 danger" Another member of our tour began jumping up and down on the stump saying, "How could this be a level 10 danger?" I believe my dream was warning me that my challenges from burnout, bankruptcy and student loan issues could be the greatest threat I had ever experienced.

The dream continued. Just then the edge of the stump gave away and he began falling into the abyss in the middle of the stump. As he tried to free himself the man became more and more entangled, being swallowed up by the stump and its branches and twine. By now I could see it was dark and went very deep into the earth. I believe that the branches represented thoughts and issues I was trying to entangle my self from in life.

In the dream, with everyone standing around in shock, I realize that this person would die if I did not help him. I took action and reached over, grabbing his hand and arm and pulling him over the lip of the abyss with all my body weight. Although he was still slightly tangled, it was obvious that the danger was over. Though there was still some work to be done to free him, the sense of danger was over. He got up, and in humor I joked, "Do you still think it's not a level 10 danger?" The humor broke the sense of tension and relaxed everyone. As the group got up to walk further up the path, I realized that I had saved this persons life through my action, yet he seemed unaware of this and did not openly thank me. As the group got up to continue unencumbered on our journey, he walked past me and touched me on the arm. It was his acknowledgement of thanks, his soul acknowledging mine. Clearly the event had shaken him at a very deep level.

In interpreting the latter part of this dream, I realized that the person who had fallen into the abyss was in fact me. I was depressed, discouraged and had lost hope. What I took from the dream and what my real life confirmed was that if anyone was to pull me out of this depression it would be myself through my own intervention. I needed to help myself.

In dealing with these troubles I found that my understanding of adversity and recovering from difficult times was profoundly deepened. I recognized that a rut is sometimes the highest mountain to climb, and developed a greater capacity for self-perseverance, hope and self-guidance. I was also able to reflect on my previous lessons and develop a deeper understanding of what I had learned. I had learned of the power of forgiveness, hope, gratitude, self-care and that we always have the power of choice.

To recover from my deeper troubles, I began learning to accept my situation as temporary and began doing things to take care of myself, one day at a time. Slowly I began to emerge from a depression, learning to exercise my mind to be more positive, to be creative in my thoughts and to visualize a positive outcome. I began meditating regularly, exercising, and eating more healthily. I also learned how I had lost my faith in God and restored it by beginning to pray and to trust that things would work out. Soon things did clear up. My finances and health improved greatly as soon as I began working on the real problem, my attitude, lack of faith and ability to help myself.

In this period I also had a number of difficulties occur that challenged my concept of control. By surrendering my will to a greater plan, I released a number of deep-seated fears and frustrations that held a great deal of energy in my throat and neck area. I began having a greater sense of health and a quickening of synchronistic events. Looking back I can now see that some difficulties were opportunities for growth. I learned that I had always feared giving up control, and had always refused to surrender to anyone or anything. I found myself having to surrender to things, to admit that I had not been able to accomplish what I had attempted, but also recognized that I had done my best. I could now turn it over to God. In this period I realized a purpose of helping others by setting up a website for Canadians with student loan issues. The site ended up drawing thousands of people each week and was featured on national television and in many newspaper articles. As our community grew, we helped each other and provided valuable resources and support.

While I am not a religious person, I definitely am a spiritual person. In this time I came across a theory by nineteenth century writer Ernest Holmes who stated that the subconscious mind is actually divine law and that your conscious mind accepts commands and acts on the commands you give it. This is the reverse of what Freud and other analysts would have us think. I put it into practice by imagining new social situations, happiness and a joy of living. Even with huge a student loan debt and health problems, I began to develop a calm sense of enjoyment of daily life.

Essentially, I learned at a very deep level that I have a great power of choice as to how I respond in action, thought and feelings. I can choose to base my future projections on past history, or envision a completely new future! This is easier said than done. I learned that although I had learned to express and heal pain, I had yet to develop control over my mental energy and I had certainly not learned to develop healthy attitudes to deal with resentment and anger. And so I began a journey to do this. This alone was probably the greatest and deepest healing that I have experienced in my life so far.

The Gift - Opportunity Knocks Loudly!

While things had improved for me and I had learned a great deal more, I still felt tired from my work and was still in great pain from my whiplash injury. Magically, I was offered a chance to go to China where I received special medical treatment and an opportunity to learn more about Buddhism and ancient Chinese wisdom. The synchronicity of this trip was absolutely astounding. I dated a woman named Sherry who was Chinese, and tried to impress her by trying to speak some Mandarin. She wasn't romantically interested in me, so a few weeks later at the suggestion of a friend, I picked up the phone and tried the telepersonals. I connected with someone nice and as we chatted, she mentioned she was going to a dance that night and perhaps I would meet her there. I went to the dance but she didn't show up as we had planned. While there I spotted an attractive woman. I noticed numerous men ask her to dance, all of whom she turned down, while talking to her friend. I waited until she finished her conversation and asked her to dance. She obliged, much to the dismay of all the other men, and we chatted for a while. We became friends, and later in the month I invited her to an outdoor festival. She had a friend visiting from Beijing and invited her along. Her friend had just arrived the day before and had been given a ride to her home by a friendly Chinese man at the airport, who just happened to call to see if they were going out that evening. He was invited along too. When I met all three Chinese people I said the only words I knew in Chinese, which I had learned to try to impress my original date. Those words were "Ni hao, wo shi laoshi," meaning, "Hello, I am a teacher." Wei, the Chinese man said, "Oh, I'm looking for teachers. Would you be interested in coming to china in 4 weeks to teach for four months? One hour later I had the details and a few days later the formal offer came in by email. Due to my fear of being in such a foreign place, I almost didn't go. Fortunately I listened to friends who said I should jump at the chance. But things started to fall apart as I couldn't get a return flight to be back on time for my regular teaching job. As I was about to give up, Sherry, who had become a friend, called to see how plans were progressing. I told her of my predicament and immediately the problem was solved. She was an airline stewardess and had just gotten notice of additional flights being added. She told me that within half an hour I'd be able to book my flight! It was a life changing experience! I was able to obtain excellent medical treatment for my whiplash injuries at a Chinese massage hospital. I met great friends, and met a great person, Estelle, who designed the cover for this book. We also began working on two children's picture books together.

Estelle took me to many Buddhist temples. I was able to learn about wisdom that originated centuries ago. I was able to combine my knowledge and work out my own difficulties and then incorporate this new found wisdom into the Feeling Soul for the benefit of myself and its readers. Like a final puzzle piece, the new information fit into this book making the work feel complete! I learned later that the woman on tele-personals was at the dance, but for some reason forgot the time and missed meeting me, all of which changed my life permanently for the better. And the woman at the dance I met had been in a near fatal car crash a few years earlier. At the time, they didn't expect her to live, but she did, and moved to Vancouver, and came to the dance, which changed my life. I am in awe and simply humbled by the synchronicity!

My Offering to You

Through my journey I have learned a tremendous amount about the nature of emotions and what happens when they are suppressed. I have also read countless articles and papers regarding the effects of emotional, physical and sexual abuse on the lives of the victims. The incidence of addiction, depression and mental health problems are clearly linked to these distressing situations. However, I have also learned that you do not need to experience extreme traumatic events to end up being emotionally numb, out of touch with your feelings, and rationally impaired. Stressful life events, unsupportive family environments, or growing up in addictive or dependent families can lead to similar conditions.

While I had gained a tremendous amount of knowledge and practice in healing, I also realized that I had come into a new period of learning and growth that taught me about faith, the power of self care and nurturing, the need to balance emotions and thinking, as well as the need for being positive and patient.

For the benefit of myself and readers of The Feeling Soul, I have experienced the reality that the effects of emotional distress and life challenges are not permanent and that healing can take place. Through some trial and error, the support of others, seemingly chance meetings with people, and reading the appropriate book at the appropriate time, I experienced a major shift in my emotional, physical and mental health. I worked hard and diligently at getting in touch with my emotions, thoughts and body memories, releasing them to the universe, and experiencing healing that will last for my lifetime. The work has paid off! I developed a much deeper understanding of myself, my past, and the emotions I was feeling in the present. With this work came new understanding and insight and a better way of being in the world. In my healing process, I developed new friendships, changed careers, developed a healthier approach to myself and improved my decision-making. I value my friends with less disappointment and recognize what I have to offer and bring to others. My self-esteem has improved. I am more assertive, and I experience a greater degree of joy in my life.

Over time, I have learned that it is possible to safely express and resolve emotions and to heal emotional hurt and pain, and in doing so experience a sense of renewal and revitalization. I am now more energetic, have achieved better relationships and friendships, and definitely have greater joy and excitement in my life. Friends tell me that I smile more often and walk taller. I no longer have a lingering sense of pain and weariness hanging over my shoulder! When issues arise, I am dealing mostly with the current situation rather than my emotional history. Without emotional baggage, others find it easier to communicate with me. When issues come up in a relationship, I can deal with them more effectively, having dealt with my past. Of course I still have difficult days, but I have successfully resolved a great deal of what is commonly referred to as emotional baggage and have begun to live my life in the way that I believe is a dream come true. Simply reminding myself of these improvements makes my day better!

The events that brought about the creation of this book seem humorous now that I look back. Originally I started to write a how-to book on buying a house! I rented a laptop computer to do some writing at my brother's isolated, rural cottage. During the daytime I worked on a few projects around the cottage, and wrote during the quiet evening hours. One of the projects I took on in addition to my writing was to make improvements at the cottage. My father had dug a well at our cottage years before, with only a shovel. He got two hernias building this well! Each spring, however, pine needles and other debris would find their way into the well and an annual cleaning was required at the beginning of each cottage season. As I began this project, I noticed that my father had taken a number of shortcuts in building the foundation of rocks that lined the well. I ended up removing all the original work and rebuilding it from the bottom with a new and stronger foundation. This was so much like an analogy of what I had done in my own life that I wrote a short essay on the subject. Then I wrote another essay on another topic, and another and so on and so forth. As

I read the words I had written back to myself, I found a new calling to write, finding myself totally immersed in a different direction.

With my new goal of writing a book and having experienced a great deal of positive change, I wanted to ensure that I fully understood the process that I had moved through and also wanted to identify the key elements that facilitated my healing process. In doing so, I believed that I could pass on valuable knowledge to others. And so I began writing, which in itself was positive and cathartic. Spending considerable time collecting information on the topics of healing, health, and resolving emotions, I searched for articles on the effects of emotional release. Collections of notes scribbled onto napkins, scraps of paper, match covers, and concert programs, were transformed into a manuscript.

This book is the result of my healing process and describes what I have learned during that time and my ongoing desire to learn. I hope the information and techniques in this book will help you in your goal of emotional healing. In reading this book, I would like you to keep in mind that there is no right or wrong way to go about healing and letting go. Each of us is unique and therefore the techniques or solutions that you choose may be different from those someone else would choose. The images and experiences you relate to will also be unique. As a result, I have not included case studies in this book, as it would not be possible to include the depth and subtleties of any one individual's experience. I have however, included my own personal experiences and examples wherever possible. In reading about the ideas and techniques I present, I suggest that you examine your own life to see how they apply to you. Try to apply them in your own unique way to your own life and situation. I hope that you create your own experience from reading these pages.

In doing so, I believe that your emotional healing will allow you to feel more joy and to be more expressive. It will unlock your creativity and spontaneity and lead to better family relationships, friendships and a greater degree of understanding of yourself and others. One of the greatest challenges to which you can rise is healing yourself. The ideas in this book have helped me tremendously. I hope to share those insights so that you and others may benefit from what I have learned and begin to experience more joy in your lives as I have. If the concepts in this book help you, then please lend this book, or tell your friends about "The Feeling Soul" so that they can learn to heal too.

Healing is an act you do for yourself that can have profound effects on your life and your future. Every bit of healing that occurs moves us closer and closer to a healthier society! Anything is possible!

Part 1 - Learning

1. The Guiding Principles of Healing

Developing a Positive Healing Attitude

Many people have come through difficult times. Gary Faris is one of those people. When jogging along a road, Gary was severely injured when struck by a truck going sixty miles per hour. Gary was thrown into a farmer's field and sustained severe injuries. In his effort to recover, Gary applied his training in business coaching to his own personal journey back to being able to walk again, let alone run. He observed that people who are successful in healing share six core characteristics.

The first characteristic is a desire to move towards a positive outcome rather than avoiding a negative outcome. Simply put, you might consider exercising due to the fear of poor health, or exercise because of the benefits it provides. The first reason is fear based, while the second reason is more positive as it moves towards a healthy objective.

The second characteristic is a desire and dedication to regain full strength and health and surpass one's previous level of health. In other words "that which does not kill you shall make you stronger." It is important to acknowledge this truth and incorporate it as a positive attitude in your healing process.

Another characteristic includes the ability to take small steps and to recognize progress one day or step at a time. This is an anchor phrase in most self-help support groups. It is also a fundamental business practice to take a large project and break it down into its small steps and individual tasks. Even though you might be in physical or emotional pain, it is the individual steps you take on your journey that get you to the destination. I remember a mentor asking me "How do you eat an elephant?" "One bite at a time!" was the answer!

Gary observed that the fourth characteristic of a core positive attitude is to "be in the present." This statement is used over and over again in literature. On a deeper level "being in the present" means to be emotionally and mentally present and look positively to the future while acknowledging the past. It means to notice one's thoughts and be careful in times of doubt and fear. A helpful tool I use is to imagine that I am on a staircase. Going down the staircase leads into despair. Going up the staircase leads me to health, both physical and mental. I must carefully notice whether my thoughts are leading me down the staircase or up. If I'm headed up, that is great, but if I am heading down the staircase, I must reverse direction with some positive thoughts and positive visions of the future, while living in the present.

Personally, the fifth characteristic has been extremely important for my own healing from a number of injuries and financial difficulties. This characteristic involves avoiding comparing yourself to others and judging yourself according to the life stages, accomplishments and situations of others. As I have mentioned, prior to the publication of this book I went through loneliness, bankruptcy, and five years of very high health costs due to my whiplash injury. At the same time most of the people I knew had gotten married, bought houses, had children, all the while I was focusing on my health recovery and was still basically broke. I had to remind myself that I was still fortunate and had blessings of my own. If I began a spiral of comparing, I had to stop myself in my tracks and begin thinking positive thoughts about myself and focus on my hope. Things eventually did change!

Now we get to the sixth characteristic which is all encompassing of your healing. This characteristic states that you need to develop a personal involvement in your own recovery. This been a foundation of the popular "Living with a Chronic Condition" workshops that are now offered all over the USA and Canada and other parts of the world. These seminars teach people the skills of self-management and involvement in their health. They learn to ask the questions they need answered, communicate, set reasonable goals, research their condition and reduce thoughts of helplessness. Results of this program have been very positive. Getting involved in your own recovery means to understand what steps you can take, develop a workable treatment plan, and to encourage yourself to develop the other five core characteristics!

Establishing a Connection with Nature

In the last one hundred years mankind has lost most of its opportunity to experience nature as previous generations have. Few city people have seen the millions of stars that light up the sky on a clear night, away from the light pollution of the city. Fewer have experienced the quiet, non-judgmental, peaceful sound of nature. Try to find a place that you can go to - a park or arboretum. Try taking a day trip now and then. If getting to nature is not possible, then perhaps you can bring nature to yourself. Get some plants or put up posters, or purchase a meditative sound recording that will remind you of the beauty of nature and its healing properties. Nature does not judge our pain, sorrow, anger, or joy.

Respecting Others

In your effort to heal emotionally you may uncover anger that will need to be dealt with. Sometimes it will be necessary to express your feelings by writing a letter or telling how you are feeling to someone. In your healing process it is very important to respect others' feelings and wishes as well as your own.

Others may not be ready to hear what you have to say about them therefore you must make certain that you keep the focus on yourself. You may think it is necessary to confront someone if he or she has harmed or hurt you, but if they tell you that they do not want you to communicate with them then you must respect their wishes.

The old adage "two wrongs do not make a right" is critical in achieving emotional health. Attacking someone verbally or writing a scathing letter only serves to vent emotion not resolve it. It reduces your personal power and worth. If you are to communicate your feelings to someone who has hurt you, you must do it with compassion and respect. I do not mean that you must be under that person's control, but if the other person indicates that he or she does not want you to contact them, you must respect this. This is particularly true in dating relationships. You must respect boundaries that other people set. If someone does not wish to communicate with you then there are other ways to resolve your emotions, which are described in this book.

Developing a Support System

A key element of getting better is developing your own support system. Although you may not have discovered this before, there are many kind people who are willing to help you and be a friend to you. To find these people we need to communicate your needs. If you are hurting you may need to take a perceived risk and let someone know that you are hurting. Even if you are very perceptive of other people's emotional state you must accept that others are not mind readers. If you are hurting and need comfort, you need to communicate these needs to others. Be honest. If you want someone to go out for a coffee with you or to spend some time with you, ask him or her; but also give the person the freedom to say no.

If you are lonely, find a support group you can join. In a support group you can share ideas, hopes and thoughts with others who are working on similar issues and you can also listen and learn from others. Most groups usually have a list of people to call should the need arise. If you are not sure of whether you like the group, go for a few times (six meetings are suggested). If you do not like it, you can always stop, but if you do not go at all, you will miss finding out what a group can do for you. For many of us, joining a group is a big step; therefore it is important to find a group that you are comfortable with. If the group seems inappropriate, then try another one until you find the group that you are comfortable with. The important thing is to at least try a group for a while and then, with first-hand knowledge and experience of the group, you can decide if you wish to continue or not.

Try also to find one or two friends with whom you can talk to openly and honestly. This may take some time to develop, but if you have a friend who will listen and help guide you, your healing process will be greatly enhanced. Most support groups provide telephone lists of people willing to discuss issues with members. The sharing among members helps them to learn from each other and provides comfort in understanding that they are not alone in their problems.

Keep in mind that although your healing process is a very personal thing, sharing your feelings during this time can lead to greater trust and better relationships later on! Sharing and allowing others to help you will enhance the healing of yourself and others. In an article titled *The Broken Heart*, James Lynch describes how communication plays a vitally important role in our health. He writes, "The rhythm of a heart beat of a patient in a coronary care unit can be altered when the patient is touched by another human being. This occurs in patients in deep coma as well as in those who are fully conscious." Communication allows us to share thoughts, ideas, hopes, and feelings.

The Power of Hope

Whenever you undertake a project or task it is usually done with a sense of hope that there will be rewards for your efforts. In an emotional healing there will be times when you are making progress. At other times you may seem stuck and feel that you are making little progress, if any at all. In revealing your pain to yourself and releasing it, it is easy to lose sight of the fact that things will get better. In times of trouble you must remind yourself of the progress you have made.

Often, you may feel overwhelmed by your problems. At times some people may even feel suicidal. If these thoughts occur, then it is helpful to try to alleviate the feelings of being overwhelmed. This can be accomplished by trying to identify the issues that are causing the greatest amount of stress in your life, discovering alternative ways of dealing with distress, reducing the amount of self criticism and "shoulds" you generate, and breaking problems down into their smaller components. You need to remind yourself that these problems shall eventually pass.

You must make an effort to notice that although you may have a lot of work to do and things may seem bleak, there is a light at the end of the tunnel. You can recover from your past injuries and begin to feel joy again. When times get tough you can reach out to a friend, or if necessary call the local distress center. There is always hope, even if you must look for it. Others have gone through difficult processes such as yours and are willing to help. Healing and growth are possible when you maintain a sense of hope. However until recently there has been very little understanding of what hope is and how you can cultivate it.

First of all, hope gives you strength against stress, motivates you to overcome difficulties, and lessens the burden on your mental health when you go through difficult times. Hope allows you to stretch beyond your current situation. Hope for the future is the most powerful thought you can have, next to being present and knowing you have the freedom to choose how you react to unfavorable circumstances. Hope is usually a protective factor, allowing you to look to the future in a positive manner expecting things not to be perfect but to somehow improve.

Types of Hope

Many people talk about hope and its power but what exactly is hope? From reading through many articles on hope, I noticed numerous definitions. It seems that hope is part emotion, part constructed belief, part faith, part intellect, part against intellect, or simply a body sense of the future that things will get better or at least that life will have some purpose and meaning. Despite many rejection letters for this manuscript from publishers, I always had hope that it would be published. Without my having hope you would not be reading this book. Hope also involves a sense of persistence in spite of rejection and setbacks.

From a logical point of view, hope is a correction in your thoughts. When you start to have thoughts such as "maybe it won't happen" you can change your thought pattern simply by saying "It can happen. I have hope!" Hope allows you to weather setbacks, and in times of discouragement, pick yourself up and keep on going.

Another aspect of hope is the time frame for the outcome of the thing that you hope for. There are actually different types of hope. The first type of hope that you should understand is daily hope. Daily hope provides you with meaning and a sense of purpose to your day. It motivates you to get up in the morning and enjoy your day through simple daily pleasures.

The next type of hope is goal oriented, such as completing a course or program, finishing a project, taking up a new hobby, or a trip coming up in the future. This type of hope helps pull you through challenges and routine work that needs to be done in order to obtain a reward in the near future. This hope is similar to the character building practice of delayed gratification, where a good thing is postponed so that you can get work done.

Long term hope is a type of hope that is life sustaining and helps you to understand that despite difficulties, your life has meaning and purpose, smoothing out the peaks, valleys, downturns and upturns. It is a deeper soul feeling that gives you the power to effect change over a long period of time. It takes a long time to turn a heavy, slow moving ship around. When faced with tremendous challenges, long term hope gives you the courage to work hard, knowing that individual steps and effort will lead to long term benefits.

Now we turn to the possible dark side of hope - false hope. As many have said, there are two sides to any coin, and the same can be said about hope, as hope can be used as a tool of denial when you refuse to believe the facts and cling to an idea that something else will happen. Yet sometimes the hope that these people hold does come true against all odds! This is what is called miraculous hope. The factor that distinguishes miraculous hope from other types of hope is the probability of the event occurring and the emotional investment in wanting the event to occur. If a loved one has a terminal illness, you can hope for a miraculous cure. If you are unprepared for the possibility that the cure does not occur, then the loss of the loved one can bring much greater pain and a sense of betrayal. Yet there are many cases of miracles occurring, of astonishing recoveries, and triumphs of the human spirit. If you have hope, don't let anyone take it away from you!

Finally, a powerful type of hope that I have experienced is phoenix hope. It is a hope that motivates you to rise above your current situation, to begin and endure a path of recovery, to strive for a better life. As you may recall, the phoenix legend tells of a bird that is consumed in a fire, to be reborn as a greater spirit. Many of us, after getting a sense of this type of hope, are compelled to move forward, and to make things better. It is often not an easy journey,, but the image and legend of the phoenix and its rebirth will keep you moving forward on your path.

How to Develop Hope

You now may be asking yourself "How can I develop hope?" I think the answer is quite simple. First and foremost, hope is a choice. It is a desire to have positive thoughts. There are times when it is healthy to have a yearning for something better, for happiness, even though we realize that happiness comes from within. You can choose to start to have the smallest of hopeful thoughts, such as "I will wake up in the morning" or "I will hope to make positive choices." You can also blend your hope with a feeling of being realistic and not discouraged when things don't go your way or when you have a setback. In observing my own progress with developing hope, I noticed that hope came from within and from outside of myself, although the feeling always resides within my self regardless of the source of inspiration. Inspiration is the key word for developing hope. While inspiration can mean "being drawn into high levels of feeling or activity" it also refers to "drawing air into the lungs." You can instill hope by drawing it in from others or from your inner spirit. Hope can be instilled by visualizing a compelling future, recalling uplifting memories, or through inspiring movies, leaders, speeches, or music. One good thing about hope is it is contagious! Find the things that help you hope and inspire you. Put these reminders around you where you will often see them - on your desk, on your bathroom mirror, on your fridge. Make sure you have daily reminders of hope. Make time for hopeful inspiration!

"I can lay bare her troubles because I have not lost hope"
– Lin Yutang

2. Emotional Training Wheels

The Child's Natural Expression

I am always amazed how a whole room of activity will come to a grinding halt when a baby is brought into the room. Everyone stops whatever activity they are involved in and a collective "ooooohh!" fills the room! The same thing occurs when someone presents a collection of baby pictures. What is it that so strongly catches our attention? The next time you encounter such a situation, I suggest you study the facial expressions of a little one! You will likely notice the unrestrained expression of joy, discovery, and laughter on their little faces. If feeding or changing time is missed, or a parent leaves the room, you will quickly encounter the expression of pain, sadness and even anger.

Young children are exuberant and uninhibited in their emotional expression and at one time you were too! In their faces we see the full range of emotions - from sadness and anger to joy and excitement -all within the space of a few moments. Their facial expressions clearly reflects their true emotional state - free of any emotional encumbrances. Each child born into this world is, at birth, lovable and emotionally expressive. Although the thinking processes have not been fully developed, the child is capable of developing rational thoughts and will develop the ability to reason. As humans we are born lovable, vital, vibrant, confident, emotional, loving and rational beings. This natural ability to be loved, to think clearly, and to reason clearly is what is sometimes referred to as our own "inherent nature". You are born with it; it is a natural state. In this sense we are all born equals.

Harvey Jackins, the founder of the re-evaluative counseling movement, writes in *Fundamentals of Co-counseling*:

> "After being hurt, an infant will cry loudly and continuously and, if permitted to do so, will seem to recover from the hurt very quickly. After being frightened badly, an infant will scream and shake and perspire. After being angered, a yelling, vigorous tantrum will result, unless interfered with by others in the vicinity. A child, given friendly attention after an embarrassing situation, will talk and laugh about the experience spontaneously until the embarrassment is dissipated. These discharges - the crying, the trembling, the angry shouting, the

laughter - are the ways in which human beings release the tensions which the experiences of hurt place upon them. Apparently babies - given a chance - would keep themselves free from hurts simply by their natural discharge of painful emotion. In our culture, no baby gets very much of a chance because, with sympathy or with harshness, the discharge of painful emotion is interfered with and shut off so repeatedly that to shut it off becomes an automatic pattern accompanying the hurt."

I found this same view stated by T.J. Scheff, in his book *Catharsis in Healing, Ritual and Drama*. Scheff suggests that as humans we are born with the innate ability to express emotions. As we progress through the years into adulthood, society trains us to suppress our emotional side, resulting in fewer genuine facial expressions and less spontaneity. As we grow older, it seems we reduce our level of creativity as well. We no longer sing, dance or freely express ourselves as openly as we once did.

As a child begins to grow, he or she will experience day-to-day life events that will bring about emotional experiences. Although you may think of children as being carefree and living in a special fantasy world, children are faced with problems of their own. When they face these problems, they need to be listened to and helped in identifying their feelings just as adults do. Yet, how many of us have heard someone yelling, "Stop it, stop it now or you will really have something to cry about!" While camping recently, I overheard a mother telling her daughter that the adults wouldn't like her if she continued to cry!

Due to the environment that the child grows up in, the child may be nurtured in expressing emotions or the child may be taught to curtail emotions. The nurturing of emotional expression will aid the child in maintaining his or her inherent nature of rational thoughts and reason, and will continue to experience him or herself as lovable. In the event that the child's emotions are shamed, or that the child is taught to suppress emotions, the child's inherent nature will be clouded over with negative messages about him or herself.

In my own childhood environment, I was certainly not encouraged to express myself, nor was I reassured, validated, or even listened to when I experienced difficulties. The nurturing of my emotional expression would have allowed me to maintain a sense of balance and self esteem. As an adult, learning to value my emotions, to healthily express my concerns, and to listen to others, has brought me out of victimization and shame into a more positive and self-responsible state.

As adults, many of us have lost the connection between our heart and our head, the ability to identify and express our emotions, and the ability to regulate and disperse emotional energy. The loss of this skill is not something that usually happens overnight, but something that creeps up on us over a long period of time. In your childhood, teenage or adult years you may have been unsuspectingly taught to hide and suppress your emotions due to cultural expectations or due to a fear of being ridiculed by others. Quite often these were not formal lessons or directions, but messages you were given through the behavior of others. If you were angry, perhaps someone would walk away. If you were upset, perhaps someone ignored you. In some cases, emotions were just not tolerable by others in your environment. You may have been told to stop crying or rewarded for stifling your feelings. In my particular case, I remember instances of stuffing down my feelings and being very fearful of letting anyone know how I was feeling. It was just too scary!

The negative messages that children receive about emotional expression are numerous and sometimes confusing. Quite often these messages are the result of the adult's inability to tolerate emotion in themselves rather than anything to do with the child's behavior. For most of us, the expression of emotions has decreased with age, however it is clear to me that the moderation of emotional expression appears to be a learned behavior rather than a biological or personality trait. The young baby mentioned earlier learns from its environment about the effects of displaying emotion. Many parents attempt to train their children to stop crying although this is changing. Children are often scolded, called crybabies, and are given negative messages about crying or expressing anger.

There is a positive movement in this area though, and not all is gloomy. Recently, while in a hardware store, I observed a young couple dealing with a young crying boy. Both the mother and father were actively participating in reassuring and encouraging the young child to express whatever was upsetting him. They did not attempt to get him to stifle his tears but encouraged them! A few moments later, the cashier told the little boy "I'll give you a candy if you stop crying" to which his parents replied with a warm smile "Could he have the candy even if he continues crying?" The cashier smiled and gave the boy the candy while he continued to cry. This story reminds me of the fact that males in particular have been taught to repress crying, while females have been traditionally taught to repress anger. Perhaps we might consider the cost of rewarding children for stifling their emotions!

It seems that there are also differences between men and women with regard to how people cry. While both men and women tend to cry more often when alone, generally women tend to cry more often, for a longer period of time, and with greater intensity. According to a study at the University of Sussex, women also tend to be more likely than men to cry when criticized, when they are having difficulty dealing with work or when they have difficulty expressing anger.

With regard to gender, there have been a number of differences in how boys and girls are treated with respect to emotional expression. These differences cannot only bring about patterns of behavior, but can also generate gender stereotypes. While females are often thought of as being more emotionally expressive, I believe this to be a stereotype. Although crying is more prevalent among women, this may only be a factor of culture. It may not be a sign that women have a greater emotional capacity, but simply that the expression of emotion in males has been suppressed or trained out of them, while accepted in females. Women are generally fearful of expressing anger, while men have been taught to "swallow their tears" which is far more than a figure of speech. I learned at a very early age that the action of swallowing helped me to literally stuff my feelings down. No wonder I developed vocal problems due to tight throat muscles!

There are a few areas where men and women seem to react differently, resulting in higher incidents of depression in women. In one study, women were found to ruminate or go over situations in their mind much more than men, often contributing to their depression. In addition, women are more likely to exhibit certain behaviors that contribute to depression. In her book *Silencing the Self* author Dana Crowley Jack describes how women refrain from speaking to their partners, attempt to fit into an image provided by others, and generally try avoiding conflict. Often women will lose their sense of self and develop repressed rage. In this mode of self-repression, many women experience a "loss of self" that results in depression.

While I am concerned that both men and women may be unable to express emotion, I am further troubled regarding societal norms and expectations. Rarely do you see films or TV shows in which males cry. Typically, male crying has been identified as a sign of weakness resulting in males being fearful of expressing themselves. This is changing however, as society begins to learn that our emotions are a normal part of being human and as the roles of males and females change. While males have typically been stereotyped as non-expressive, this is not in fact the reality. We find many males openly discussing and expressing emotions in art, self-help groups and in close friendships. While some studies have shown that females will often score higher on adjustment tests, this may only be reflecting a greater willingness to accept the expression of emotion.

In a recent study of brain use patterns, it was shown that there is a biological basis for the difference in female and male behaviors. The study showed that on average, women are more inclined to exercise a portion of the lower brain that helps refine the way emotions are expressed. The author of the report, Ruben C. Gur, states, "Our findings do not answer the question of whether the differences are genetic or cultural in origin. After all, culture shapes the brain just as the brain shapes culture."

Regardless of gender, many people have learned various methods of expressing their emotions and many have developed methods of withholding or denying their emotions. In the course of writing this book, I have encountered numerous males and females who were experiencing emotional numbness and who were looking for ways to connect with their emotions. We should not generalize about these gender issues. Both males and females learn to hide their anger or provide a smile when they greet someone who has hurt them. All are behaving in ways that block or hide their true emotions. This decline in expression does have its price. These people are all robbing themselves of the value of emotional expression.

As in my case, the suppressing of emotions often leads to greater problems. Many children, adolescents and adults have suffered through painful experiences such as abandonment, and emotional or sexual abuse. As a result, their ability to function in other spheres of their life has been impaired. At the heart of every addiction lies a wounded soul. Yet when someone gives up the addictive behavior, they must face the part inside themselves that started drinking or taking drugs in the first place. The key to long term resolution of addiction and other destructive behavior is found by developing new ways to handle anxiety, by accessing and resolving the underlying problem, and by developing greater self-esteem. Identifying and disclosing the nature of the emptiness in the soul and releasing the pent-up emotional pain assists in giving up the addiction or compulsive behavior.

In many self-help programs, the process of hitting bottom, and subsequent release of emotions within a spiritual context, is a common occurrence among participants. The reappearance of positive feelings, allowing them to experience the joys of life, have been observed and documented. While it cannot be medically explained, it often occurs in life and is considered a mystery of spiritual phenomenon. Perhaps this re-experiencing of emotions fosters a connection with others, for emotions are the basis of the strongest form of communication we possess.

Emotional Myths

Typically, emotions have been labeled as either positive (such as joy and happiness) or negative (such as sadness, anger and depression). Love and contentment have been viewed as the opposite of anger and rage, while joy and happiness have been viewed as opposites of sadness and depression. I sometimes think that we need to re-evaluate this language and begin to view emotions as neither positive nor negative but simply as a reflection of our response to the events and internal processes that are occurring in your life. A more appropriate and healthy scale of emotions would involve classifying depression, fear, anxiety, rage and love as states of mind rather than emotions. Anger, fear, joy, and happiness occur in everyday life and are not necessarily negative or positive; however the outcome of your actions and how you deal with emotions can have a positive or negative impact on your mental health. Each unpleasant emotion has its own unique value in your life as a warning sign of needed personal work.

Some of our myths about emotions lead us to believe that experiencing anger towards someone means that we do not love the person. Furthermore, very few people have learned to discern the difference between anger and aggression and they confuse the two terms. Anger is an emotion that occurs within the body, while aggression is acting out behavior that attacks another person in some way. The experience of anger is an important internal signal yet in most cases it is the outright expression of anger that causes damage in relationships. When someone expresses anger it must be done in a manner that conveys that they care enough about the relationship to express the need that is not being met. It is rare that problems can be solved in the heat of the moment. A calming down period is usually required prior to initiating a discussion with the person you are angry with. Obviously, the raw expression of anger will usually have negative consequences unless you learn to assertively describe the offending behavior, how it is affecting you, and what your needs are.

This links to another emotional myth, that the raw expression or venting of anger is healthy. Unless the underlying thoughts are examined, and the cause of the anger dealt with, venting does not bring about healing. Venting anger simply doesn't work unless the ideas underlying the anger are examined. Current thinking by most Buddhist leaders is that the venting of anger only reinforces your anger. Instead of venting, you need to learn how to be compassionate and forgive. Forgiving is an ongoing process for which you become better skilled at.

One of the most common myths about emotions is that we believe we have the ability to selectively block out certain emotions. We tend to believe that we can avoid anger, yet still feel love and that we can block out sadness and still feel joy. Perhaps you may have numbed out some of your emotions and still feel a degree of love and joy. In fact, your capacity for joy and love is limited when you suppress your emotions and build up tension. The truth about emotions is that you do not truly have the ability to selectively block out only a spectrum of emotions. If you block sadness or anger you also end up limiting your ability to feel joy.

If the logical Mr. Spock of Star Trek fame is your role model, you might want to reconsider this! I recently read "I Am Spock", the autobiography of Leonard Nimoy, the actor who portrayed Mr. Spock. I was fascinated to learn that Mr. Nimoy found it quite emotionally challenging to stay in character for long periods of time without an undesirable impact on his mental health. Nimoy describes that his Spock character "took on a life of its own" and remaining in character became very stressful. Nimoy states that "repressing one's emotions, after all is an unnatural condition." He found that he became prone to "eruptions of emotion" and at times broke down and wept –the exact opposite behavior of the character he played!

One of the benefits of working on your emotional healing is that you generally find a greater capacity for joy and for sharing in your life once you begin to resolve your emotional baggage. A "put-on" smile is replaced with a more genuine smile that comes from the heart. A greater degree of closeness develops with others as your thinking becomes clearer and as you become less fearful of others discovering or opening up your pain. The path to joy is found by facing your pain and accepting that life is difficult. Life is a series of ups and downs. Rather than believing that you can always be happy, perhaps a measurement of mental health is your ability to experience the full range of emotions that occur as a result of events in your life, and your ability to nurture yourself and lift yourself out of troubles and into happier times!

Emotional Role Models

In recalling my childhood, I remember a number of adults who impacted my own emotional well-being. Some of them listened and encouraged the expression of my ideas, while others were too lost in their own problems and discomfort and provided discouragement. In my adult life, and particularly in 12-step groups, I encountered people who were nurturing and supportive. All of these people have been role models in some way or another to me - some positively and some negatively. Your role models can have a tremendous impact on your emotional well-being and awareness.

Observing the behavior of your emotional role models develops patterns of emotional expression or non-expression. These role models may be parents, teachers, extended family, scout leaders, daycare workers, or anyone who has contact with you. Your family emotional patterns can greatly influence your ease or unease regarding the display of emotions. Some families may encourage emotional expression and creativity but many families do not tolerate it. Some may accept emotional expression in children but not tolerate it with adults. With many families the rules are not clearly spelled out in directives, but are defined by the examples of others. My own father never gave any indication as to what he was feeling. He was impossible to read. Questioning him about how he was doing was treated as an intrusion. While most people appreciate the concern of others, my father's behavior led me to believe that asking questions was inappropriate. For me, this replicated behavior pattern appeared to others as disinterest. Once I learned that questioning was OK and normal, and began practicing it as a social skill, my social and work situation began to improve. I still have to catch myself sometimes though, and remember to ask how the other person is doing!

As described above, quite often the emotional maturity of the parents will greatly affect their ability to tolerate emotional expression in their children. If the parents have worked through issues and healed from their own losses, then they are more likely to encourage emotional expression and healing rather than hinder or shame the child for being emotional. Shame is experienced when you are given the message that you, rather than your behavior, is bad or inadequate. There is an important distinction between behavior and the individual. When a child behaves improperly, the child needs discipline and guidance, not shaming.

Often children are shamed for getting angry with their parents. Children get angry and have a right to express it, yet many parents fear this expression as a challenge to their authority. However, anger can be a catalyst for understanding your needs and the subsequent learning to communicate these needs can be a pathway to better communication. The expression of needs can facilitate feedback and dialogue of consultation and compromise in getting your needs met. True communication follows when you are emotionally expressive. If your parents have a great backlog of emotional issues, then true expression may be difficult due to a greatly enhanced fear of criticism, and the fear of their own issues being exposed.

Honest communication is unlikely to occur if the parent is overwhelmed by unresolved self-criticism, missed opportunities and defeatist attitudes. In this case the child cannot feel free to express his or her self without fear of upsetting the parent. The child can then develop an improper responsibility for other peoples' feelings when it is the adult who has the emotional coping problems. The child will become fearful of expressing emotions due to the consequences and patterns that appear when communication is attempted with the emotionally clouded adult. An adult who experienced this type of childhood will need to learn that emotions can be expressed without causing harm or hurting others. Many children learn at an early age that they must perform an emotional dance around their parents so that they don't upset their emotionally fragile parents. In my own situation, this led me to being shy and very timid. Children may unfortunately develop an overwhelming shame and improperly placed sense of responsibility for the feelings of their parents or caregivers.

A great hindrance of emotional expression can occur when one or both of the parents assume a "peace at any cost" role. To avoid conflict, a parent may try to deal with issues by doing anything within their power to placate the parties with the conflict. Covering debts, speaking to the parties individually rather than together, or caretaking can be ways of avoiding conflict. This usually results in the issue being cleared up but without any actual communication between the two. As a result, the emotions are not expressed and the parties do not learn to resolve their issues through communication and expression. This can lead to a fear of bringing up and confronting issues as adults. It usually also results in a sense that you are not part of a family team.

Another factor that affects both adults and children is the perfect family image that many parents try to maintain. This results in the denial of family problems and makes many topics off limits for discussion. Again, the lack of discussion and resolution of issues creates emotional tension and isolation in the family. This tension will manifest itself in the family behavior patterns unless an awareness of the habits is developed and worked on.

In many religious circles, showing anger towards God is considered sinful. While I used to fear my religious God, my sense of faith has truly changed. I now recognize that it is acceptable to get angry, yet it is usually because my needs are not being met, and because my faith is not strong. At one point in the writing of this book I discovered that I had to move. This would have been the third time I was forced to move in five months. I was angry, frustrated and tired of searching for an apartment yet I had to begin the process all over again. I felt that God had let me down. I was angry about the life circumstances I was experiencing. But one lesson I have learned is to ask for help, rather than venting. While driving around searching for vacancy signs I looked up to the sky and said, "It's my turn God. I've heard of people finding great places to live by chance. It's my turn to be helped out." I felt safe in my anger, yet acted differently by asking for help. It turned out great. Within five minutes of getting home, my phone rang. A friend called to say that due to a call from his former landlord, he knew of an apartment to rent. I took it immediately. It was literally a godsend -quiet, lots of windows, nice fellow tenants and a spectacular view of sailboats on the water, parks, and mountains. Six years later, my dear friend and landlady passed away, and the building was to be put up for sale. Instead of spiraling down in worry, I knew that no matter what, my accommodation needs would be taken care of. My neighbor in the basement apartment quickly found a nice place, and my other neighbor found a great house to live in. While I had no plan yet, I knew that a new place would be given to me at the right time that would help me in my journey if it became necessary to move.

Examining and identifying the behavior patterns of your role models, as well as your own habits that you have developed, is a necessary step in facilitating your own emotional awareness. The level of emotional acceptance in your role models may lead you to shut down emotionally or to be more expressive. Again, these patterns are learned behaviors. Healthier and more open patterns of expression can be learned to replace the old ineffective behaviors. The patterns you choose to develop and use end up shaping your choices in friends, careers, attitudes, and partners.

One of the most common issues that have been modeled for you is the way you search for happiness. In my own upbringing, the idea of happiness was a reward for living a good life. It was presented as something in the future, a goal, or a place to reach. Learning to find happiness in the present moment is one of the challenges you face in attaining serenity, or a sense of personal calmness. When you stop looking for happiness in others, or in the future, and realize that it is in your heart, you begin living more in the present, being aware of the gifts you have. You need to acknowledge the past and learn from it, but not overindulge in reliving it. You do not need to remain a victim. Your mind has the ability to recall events, but you can review and learn from each incident. You can play the movie of difficult events over and over again, backwards and forwards, but you should do so to heal and learn new things, not just to ruminate. Fortunately you are not stuck in the past. You can learn from the events and not continually relive your pain. You can free yourself from your pain, distress and unhealthy behavior by finding new role models to learn from!

The Rule Book

Each family, whether it is conscious of it or not, has a set of rules that governs how things are done within the family, and how the family and members relate to each other and to the outside world. Some of these rules, behaviors and ways of thinking have been passed down from generation to generation and are just as much shaped by the religion, careers, culture, and world view of each generation. Some of the rules were shaped by a parent's drastic attempts to not become their own parents, yet in having the pendulum swing fully from one side to another, have created new problems.

These rules are often not conveyed as commandments, but by responses you receive to your behavior, statements of belief, career choices, etc. There are an unlimited number of do's and don'ts in each family. Some of them are listed below. Try to think of any rules that might have existed in your home. How are your beliefs different?

You must carry on the family business.

You must go to university or college.

You must choose a respectable profession.

You should be introverted.

You should be extroverted.

So and so is the musician/artist/doctor in the family.

Don't get angry with your parents.

Don't get involved.

Don't invite people over.

Other families/religions are not correct.

Do as you are told.

As parents, we will choose your friends.

You answer when asked a question.

Don't draw attention to the family.

Keep up the image.

Don't ask others for help.

Not only does your healing process involve examining your emotions and thinking, you need to understand the people around you as well. Problems do not exist only in you! They exist in your family, friends, workplace and social network. A lesson to learn is that you can truly only change yourself. In doing so, others may follow, but it is ultimately up to you to examine your relationships and how you do things. You do this so that you may be more objective and better able to relate to the world you live in!

Can Others Make Me Feel?

One of the last areas to be discussed in this chapter is our responsibility for feelings. There are actually two questions or aspects to discuss. The first is whether or not someone can make another person feel a certain way. The second aspect is whether you should feel responsible for another person's feelings.

With respect to the first question, assertiveness training coaches would suggest that another person cannot make you feel a certain way. But I must ask whether this is realistic. If someone belittles us, shouts at us or even just sits and whines about how hopeless and negative their future is, it is difficult not to be impacted in some way. It is important for you to look at how you behave in these situations. Do you stick around, or do you assertively communicate your concerns. Does the other person listen or are they simply too self-absorbed to be concerned about your feelings?

In the research world, it is recognized that the simple act of observing can impact study participants. My point is that in some situations, it is almost impossible to avoid being impacted by other people's behaviors. Relationships will affect you just as you will affect them. A recent study of college students found that roommates who were living with someone who was depressed ended up feeling depressed themselves after a few months. It is important to note the impact that others have on you, given that you take in a great amount of information in a day, and that most of us seem to unconsciously respond to others rather than being in total control of our feelings and thoughts as we might think. You and others do matter in some way or another. As adults, it is the choices you make that results in having control over your situation when being impacted by another person. As children, or perhaps at times in your adult life, you were unable to affect the choices you would have liked to make. Given the study of college students, I can now be more appreciative of the roommates I had during the times that I was depressed. Part of healing involves learning to open up, but also achieving balance in choosing what we share. While feeling down at times, I've learned that being positive with people we meet does not negate the feelings we are having.

When interacting with others, especially in early years, your beliefs and judgments about yourself will be greatly impacted by the non-verbal cues of the adults around you. Other family members, children and even teachers, may pick up these parentally modeled behaviors causing further feelings of shame, guilt or excessive responsibility. Unfortunately, a child or teenager may have no situation other than his or her own family against which to compare or develop other belief systems. There is no fault in someone developing a sense of shame or guilt in a family situation that offers little or no healthy emotional and nurturing support. It is unfair to say that you chose to feel that way, as there may not have been more than one alternative. Evaluating these types of situations requires objective thinking. If you do not have other reference points, then you fall into a trap of believing the shaming authority.

Even as an adult, my father used to worry excessively and put the responsibility for his worry on me. I remember my father saying "If you don't make it home from the cottage by eleven then I'll be so worried that I won't be able to sleep." Am I responsible for my father's worry? No! What he was really saying was, "I do not take responsibility for my behavior. It is you who I will hold responsible for my feelings of worry." In this case, the worry reflected his inability to trust and his discomfort with his feelings. I have heard similar statements from others such as "If you don't come home for Christmas, it'll be ruined" or variations thereof. What is really being said in such situations is that the parent does not want to accept that their children have grown up and have their own lives, and perhaps the parent is unwilling to look at their own loneliness. The parent avoids accepting the challenge of growth and the feelings of the parent are ricocheted onto the children by suggesting that they are responsible for the situation and resulting feelings. Some adults use "You make me feel...." statements when another person is not doing what the parent asks. These are often not statements of disclosure, but are manipulative statements intended to change the choice of action or behavior of the other person. Of course, you need to be accountable for your behavior, but emotional ransom is a behavior that is difficult to extricate yourself from.

Clearly, someone might tell us that if you left, they'd feel hurt. You still need to be sensitive to the feelings of others, but you also need to consider your own needs and whether the statement is made for the purpose of communication or manipulation. It is far better a practice to say "when you behave a certain way I feel this way." In this manner we describe the behaviour and the resulting feelings.

You need to recognize the distinction between the impact your feelings have on others and the impact that your behavior has on others. Your behavior can result in feelings in others, but you cannot control what those feelings will be, just as you cannot make someone love you, no matter how hard you try. While some people take the approach that you cannot create feelings in other people, there is research that suggests that you respond in very subtle ways to the emotions and behavior of others, particularly when below the surface anger is involved. Certainly, some behaviors will likely result in a greater respect between two individuals and a greater chance of being liked, but no one can be the sole creator of feelings in another person. The other person also has the right to choose how they react, or even if they want to stay in the relationship. No one should hold you solely accountable for their feelings, however you may find that a chronic negative attitude will drive people away. There is a saying that "misery loves company" but I haven't found that to be true among healthy people. During vulnerable times it is important to choose your friends carefully, to associate with those who can receive and give support, and not fault those who are not in the space to give at that time. They are facing their own issues and are likely having difficulty separating their own feelings from being triggered by your feelings. Clearly, some situations will likely evoke certain emotions and beliefs.

The creation of a response in any individual requires the processing of communication. This process involves interpretation of messages created with an imprecise language, recalling similar experiences and examining one's beliefs. If you were emotionally abused, then you will likely feel low self esteem and have difficulty in trusting others. But as discussed later in the book, blaming does not help. When you understand the way you are, you are free to make choices and to heal. You can develop new attitudes, learn to trust and take responsibility for yourself, given the understanding you have of the problem!

On Becoming Affectionate

One of the attributes of being human is our need for affection. This, of course, is not to be confused with sex, which unfortunately many people equate with affection. What is intimacy? Is it closeness, sharing or is it sex? Many of us have mistaken sex for intimacy. Sexual intercourse between two loving communicating people is intimacy in a very powerful and special form, yet to achieve this form of intimacy requires a great deal of communication and caring between the two people all of which takes time and effort to develop. The sexual act itself will not generate the intimacy you desire.

Have you learned yet that in a relationship there are other types of intercourse with the sexual aspect being only one of them? In a quality relationship there will also be intellectual intercourse with the sharing of your ideas, thoughts and feelings. There will also be a spiritual intercourse with the sharing of beliefs and a special bonding between the two partners. All of these are in addition to the sexual aspect of the relationship.

When all three are present then you achieve a special intimacy. It is easy to mistake sexual intercourse for intimacy when you have not had a relationship that contains the other types of intercourse. But you can learn that your needs can be met in a more fulfilling way. When you learn to open up and develop spiritual and intellectual as well as sexual relationships you get closer to finding a greater sense of what being human is all about.

Each of us needs to be held, to be hugged and to be able to show our affection with others. You are healthier, both in mind and spirit, when you are able to experience the warmth of affection with another. Unfortunately, many people including myself began life in an environment where affection was not present. I do not remember my mother holding me, and I remember my father being cold and unresponsive when I was a child. I remember a time when I may have been about six years old, running up to my father and hugging him when he came home from work one day. There was no response from him, only a coldness that I remember to this day. I thought there was something wrong with me! I also cannot recall my parents ever holding hands or giving each other a hug, let alone giving my brothers or myself any affection in our childhood. As

31

children, we learn from our role models and we can develop fear around affection. We tend to develop behaviors based on the modeling of the adults around us. If appropriate affection is shown between parents and siblings then you are more likely to develop affection in your own life.

Although you may end up being unaffectionate, I strongly believe that this is a learned condition that can be unlearned, or replaced with healthier habits. The key to doing this is to overcome your discomfort and fear of being affectionate. Due to my own upbringing, I became very defensive. If someone were to pat me on the shoulder or attempt to give me a hug, I usually tensed up, giving signals that it was not OK to get close to me. This has been a knee jerk reaction for most of my life. Part of it may be the result of a heightened startle response, a characteristic of posttraumatic stress disorder. Regardless of the cause, I have trained myself to be aware and relax when someone shows affection. When people approach and touch my arm or shoulder, I welcome their contact without the fear I once experienced.

In non-threatening situations, I have no trouble being affectionate, and this too was something that I developed as a result of relearning. From my early twenties, I clearly remember a night I went with a friend to a discotheque. My friend and I spotted two attractive women and I asked one of them to dance. With the loud music it was very hard to hear each other and it seemed as though she didn't understand a word I was saying. Being in a French area of town, I switched to speaking French. She seemed even more confused! After dancing, her sister explained to me that she spoke only Polish and that she had just moved to Canada! We ended up going out on a few dates, and although we did not become sexually active, this woman was extremely affectionate in a kind and loving manner. She essentially brought out and developed a part of me that had been hidden and discouraged. Of course, at the time I was quite dysfunctional and didn't pursue the friendship. I still kick myself for that, but the gift she gave me has impacted me tremendously.

On the other side of the coin, affection without boundaries can be harmful as well. Particularly for those who have experienced sexual abuse, the ability to say no to touch has not been learned or allowed. Since working through my own issues, I find that I am much more approachable and have often encountered people who have hugged or touched me on the shoulders without asking. While in most cases I don't mind these gestures of affection, there have been times when I preferred not to be touched. Having the freedom to say yes or no to affection is a healthy boundary that many of us struggle with. My own father seemed to lack this respect of boundaries. Whenever I was in the passenger seat of the car and yawned, he thought it was funny to stick his fingers in my mouth. This annoyed me to no end, yet my protests seem to fall on deaf ears. Finally I got quite angry and reprimanded him for the true issue, that he did not have the right to do this. He got the message and stopped.

I've often heard the phrase "I'm too old to learn new ways" or the classic phrase "You can't teach and old dog new tricks," yet I have seen great changes in families and parents as well. My own mother, at age sixty-two, was a perfect example! Although my family was large, my mother was in many ways isolated. Shortly after meeting the woman from Poland, I began to hug my mother when I finished a visit with her. At first, hugging her was like hugging a cement pillar, but slowly a hand reached out and patted me on the back, which was a major step for her. She slowly established safety and a sense of confidence in being affectionate. Within a few weeks she was hugging me, as well as hugging other family members. She later confessed that it was her fear of rejection that kept her from expressing affection and emotion. What a treat it was to watch her, a few months later, greeting my brother Bill with a hug as he walked in the door! I also remember a co-worker who was so intently focused on setting boundaries that he missed some genuine caring by others. Eventually he learned that not all actions of touch were misguided or sexual in nature and he began to learn to trust. These are examples of how affection can be re-introduced into our lives.

3. What Are Emotions?

Emotions – Your Natural Resource!

Feelings tell you a lot about what is going on in your life. Emotions are a common bond among us. Without emotions, entertainers and musicians would be out of work. The human race entertains each other by evoking emotions in theatrical plays, musicals, or through the visual effects of a work of art and dance. One of my favorite romantic tunes is "I Will Still Love You" by Stonebolt, which still gets substantial airplay years after it was released. David Wills of Stonebolt explains, "Many of the best songs I wrote were the result of highly charged emotional times." Without emotion, there would be no inspiration for the world's greatest works of art, nor would we have any kind of entertainment industry! Revolutions have occurred because of the ability of leaders to stir the emotions of their followers.

To a great extent, emotions add to your life, social structure and connection with others. Life would be rather boring without the resource of our emotions - a powerful human trait in communication and problem solving. Studies have shown that facial movements and the corresponding emotions contribute greatly to the impression people have of us. I can't help but notice most of the successful TV show characters are built around a variety of emotional facial expressions. Much of the dialogue is actually non-verbal, being communicated through facial expressions, and this is one of the great talents of any great actor! It has been suggested that only twenty percent of your communication occurs with words. The rest is left to body posture and facial expressions! Is it coincidence that many of the most popular TV shows feature a great deal of non-verbal communication?

Unfortunately, most people have never learned to utilize their emotions. In his book *Managing a Difficult or Hostile Audience*, lecturer and organizational trouble-shooter Gordon F. Shea writes, "Feelings (are) our lost resource. Feelings - good and bad, can be one of our primary tools for problem identification and problem solving." Many of us have lost, or perhaps never developed, the ability to read the feelings of others. Our inherent ability to be tuned into other's feelings has been lost or trained out of us. Since most people have learned to suppress feelings, we also learn to discount the feelings of others. We often listen for just the facts or details of the situation, and neglect or are unaware of the feelings involved in the situation.

Just as sight, smell, touch, hearing, and tasting are important senses, so too are your emotions. While we would not arbitrarily destroy our sight or hearing, many of us have blocked and denied our sense of feeling. Emotions are just as valuable as your other senses. As a counselor, I have found that clients often have their greatest moments of relief after simply acknowledging, restating and validating what they are feeling. This does not involve saying that their view of the situation is correct, nor do I take sides. It is a simply yet skillful acknowledgement of the clients experience. The acknowledgement of the emotions is often far more important to the client at the time than going over the facts. Furthermore, the use of empathy has been thoroughly documented as one of the most powerful counseling tools.

Instead of seeing emotions as a resource, many of you see your emotions through fearful eyes. You may be afraid of being judged as having poor mental health or that you are impulsive and illogical in your decision-making. Impulsive and illogical behavior occurs when you are blinded by the strength and intensity of your emotions or if you are emotionally numb and anxious. Emotional intensity can be frightening for many people, however if we process emotions as they are experienced, we are less likely to experience the intensity and anxiety that occurs when unresolved troubles are triggered by current events.

Even if emotion is present, many people rely solely on intellect and hard numerical data in the process of problem solving. Many successful people from all walks of life often comment on how an appropriate decision was made based on "gut feeling." This gut feeling is part of your emotional side that you many often neglect in decision-making. How often have you had a feeling or sense about someone or a situation that ended up being correct? As you become more aware of your feelings you can use them as a gauge to measure the impact of other people's behavior as well as your own. You can also use your feelings to rate various career choices or to identify needs that are not being met in your life.

With little understanding of each other's emotions, it is no wonder that there is such a degree of conflict and misunderstanding in the world on international and personal levels. Once I became more in tune with my own emotions, I experienced an increased awareness of others feelings and moods as I became less and less focused on my own troubles and became a better listener. Understanding and listening to the hurt, the sadness, the abandonment, and the fear of others helps establish a basis for understanding and problem solving. The rewards are multiplied when you can share in their joy and happiness!

Mark Linden O'Meara

A Definition of Emotion

Developing an all-encompassing definition of emotions is a great challenge and one that may not be met for a number of years. A scientist might wish to measure emotions in terms of physical changes or energy. A medical doctor might wish to measure heart rate and skin temperature, while a psychiatrist might measure chemical levels in the brain. A massage therapist might measure muscle tension, while a yoga teacher would lead you to concentrating on life forces or chakras. Arriving at a definition of emotions is not likely within the scope of any one profession.

What are emotions? What is the essence of the feelings? How are they created, released and resolved in our minds? What happens when we do not express them? Do they simply disappear or are they stored in some other form? Most of the things in this world can be described in terms of color, shape or form however emotions seem to escape these types of measurements and descriptions. In the following pages you will discover some things that you may already know as well as some new things about emotions. In writing this section, I have tried to convey the concepts of various research and studies. I believe the information is valuable in that you can build a foundation of understanding from which you can learn to accept your emotions.

The study of emotions and how they manifest themselves in our bodies is far from complete but is definitely evolving. Earlier research has shown that your emotions do evoke physical responses in your body. The earliest and most cited study of these responses was done by Ax in 1953. Ax elicited fear in his test subjects by telling them that there was a possibility of a short circuit in his recording apparatus. He then measured face temperature, blood pressure, and galvanic skin response as well as other physical measurements. Ax was able to prove that emotional responses do affect blood pressure and heart rate.

Generally, emotions are thought of as having three distinctive components: a feeling aspect of the emotion; bodily changes such as increased blood pressure, heart beat, as well as hormonal changes; and bodily changes involving the level of muscle tension.

Years ago the view advanced by scientists was that the bodily changes were in fact the emotion and that the feelings involved in an emotion were not observable or verifiable. The only way to verify that an emotion was occurring was to ask the person having the emotion. If emotions are to be defined as only bodily changes (such as visceral and skeletal reactions), then artificially produced bodily changes should result in the emotion; however this is not the case. Someone who is artificially stimulated does not experience the tone or feeling.

It is now more accepted that the three aspects (feeling, bodily changes and increased muscular tension) need to be present.

In addition, I would argue that a person's values and beliefs at any given time would influence the process of emotional stimulation. A person's belief as to what constitutes a threat or perceived hurt will vary a person's emotional response. Some people are more sensitive than others, resulting in variations in levels of emotional response. Carl Jung proposed that there are sixteen basic personality types. One of the measures of personality types is the Feeling/Thinking component of the Myers-Brigg measurement test. Some of us relate to the world through thoughts and logic. Others relate to the world more with their emotions.

In recent years, new technology has led to a greater understanding of emotions. New scientific advances such as Magnetic Resonance Imaging (MRI) have allowed the medical field to record and review areas of brain activity while emotion is occurring. The identification and description of the emotion is still required from the subject.

Some theories suggest that Central Nervous System activity is intrinsic in emotional experience. Emotional behavior releases a substantial number of chemicals and hormones. Other studies regarding the regulation and production of hormones, as well as the secretion process in other glands have put emphasis on inter-relating central nervous subsystems. Some hormones seem to play an important role in memory, learning and selective attention. Other hormones, such as serotonin, have been linked as well to heightened emotions. There is a clear link between serotonin and depression. I keep wondering though, "Which comes first?" Does the lack of a particular hormone result in a depression or is the lack of a particular hormone the symptom of a depression?

In a research paper investigating the emotional experience associated with running and meditation, Jane Harte states that "A well tested, comprehensive, neuro-anatomical map of emotional experience has not yet been found," however our understanding is growing in leaps and bounds. It is important to note that emotion, behavior and thoughts are linked in a complex system. One study reported in the American Journal of Psychiatry, showed that as we become more emotional, the blood flow to our logic functions is reduced. This may explain why it is often difficult to heal until the emotion is dealt with, as it is usually an incorrect underlying belief that needs to be resolved in order to heal. It may also explain why we often see things more clearly after an emotional release!

One aspect of emotion that is often overlooked is that much emotional information is conveyed through your eyes. It has been said that the eyes are the windows to the soul. In attempting to read the emotions of others, it is usually the eyes that either confirm or betray what they are feeling. Also, it is important to note that none of the current theories can explain where the sense of life comes from, our essence of our being, or as in religious terms, where our soul resides in our body.

Humans have sometimes been described as walking chemistry sets, but we are also much more than that. Our bodies are much more intelligent than science realizes or can presently measure. In a video series on the nature of the mind, Dr. David Suzuki states, "If the doors of perception were cleansed, the world would appear to man as it is.... The door to perception is the brain's own chemicals."

Emotional Energy

Although we may now be able to measure chemical, hormonal, and physical changes in the body as a result of emotions, we still are left with the trouble of defining what the actual feeling of the emotion is. How does it enter consciousness? How do we resolve it? What process occurs when we grieve or talk things out with a friend? How is the subconscious created in this milieu of chemicals and hormones? Perhaps these answers are still unattainable. Our bodies are very complicated systems. We have yet to understand how the brain generates ideas, or how your brain creates your dreams. We are learning about the power of the subconscious mind and its powerful abilities to assist in problem solving, yet we still do not have an understanding of where conscious energy comes from.

Most of us would agree that just as emotions can at times drain us, they can also produce vitality and energy in us. In times of joy we feel light, alive and invigorated, while during times of sadness we can feel lethargic. An emotional experience always results in a change in the energy state of the individual experiencing the emotion. Anger or fear tends to raise the energy level of an individual, while we can feel exhausted after a good long cry.

Let's look at the composition of the word "Emotion". Breaking it into two components, we have the letter "E" and the word "motion". In scientific equations, "E" is used to represent energy. The word motion describes an object or entity that is moving and not resting in one place. Your emotions exhibit the same characteristics of energy and motion. The emotion is a form of energy that is not meant to be static. Your emotions are processes through which you move and reach resolution. You are not meant to stay stuck in a particular emotional state. To move from a particular state you must release the energy associated with the emotion.

This emotional energy cannot yet be measured with scientific instruments, but it can be measured in terms of the transfer of the energy into behavior and emotional expression. This energy seems to be created as a reaction to events or circumstances in life. If you have been injured then you will feel anger or sadness. If you experience an uplifting moment you can feel joy. The emotions you experience are created and, as you experience these feelings, the energy associated with them is released. Each emotion you experience and express has a beginning and end to its energy life cycle. Through the expression of emotions you release that energy and become free to move on.

I have often been asked about the difference between a feeling and an emotion. Since the word emotion comes from the Latin word "emote", meaning to express, I would therefore suggest that feelings are vague sensations within the body while emotions are the feelings that are ready to be expressed.

While the difference between feelings and emotions may become a point of argument for the scholars, it is important to remain focused on the cause of the concern, namely that the experiencing of emotions can have a tremendous effect on your daily life. Think of a time when you were happy. Your body felt active and vibrant. At times when you feel sad or depressed, you tend to feel listless and lethargic. Emotional energy can either add to your daily life or drain your energy levels. As you release your emotional energy you maintain a sense of balance. Simply put, emotional energy can either tire you or add zest to your life. If you repress your emotions, you alter and block a vital flow of energy and a process that maintains stability in your mind and body. In my own situation, I think of a balloon as a metaphor for the emotional state I ended up in by not allowing my emotions to be released. Imagine a balloon that is completely full. It is easy to burst with a simple jarring. I was like that full balloon. I was fearful of any vulnerability, and like the balloon I had to protect my emotions from being burst. Slowly through my healing process, I was able to untie the knot at the bottom of the balloon and slowly let the pressure off in a safe and healthy manner. Soon the pressure in my emotional balloon returned to a level where my emotions could be celebrated and enjoyed!

Some members of the alternative medicine community have held the belief that unexpressed emotions are stored in muscle tension and that releasing the muscle tension through massage will result in discharge of the emotions. It is evident that emotional expression fully involves many muscle groups. Frederick Perls, the founder of Gestalt therapy, says, "Emotional excitement mobilized the muscles, the motoric system. Every emotion, then, expresses itself in the muscular system." It is not possible to be angry without muscular tension and movement. Even if you do not express anger, there is an increase in muscular tension as you hold it down or as described above, fill your emotional balloon.

In attempting to research and resolve my singing problem of a restricted range and throat tension, I came across a study that measured jaw tension with uncommunicated anger. The study showed increased jaw tension in those who repressed their anger, and a return to normal tension for those who resolved their anger. Perls aptly states, "Any disturbance of this excitement metabolism will diminish your vitality." A foundation of Gestalt and other therapies is that the denial and repression of emotions lead to a state of anxiety.

If your emotions are numbed or denied, particularly through the avoidance of crying, then we must raise the question of what the long term effects of not crying might bring about. Adults may learn whole new repertoires of action or patterns that may serve as substitutes for crying. Often people will use sports, talking or other forms of expression to release their emotional energy.

Emotional Maturity

Achieving emotional health and maturity involves the integration of emotions into your life. There are two polarities that can indicate a lack of emotional maturity. On one extreme you may run from your emotions. The opposite occurs when you are run by your emotions. Neither of these two states is conducive to emotional health and well-being. What is needed is a sense of balance and the ability to integrate emotions into daily life so that your emotions do not overrun your mind and behavior.

So, how would you define an emotionally mature person? The following words describe the emotionally mature individual:

accepting	expressive	integrated
balanced	constructive	secure
appreciative	self-aware	free
forgiving	compassionate	aware

To be emotionally mature means being appropriately expressive, being aware of others, and being secure in your identity. It also involves having a sound understanding of self and a set of skills or patterns that you use to deal with everyday challenges as well as other difficulties. Being emotionally mature involves being open-minded and having a realistic view of self and others, and knowledge of what you will or will not accept. The emotionally mature person can maintain control and refrain from hurting others in emotionally stressful situations. The emotionally mature person will also be able to handle negative comments from others and evaluate their truth without becoming aggressive.

As a result of these traits, the emotionally mature person can accept that life is difficult, yet derive a satisfaction from life through contributing to the goals and needs of themselves and others. Improving your maturity level is a lifelong goal. Increasing your level of maturity begins with accepting that you have emotions but they are not the totality of your experience. You also take responsibility for your actions and consequences. Living an emotionally mature life allows you to see things as they are, to experience connectedness with others, and to give selflessly to others.

Emotional maturity also means to be free of shame and to be able to express yourself without hesitation. You may ask the question, "Who am I?", but answers can be clouded by shame and fear of being rejected. A great deal of change and personal growth can result in the loss of a sense of self, yet through time and healing work, a new definition of self will emerge. As you let go of the emotional backlog you learn who you are without the baggage. The process of self-discovery involves answering the question "What are my interests and how do I express myself when I am rid of my shame, fear and sadness that has haunted me for so long?" Can you sing and/or dance when alone yet clam up when someone is watching? Do you express your opinions or agree with others to avoid rejection? When you start to express your creativity, you will begin to know who you truly are. But first you must let go of the shame and the embarrassment of being who you really are. You might find yourself feeling awkward showing others your true self, but you may also find that letting others know who you are and what your talents and interests are will be rewarding. Maybe some genuine people have been waiting all along for you to show your true self. Deep down you are a genuine person interested in meeting genuine people. But the genuine people you met weren't interested because you had hidden behind a mask that they could so readily see! But the future can be different. You can reveal yourself to those you choose and be a little more genuine with some genuine people!

Some questions to ask are "Do people really know who you are? Have you shown your true self to the people you have met" or "Have you been afraid to let others know who you really are?" "Have you told them about your interests, your desires, talents and weaknesses? If you have not, how can they decide if they connect with you or not? How can they learn about you if they do not know the true person behind a mask? If they accept you, are they accepting the mask or the true you?"

You may be afraid of letting people know you, but if you do, then there will be a greater chance of attracting people with similar characteristics and interests. You need to let go of your fear, to suspend it and to begin to let people know more about you. You may not be used to doing this, but it will become easier.

In the Princeton Language Institute's *Synonym and Antonym Finder*, I searched for words that can be used in place of the word "emotional". Some of the words from the list are as follows: ardent, enthusiastic, excitable, feeling, fervent, heartwarming, impassioned, moving, passionate, poignant, responsive, sensitive, sentient, sentimental, spontaneous, tender, touching, warm, and zealous. For words to replace "emotionless", I discovered these adjectives: blank, chill, cold, cool, detached, dispassionate, distant, flat, frigid, icy, impersonal, indifferent, remote, unfeeling, and unimpassioned.

A question you might ask yourself is, "To which group would we like to belong?" I know I would like to belong to the first group! The first list describes someone who is living and experiencing relatedness with others. The second list indicates a sense of dissociation and disconnection with others.

Frederick Perls writes, "the center of personality is what used to be called the soul: the emotions, the feelings, the spirit. Emotions are not a nuisance to be discharged. Emotions are the most important motors of our behavior."

To become emotionally mature requires changes in your thinking and behavior. You need to learn to be comfortable with the emotional aspect of yourself and you need to unlearn some of your behaviors. This can be accomplished through a number of ways. Perhaps your healing work, along with support from a counseling group or counselor, will help you gain greater emotional health and maturity.

Depression, fear and sadness can be resolved if you are willing to do the work required. By releasing your pent up emotions you can experience joy, happiness, clearer thinking, and better relationships. You may find health problems are lessened due to the extra energy that you will have available. Your eyes may become clearer and your posture may improve, since you will no longer be carrying around the weight of the world on your shoulders. In my own experience, as I became more emotionally connected I found I was receiving feedback that I was becoming more genuine, warm and caring.

With emotional resolution, you will likely find a renewed joy in your life. You will begin to cultivate a relationship with yourself and begin to discover who you really are without the emotional baggage. You will discover new interests, hobbies, develop new friendships and end your isolation. You will also begin to remember your past in a clearer more accepting manner. You will begin to forgive yourself as well as others and begin living with more serenity, warmth and love in your day-to-day living. Let go!

4. The Many Layers of You!

I remember a time in grade eight when our teacher, Mrs. Hendricks, gave a few lectures and exercises for us to do to help us answer the question "Who am I?" At the time, the questions and exercises didn't have much meaning for me, but looking back, I wish I had paid a bit more attention to these lessons. Like many people I have at times heard the phrase "discover who you really are!" While this has become a bit of a cliché phrase, there is a great benefit in going on a journey within to learn about you. Fortunately the ability to learn about yourself has grown immensely within the field of psychology and the tests that have been developed to help you learn about yourself. I have also come to believe that "who you really are" could be more productively rephrased "who you are on a deeper level, given the choices you have made, the people you associate with and the personal history you have experienced!

While in China I came across a wonderful book called *The Importance of Living* by Lin Yutang, a distinguished scholar and Nobel Prize nominee. According to Lin,

> "The thing called "self" or "personality" consists of a bundle of limbs, muscles, nerves, reason, sentiments, culture, understanding, experience, and prejudices. It is partly nature and partly culture, partly born and partly cultivated. One's nature is determined at the time of his birth, or even before it. Some are naturally hardhearted and mean, others are naturally frank and straightforward and chivalrous and bighearted; and again others are naturally soft and weak in character, or given over to worries. Such things are in one's 'marrow bones' and the best teacher or wisest parent cannot change one's type of personality. Again other qualities are acquired after birth through education and experience, but insofar as one's thoughts and ideas come from the most diverse sources and different streams of influence at different periods of his or her life, his ideas, prejudices and points of view present a most bewildering inconsistency. One loves dogs and is afraid of cats, while another loves cats and is afraid of dogs. Hence the study of types of human personality is the most complicated of all sciences."

There are popular songs that say "we are all the same" and there are beliefs that we are all created equal, but given my understanding of psychology, people, and my own likes and dislikes, I would debate this. Certainly we should all be treated equally under laws and by each other, but it is clear that each of us possess certain likes and dislikes, as well as special talents that others may or may not possess. Some of us are more sensitive than others, while some spend more time thinking while some are more involved in their emotional side. It is not to say that any of these are better than the other, but accepting the basis of your personality traits can do wonders to help you understand the root of dissatisfaction in your life, or to gain an understanding of why you may not feel fulfilled.

The Nature/Nurture Dilemma

One of the popular questions asked in the field of psychology is whether the behavior, thoughts and feelings are the result of nature – the genetic characteristics of a person, or nurture – one's upbringing. I believe that sometimes we have to look at not only the suggested answers but also the fundamental question being asked. I believe the nature/nurture concept is fundamentally flawed in that it does not address personal responsibility for your actions and your ability to change your behavior. The nature explanation relies solely on genetics to explain behavior, while the nurture model can be used to blame parents and caregivers. It is clearly important that you must examine your own contribution to problems and issues and recognize the ability to choose a new path in solving problems and healing. Clearly, nature and nurture play a role, but I believe that a more comprehensive model is required to help us understand the nature of your actions, your personal choices, the power of your dreams and your ability to forgive.

In this area I have found my combined knowledge of computers and psychology to be helpful. I remember sitting on a beach during a vacation in Australia, and mentally going over my career path. I was thinking about the different levels of what is called the Open Systems Interconnect model, which is basically a seven layer model of standards for the transmission and display of data. I made the connection that although we are far more complex than today's computers; we share similar layers of complexity. While at the most basic level we are just atoms and chemicals; there is a communication network and various layers of traits, personal history and experience, as well as a higher self that makes up who we are. I jotted this idea down in my travel journal and when I returned from vacation I presented the concept at a counseling conference and present it here for you.

Genetics and Physical Characteristics

As a result of your father's, mother's and their parents genetics, you are born with a genetic structure that is dealt to you at conception. We all share at least a basic genetic system that differs only very slightly from person to person. I have read that the genetic differences between a basketball star and a midget is less than .03 percent! Our ancestry determines our genetics. There is not much we can do to change this part of our self, but fortunately this is only the first level of the many layers of being human!

Mind Body and Psychoneuroimmunology

Superimposed on this genetic basis is a communication network of neurons, neurotransmitters, synapses, hormones, chemicals, and signals that give you the sensation of being in your body. It is a complex system of neurotransmitters and receivers that adapts as you respond to stressors and other events. Some neurotransmitters such as acetylcholine are associated with the memory process, while others such as norepinephrine act as excitatory or inhibitory functions depending on the site in the body. Another neurotransmitter is serotonin, which has implications for mood, sleep, arousal and eating. This electrochemical process of communication within the body is the basis of the central nervous system. The nervous system interacts with the endocrine system, which in turn impacts our immune system!

It is an accepted principle that what you believe also impacts your central nervous system. In medical research, the placebo effect occurs when someone is told they are taking a pill and a measurable outcome takes place, even though the patient was given only a sugar pill rather than the actual medication! One of the foundations of research for new drugs is the requirement that to be proven effective a new drug must show that it shows significant changes above and beyond the placebo effect of the drug. It has now been discovered that placebo medication can induce changes in brain functioning of individuals with major depression. "People have known for years that if you give placebos to patients with depression or other illnesses, many will get better" states Dr. Andrew Leuchter. What you believe has a powerful impact on your mind and body right down to the chemical level.

While it has also been stated by many theorists that thoughts create our emotion, there is now scientific evidence that questions whether that statement is the complete picture. Obviously your thoughts and beliefs have an impact as evidenced by the placebo effect, yet new studies show that the emotional parts of the brain will react to perception far more quickly than the parts of the brain associated with thinking. If someone comes toward you with a scowl on their face or even a smile, your body has responded long before your thoughts surface! While some have suggested that love is simply a series of chemicals and neurotransmitters, I would refute that statement, as it is only looking at one level of the process. The same could be said for art, music, or the best works of fiction. At some level they are all just waves of light or sound bouncing off matter! Continue on to find out how complex you are!

You've Got Personality!

Going to the next level, we also seem to be born with a set of interests, likes, dislikes and talents. Why is it that one person can visualize an image and recreate it on paper, while another person like myself, seems to lack that ability, yet I have the uncanny ability to name a tune hearing only a few bars of a song? Newer research suggests that you may be born with a set of interests such as an interest in classical music or literature as opposed to more pop oriented music and reading tabloids! Of course you can learn to nurture and develop interests, but you often find that in some areas you excel while in others you do not. The challenge is to try to discover what your talents are. Life might be a lot easier if you were born with a little tag that gave you a hint as to your talents, however it would take away the challenge of self-discovery! In the model I am suggesting, this next level consists of your combination of personality types. Many mothers and fathers will report that their babies seem to have a distinct personality right from birth. This phenomenon is more noticeable in the birth of their second child, as the second child seems to respond in different ways than their first child. It seems that our personality type and learning styles are set at birth. Some of us learn by watching, some by listening and others by doing. Others are more emotionally sensitive. There is no concept of one being better than the other but learning about your personality type and learning style has clear implications for how you need to be treated and nurtured.

There are now indications that personality type impacts how your brain responds to emotional stimuli. Previously, this concept had been disregarded in research but is now being given more attention. Dr. John D. Gabrieli of Stanford University states "Depending on personality traits, people's brains seem to amplify some aspects of experience over others." It is now thought that emotional reactions are highly personal and individual based and as a result, therapy should be tailored to the person rather than applying a general set of principles to all clients.

Your personality type impacts your career choices as well. I remember how, as a computer programmer, I kept experiencing dissatisfaction in my job, even though I was competent. I received positive review for my work at the start of my career, but gradually I lost interest. I realized that a career change was necessary, and went for some career testing and counseling. As described in Richard Bolles' *What Color is your Parachute* I completed a test that describes my Holland Codes. Basically, this theory suggests that there are six basic groups of work: Social, Artistic, Conventional, Realistic, Enterprising, and Investigative. The Socials like working with people, the artistic are creative, the conventional like working with numbers, realistic types like programming, fixing or constructing things, the enterprising are the business owners, investigative types like analyzing data. The Holland Codes system helps determine your top three codes.

In completing the test, I learned that my top three codes are Social, Artistic and Realistic. This helped explain my dissatisfaction with my career as a programmer as my work was non-social and not very creative. I was basically looking after only the third rated code in my test results. Continuing on with the counseling, I realized that I could utilize my computer skills in a teaching environment, and therefore began teacher training. I started teaching night school programs and eventually got a job at a community college. I began teaching a variety of programs for jobless people, leading to taking courses in career counseling and psychology theory, and ended up doing a masters degree in counseling, and writing this book. As you can see, a little bit of self-knowledge can have a substantial impact on career and personal choices! I encourage you to read Bolle's book to gain a deeper understanding of your own personality traits!

Another personality measure is the Myers-Brigg indicator. In a quick summary, this test helps to categorize one's personality based on whether they are an introvert or extravert, thinking or feeling type, intuitive or sensing, or a perceiving or judging type. Introverted and extroverted people differ in how they interact with their world. The introverts energize themselves by looking inward, while the extroverts get inspiration from exterior forces. The sensing people gather information through their five senses, while the perceiving types rely on intuition or an inner sense. Thinking people form conclusions through logical deduction and relying on facts, while the feeling types rely on personal values, and the impact of a decision on people. Both methods are valid. Judging types tend to bring structure to their lives and move on, while perceiving types tend to leave options open and are considered to be more flexible and spontaneous.

It is important to note that personality types are not either or but are measured on a scale. You are not completely one or the other but a combination of both. One of each of the types will usually appear to be more predominant. Some theorists suggest that the type on which we rate lower often needs attention. For example, if you rate as a feeling type, work may be needed to strengthen the thinking aspect and vice versa. I would also highly recommend *Please Understand Me* by David Keirsey and Marilyn Bates for further study.

While most of these measurements and descriptions have been used mostly for career counseling, they are very valuable tools in the development of your self knowledge and understanding of others. Imagine if the personality types were taught in grade school and everyone introduced himself or herself as, "Hi I'm Mark. I'm an intuitive, feeling, extroverted perceiver!" The other person introduces themselves as, "Hi I'm Bob. I'm a thinking type and an introvert." We'll have to adjust to each other's ways of being here." It would help greatly in understanding why people behave, think or feel in certain ways and probably help us avoid a lot of conflict!

Another area of self-discovery that can impact our success is your personal learning style. Social scientists have known for ages that people learn differently. There are active learners who learn mostly by applying their new knowledge and doing something with it. Reflective learners prefer to think about what they have learned. Similar to the Myers Brigg types there are sensing learners and intuitive learners. Sensing learners like facts and figures, while the intuitive learners prefer possibilities. Some people are visual learners and learn by watching, while others learn by listening. I easily get bored listening to a teacher but can follow easily when there are slides and notes. I am likely a visual learner! What type of learner do you think you are? Does it make sense to you that it can be harder or easier to learn in some styles of classroom?

Personal Development History

Now that we have established a basic framework that was likely given to us at birth, you can now incorporate your own personal history as the next level in this model. As mentioned in the nature/nurture model, your upbringing can have an impact on your current situation however the nurture level should include your complete personal history rather than just your family upbringing. Your history of relationships, friendships, mentors, teachers and even your personal choices all form into a sense of who you are. Collectively, your conscious and unconscious memories form part of your personal history as do your unique set of interactions with other people. This personal history may include some relationships that were painful, joyful and everything in between. You may have ended relationships years ago, or have unresolved difficulties with certain people, or even are presently in long-term relationships, yet all of these form your personal history.

Other factors that contribute to your personal history are friends at various ages, your spiritual influences, mentors, teachers and your family background. While counseling theories have focused on family history, I believe it is equally important to understand the impact of childhood and teenage peer relationships as well as your circle of friends at various times.

Another major factor of your personal development is the culture that we were born into, as well as exposure to other cultures. Culture consists not only of race but also time, place, gender, age, and natural events. Each region of the country has its own regional history and characteristics. Someone who has grown up in a rural area will have a different experience of nature than someone who grew up in an inner city. Similarly, someone who has grown up in a smaller city will have a different development history than someone who grew up in a rural community or a large city.

Culture shapes us in many ways. It is also time dependent, as our laws and standards of social morals change with the decades. Growing up in the nineteen sixties was very different from growing up in the nineteen eighties. Your grandparents' experience may have been quite different from yours with careers expected to last a lifetime. Nowadays it is expected that you will have two or three different careers in your lifetime. Understanding the culture that you grew up in can help you understand why you do some things. Being aware of your own cultural experiences is important to understand the influence it has had on your development.

Daily Living, Emotions, Thoughts and Choices

The next level is a challenging level that many people never really look at! This level involves emotions, thoughts and choices. While you may naturally have strong feelings as the result of difficult times, and you may have troubling thoughts as a result of those emotions, most people don't really like looking at their choices and the fact that they can make changes. You don't have to be stuck with the feelings you have, nor the thoughts! It is also very difficult for people to accept some decisions they or others made in the past and forgive themselves or the other people involved. As discussed earlier, the advantage that you have over computers is that you can write and rewrite your own mental and emotional programs. While this layer of the model may feel threatening to some, it is also the key that gives you freedom!

The Presenting Me

How do you appear to others? As you move up the levels of our model, you reach what I call the presentation level. This refers to how you present yourself to others, how much you disclose to others, and how much of your personal history you share. It is also impacted by your degree of emotional health, as it is often difficult to share emotion if you have not dealt with the darker issues that you have buried away. Your presentation may be impacted by things such as unresolved losses and fears of intimacy. The lower layers of this model also will impact your presentation to others. Imagine how a child who is an extrovert will present him or herself to others, if the child's natural expression has been discouraged or even ridiculed. The true personality will not emerge due to a state of fear. Fortunately through your healing work, your true personality and gifts can reemerge!

Your Insightful Higher Self

Finally we reach the highest level of the model, the higher self, which may be the most intangible. This highest level represents a knowledge greater than yourself that includes the healing and symbolic messages in dreams, your intuition, and the synchronicity of life events that brings to the place where you need to be at a given time. It also includes your desire and motivation to do better and create a kinder world. When I started writing this portion of the book I had difficulty figuring out how to incorporate the concept of subconscious mind yet this answer came easily when I learned that our subconscious is impressionable and responds to our creative thoughts and ideas through meditation and positive thinking. Since it seems to be a force that is far more powerful than your personal nature or nurturing history, I found myself compelled to include it as a higher function that connects all of us to a consciousness that is greater than ourselves.

The Higher Self compels you to try to do better, to improve yourself and to make things right. It is the part of your spirit that recognizes when an improper compromise has been made, a relationship that doesn't feel right, or helps you recognize injustice. On a deeper existence, the Higher Self brings to you the lessons you need to learn over and over again until they are learned, tested, and became part of your way of being. The Higher Self is involved in synchronicity as well as helping you to remember important dreams, both the sleeping and waking daydreaming kind!

Who Can I Be?

In summary, people are different. You may want different things in friendships, relationships, careers and hobbies. Once you become aware of the differences, they are easier to identify in your relationships. With a greater understanding of what motivates people, you can increase your compassion and acceptance, and reduce your anger and frustration by accepting others without the expectation of having others behave the way you would like them to. You can learn to let people be themselves.

As with any model, there has to be a purpose in creating it. I hope that you will have developed a greater understanding of yourself by going deeper than a simple model of nature/nurture. Also, I believe it is important to understand as much as possible about yourself so that you can make informed choices! In looking into your own situation you can look at what you can change and what level needs work. A person who last lost connection with his or her higher self is in just as much trouble as someone who has denied the pain of their past. I have learned that restored faith and believing that things will work out is just as important as understanding and working through difficult emotions or thoughts patterns.

In the last few years I have also learned that I can be much more than I currently am and that my history does not necessarily determine who or what I can be, although I can recognize my personal limitations. I think this is a sign of good mental health. I don't get angry with myself or disappointed when I realize I don't have a particular talent. I know I am not good at sports, but I am a good listener and have a good singing voice. More importantly, by learning about and acknowledging my past, my personal traits and the choices I have made, I can grow into the person I really can be, regardless of the messages I may have received as a child or young adult! Essentially, I begin to accept the past, and begin coaching myself in the present moment!

One of your life challenges is to rise above the narrow view that you can easily develop when you are immersed in your own culture and family upbringing. There is a Chinese phrase "zuojing-guantian" which means "Sitting in a well and looking at the sky, you will have a narrow perspective." The definition and wisdom of these words goes on to say that "you need to see the trees and the landscape otherwise you will be restricted in what you see."

Edward Hall states "We can not thoroughly understand our minds until we experience another culture." When it comes to viewing problems, we should not do so "from the bottom of a well' but should rise up to another level. People who view the world from a limited perspective have no way of comprehensively and correctly perceiving the objective world.

A key to self-understanding is to learn how you talk to yourself. Try to develop an understanding of how your mind works, how you perceive things, places, and people, what beliefs you have, and what values you hold. As an exercise to understand yourself better, try drawing a timeline of your life so far, from your birth to present. Include major events as well as the things you did at each year. It is also helpful to map your happiness level at each stage in your life, as well as your spiritual satisfaction, emotional health and community!

5. Mind, Body, and Emotions!

Stress, Emotions and Physical Health

Time and time again you hear how your physical health is interconnected with your level of stress. How big a role then, does your emotional health play in your physical health? What happens to you if you do not allow yourself to release and, most importantly, resolve your emotions? What happens to your life expectancy? At various times in my own life, stressful periods have often been followed by times of muscle aches, lethargy, colds, or insomnia. Once the stress was dealt with, these symptoms disappeared. The latest research has shown a great number of links and trends between emotional expression and health.

For starters, hostile and cynical men and women tend to live shorter lives. This is not to say that people who experience anger can expect a shorter life, but those who do not resolve their anger and stay hostile have a shorter life expectancy than those who do resolve their anger! Many studies have shown a direct link between unresolved anger and heart disease. If we consider the physical responses that occur when someone is angry, it becomes easy to understand the strain placed on your heart when subjected to prolonged anger. When you are angry, your blood pressure increases and your heart muscles contract. If you remain angry, your heart is continually under this strain, which can lead to heart disease. Most doctors and nurses recognize that emotions play a large role in a patient's blood pressure and heart health.

Links between expressed emotion and glucose control in insulin-dependent diabetes have been identified, as well as a decrease in asthma, after crying. In animals, research has shown an inverse link between coping and tumor susceptibility.

In studies involving the bereaved, widowers showed a decrease in the functioning of the immune system. The immune suppression continued for as much as four months after the initial bereavement, eventually returning to normal with the expression of the grief. The results of the study suggested that those who express their grief are less likely to suffer from disease than those who hide their feelings and loss.

Even smoking can be linked to your emotional state. A recent study has shown that having a cigarette results in certain hormones being released in the brain. These are the same hormones that affect levels of depression. Smokers who cannot quit are more likely to be depressed. Not only does it seem that the nicotine is addictive, but a smoker who is feeling down will actually get a hormonal lift from having a cigarette! Doctors are now looking at helping these smokers kick the habit by alleviating the depression.

It has also been proposed that difficulties in experiencing anger and difficulty controlling intense emotions are factors that can pre-dispose you to depression and chronic pain. In an article summary for the Journal of Consulting and Clinical Psychology, the authors state, "Chronic pain and depression may be disturbances or failures to process intensely emotional information, with concomitant disturbances both in the body's immune system and in interpersonal relationships." In my own case, a period of considerable stress led to severe neck pain and tension. By using some vocal expression and relaxation techniques, I was able to reduce the tension and improve my health. Most of the problems were due to my lack of emotional expression, rather than any physical disease that could be diagnosed by my doctor!

It seems that suppressing emotions does affect your ability to fend off illness. Using energy to suppress your emotions results in a drain of the resources you normally use to fight colds and other health problems. With less energy you will be more susceptible to stress and fatigue. This explains the fact that when you are under stress, you often tend to get sick. Resolving emotional issues often brings about the reduction of health problems.

Allergies have been attributed to unresolved grief and the allergy symptoms have disappeared upon the release and resolution of the emotions. In my own case, allergy symptoms all but disappeared after the resolution of emotional issues. I now consider myself to be allergy free and enjoy the company of a wonderful cat!

Others have experienced changes in their body cycles once they began to face and express their bottled emotions. A close friend of mine began having regular menstrual periods after getting in touch with, releasing, and resolving some of her emotional issues.

In reviewing *Mind/Body Health* by Hafen, Karren, Frandsen and Smith, it is clear that there is a correlation between one's emotional state and accidents, allergies and asthma, arthritis, back pain, cancer, dental cavities, diabetes, hypertension, insomnia, irritable bowel syndrome and many other syndromes and maladies. However, telling you that emotions play a big role in your disease does not help you cope with your disease, nor does it help you get better or deal with your emotions. It is important to note that a correlation indicates only that one variable changes as the other variable changes. I remember reading in my statistics course of a study that showed a correlation between the stork population of Greenland and the North American birth rate! Although two variables may show a correlation, it cannot be assumed that the presence of one variable is the cause of the change in the other variable. Other factors or causes may be at work.

When discussing emotions and health issues we want to take care in realistically identifying the true causes of illness. Recently we have become more aware of the role that your psychological state plays in your health. Conversely, doctors have sometimes blamed illness on your psychological state when no cause for symptoms can be found. For many years, women had their diagnosis of Chronic Fatigue Syndrome dismissed as psychological, yet we now know that this syndrome has clear markers such as changed levels of melatonin. If you review the history of treating ulcers, you find that for many years ulcers were blamed on stress. While stress may have been one factor, the presence of bacteria is now known as the cause of stomach ulcers, which are now treated with appropriate antibiotics. In researching articles on emotion I came across a number of journal articles correlating emotional distress with breast cancer. I wonder if in a few years we will be describing how the correlation was simply that – not a cause of the disease as with ulcers.

We have learned through the work of Jonas Salk in the 1960's that illness is based on a multiple of relationships such as genetics, behavior, and the nervous and immune systems. Instead of looking at the causes of diseases as a simplistic model, we can now understand that they can have a number of interrelated causes. We therefore want to be careful and state that unresolved emotions are not necessarily the sole cause of the allergies, asthma, illness, or health problems. Even if stress is contributing to the health problems, this information does not seem to help patients, as it only seems to induce a sense of guilt and implies that you could whisk away the disease simply by immediately dealing with your stress. While the addition of emotional stress is likely to bring on a stronger allergic reaction or an attack of asthma, you must have compassion for those who are ill, not judge them because a study shows a correlation. Hopefully dealing with the emotional component, you can reduce some of the factors contributing to the illness.

The Healing Brain

One of the most interesting books I have come across is *The Healing Brain, a Scientific Reader.* This collection of articles regarding the brain contains a chapter titled *The Brain as a Health Maintenance Organization.* Authors Robert Ornstein and David S. Sobel write, "We need to recognize that the brain is not primarily for educating, not for speaking and thinking, but it is more like a gland, part of the body and a system to the mind and body."

Your brain works to maintain stability in countless subsystems. It controls the beating of your heart, blood pressure, the expansion and contraction of your lungs to provide your body with needed oxygen, the transfer of oxygen into your blood stream. Your brain also controls an internal pharmaceutical system, maintaining thousands of chemicals in your body. It keeps you from danger, holds you close to friends and family. It creates dreams for you, many of which can be analyzed to solve problems, and guides you through various life crises. It is also interesting to note that over ninety percent of what we know about the brain has been learned in the last ten years.

What we do know is that the brain spends a minimal amount of time on conscious functions such as preparing for communication, processing music, organizing, writing, cooking, balancing the check book or preparing for other human activities. The brain spends most of its time maintaining balance in a changing environment. The body and brain must continually adapt to change. As an individual, you are always growing emotionally, spiritually and in knowledge, and the brain must adapt and deal with these changes. The brain therefore, is attempting to maintain stability during an ongoing process of change.

To understand the brain we need to recognize that the brain can be considered as one large gland, which under various influences, attempts to return to a state of equilibrium. If we experience an event that triggers an emotional response, the brain will attempt to return to a state of equilibrium through a number of actions. These actions include the release of emotional energy through crying, laughing, trembling, blushing, increased muscle tension, or a host of other forms of energy release.

The brain consists of numerous subsystems that manage this change. Science is just beginning to obtain a grasp of the complexity and inner workings of these systems. Obviously, with the new discoveries we are making about the brain and its resistance to disease, we are at the beginning of a new era of medicine and healing. We are also more aware of the role hope plays in the health of an individual. Ornstein and Sobel also write, "Recent discoveries about endorphin, immune and cardiovascular systems, combined with new studies of brain physiology, human evolution and cognitive psychology point to a new understanding of this most mysterious organ...."

Besides being an organ that regulates and maintains our bodies, the brain is a fantastic agent of healing. It restores you to health after an injury. Almost magically, your body will heal from a cut or an infection. It protects you when the injury is severe by shutting down some systems. It is a healing brain. But the healing work that the brain does is not limited to physical injury alone. When you allow yourself to grieve a loss your brain allows you to heal from the loss. When you proceed through the emotional process of letting go, you return to a state of stability, but with less pressure on your system.

Ornstein and Sobel conclude that, "Healing does not merely restore the mind or body to its condition before the illness, but more usually it brings about a lasting change." It is a fact that even the most primitive organisms possess the ability to self-heal. While much attention has been focused on medical cures and medications, it may also be reasonable to focus more on your capacity to heal that exists at every level of evolution. This ability to heal is present in all living things. Although healing can be considered to be the process of repairing physical or emotional damage, there is often a greater aspect to the repairing process. Healing brings about a permanent change in the person or organism that allows you to cope with new situations. Focusing on the mind and body's natural ability to heal in the next stages of research is certainly warranted.

A new field that studies how the body and mind interact in healing is psychoneuroimmunology. This field is beginning to understand the relationships between neurons, synapses, neuropeptides, and cells that form the body's communication network. This field of study is learning that the brain, glands and immune system are joined and interlinked with one another. It is a bi-directional network of communication. It is now known that neurons communicate with one another through neuropeptides. The neuropeptides can produce effects in regions of the body that are different and far away from the location of the neuron that produced the neuropeptide.

We are beginning to learn that emotions do not just occur in the brain, but are linked to the whole body. This explains or correlates with the idea of a "gut feeling", that your emotional state is often reflected in your eyes, or that an emotional experience may trigger a shortness of breath. Many fields of holistic medicine focus on the whole body and mind when treating various illnesses. A sense of the body as a whole is beginning to develop in the research into healing and immunology. Instead of focusing on the area of injury, the body, mind and person must be treated as a whole. This form of treatment has been the basis of treatments such as acupuncture, massage and various other forms of healing.

Until recently, the idea that emotions can build up has never been proven by science. We are learning that emotional trauma has significant effects on the body's chemistry and that emotional expression brings about change in the body and mind state. The latest scientific research has identified a number of communication systems in the body that tend to support the notion of emotions occurring as a whole body experience. In *The Body Keeps Score: Memory and the Evolving Psychobiology of Post traumatic Stress*, Bessel A. Van der Kolk M.D.

describes some of the effects of trauma on the chemical and hormone levels in the body. It is now understood that emotional trauma brings about long lasting changes in body chemistry. I believe that one day scientists will prove that emotions are in fact stored in the body through changes in energy, chemical balance and muscle tone.

In a discussion of holistic medicine, Dr. Leo Roy stated "An emotional trauma can do more damage to the liver than six months of drinking." Our emotional traumas and hurts can be felt throughout the whole body. Muscle tension, a knotting in the stomach, backaches, high blood pressure, and sugar levels are all affected by your emotional state. Should you suppress or avoid your emotions, you end up placing pressure on your body to cope with an emotional imbalance. Expression and resolution will assist in your returning to a more balanced state. Perhaps the intrusive flashbacks, somatic symptoms, dreams and emotional distress are clues the mind presents to us to alert you to your need to do some healing work.

In working through issues you discover that your human experience is far greater than you can currently measure. As many massage therapists and other healing profession workers have found, we seem to have an energy system that responds to touch and other forms of hands on healing. We also have the subconscious or as some call it, a divine state, that sends us key answers in your dreams. Within you is a force that helps you, in its own mysterious ways, to solve your problems. While trauma and pain do harm you, you have a fundamental ability to direct your mind and body towards healing. When you do this, a powerful force kicks in to guide you and accelerate your healing. With a commitment to heal that makes use of all your resources, you begin a process that can result in dramatic and seemingly impossible changes in your life. Holistic healing acknowledges all aspects of your humanity.

The Benefits of Expression

Having looked at adverse effects of emotional stress on our health, let's begin to look at the positive outcomes of letting your emotions take their natural course. As mentioned earlier, tears are a natural response to a loss or emotional injury as well as the gift of joy. A great number of chemicals and hormones are released through your tears when you cry or laugh. Even the verbalization of your fears and anxiety can help in improving outlook and coping. A study of women with breast cancer found that those who articulated their feelings decreased their anguish and experienced increased optimism. In *It's Never Too Late to Have a Happy Childhood*, author Claudia Black writes, "Where there is loss there are tears; tears are the elixir of recovery." As with any expressive therapy, it is important to balance your thinking and behavior and avoid the pitfall of indulging in the expression and hiding in the expression rather than moving on. With the breast cancer patients, it was found that those who continually used this coping strategy of emotional expression increased their anguish later in the treatment program. It is then with a word of caution that we examine emotional expression as a singular healing tool. As discussed in this book, you need to make sure that you focus on all three aspects of emotional expression, behavior modification and restructuring your thinking! All three are necessary for healing!

Healing through Laughter

In creating a therapeutic group climate for elders, laughter is one of the top ten components. It is not possible to be depressed when you are laughing. Laughter brings about chemical changes in your body that help you fight illness and disease. One of the classic tales of curing illness by laughter is told in Norman Cousins' book *Anatomy of an Illness*. Cousins had been diagnosed with a fatal illness. He cured himself by booking himself into a hotel room, sending out for Marx Brothers movies, and watching segments of Candid Camera. Cousins' pain diminished and as he says "The more I laughed, the better I got."

Laughter has been credited with restoring balance in the body, returning blood pressure to normal, bringing about relaxation, and improving circulation. Studies also link improved respiration and heart rates to the benefits of laughter. An article called "Laughter and Health" published as early as 1928, the doctor described "laboratory evidence which established that a hearty, throaty laugh momentarily compensates for either high or low blood pressure."

In another study, two groups of college students were fed the same diet. One group of students was treated to lectures by a professional comedian, while the other group was treated to scientific lectures. Not surprisingly, the results of the test showed that the students who experienced the comedy routine at lunchtime were healthier, with a noticeable improvement in digestion.

In the journal abstract for *Laughter: Nature's Epileptoid Catharsis*, by Gerard Grumet, states that the article "depicts laughter as a symbolic triggered release mechanism that unleashes instinctive drive energies associated with survival and lowers anxiety in the process." However, another study I came across described how being able to laugh at yourself produced a far better health change than laughter that was directed at another's expense. It seems it is important not only how often you laugh but whether there is mutual respect and good intention!

The Healing Power of Tears

Shakespeare understood the power of tears when he wrote "To weep is to make less the depth of grief." In recent years, scientists have been proving that tears are beneficial to our health and well-being. My own personal experience has proven this time and time again. Scientists have known for over 35 years that emotional tears are different from tears produced as a result of peeling an onion. Tears released on account of emotions contain more protein as well as one of the body's most powerful pain killers - beta-endorphin.

Dr. William Frey of the Dry Eye and Tear Research Center states that people who cry "may be removing, in their tears, chemicals that build up during emotional stress." Dr. Alan Wolfelt of the University of Colorado Medical School states, "In my clinical experience with thousands of mourners, I have observed physical changes following the expression of tears. Not only do people feel better after crying; they also look better." I'm sure that Dr. Wolfelt meant that the clients looked better after they had cleaned up their mascara! In *The Brain as a Health Maintenance Organization*, authors Robert Ornstein and David S. Sobel respond to the question of why people cry. The authors state that recent evidence implies that crying "may be a way in which the body disposes of toxic substances." Many people believe that crying helps them to reduce tension. In the long run, a good cry makes them feel better.

Researchers at the State University of New York at Buffalo have also found that crying is common among emotionally healthy adults and that crying is not necessarily a symptom of depression. In a study of people in their late sixties, researchers found that the adults had a good cry every two or three weeks. The main reasons for crying were simply to reduce feelings of stress. In a study by the University of Pittsburgh, it was documented that there is a definite correlation between stress-related illness and a reluctance to cry. Scientists are now learning that crying seems to reduce stress levels and increase your level of health.

Tears have also been known to bring about changes in the behavior of people, even children, with seemingly disturbed behavior patterns. An article in the *International Review of Psycho-Analysis* describes how a child, completely withdrawn and with a destructive behavior pattern, broke out into a weeping fit in one of her therapy sessions. These weeping fits, which contained feelings of rage, despair and sorrow, continued for a number of sessions during which a change in the character of her appearance as well as in her behavior began. The article suggests that the release of tears was the first phase of her psychotherapy.

Other benefits of tears have been identified as well. In addition to reducing asthma attacks, studies have indicated that crying seems to reduce the occurrence of hives. After crying in therapy sessions, patients have lower blood pressure, lower body temperatures, and more synchronized brain wave patterns, as well as notable psychological improvements. In fact, the benefits of crying have been scientifically known for almost a century. A study by Borquist in 1906 reported that 54 out of 57 respondents believed that crying had positive results. A study by Weiner found that asthma attacks, which were for a long time thought to be psychosomatic, ceased as a result of crying.

The belief that crying has positive effects was developed over two thousand years ago. Aristotle believed that crying could cleanse the mind through a process of catharsis. Catharsis is a means of reducing emotional stress through the expression of emotion. Many others have echoed Aristotle's thoughts. Suggestions regarding the benefits of catharsis can be found in a variety of sources – from aboriginal literature to the writings of Freud. Aristotle believed that theater and drama serve a useful purpose in catharsis. Sobel and Ornstein write, "Many people attend movies and plays that they know beforehand are, shall we say, elicitors of psychogenic lacrimation, or tearjerkers." People may often feel comfortable crying during a movie and not experience any embarrassment or regret, knowing that the tears bring benefits.

Although we know that chemicals are present in the emotional tears, we are still attempting to fully understand what function the release of these chemicals serve. Some of the chemicals such as beta-endorphins are responsible for relieving pain. In the literal sense, crying and sobbing may actually be cleansing the mind, thus validating the original theory of catharsis. Perhaps tears and crying are the body's mechanism for releasing emotional tension and for restoring the body to a state of equilibrium.

In addition to the release of tears, crying results in a number of physiological processes. Although a person in the stages of grief may show less facial expression and muscle tone, facial tension actually is increased. In a study of facial expression and tension, it was noted that facial tension increases in the forehead pulling the eyebrows together. Increased tension can also be found in the jaw and mouth, which results in a pulling down of the corners of the mouth. Your body releases a great deal of muscular tension when you cry. Sobbing with tears will cause a reflex that reduces and resolves the muscle tension associated with grief. Emotional release, often referred to as catharsis, will lead to a reduction in tension and previously observed effects virtually disappear.

Researchers are now focusing on contents of emotional tears and attempting to identify the content and purpose of these chemicals. With this new knowledge, it is certainly reasonable to conclude that emotional tears play a very important role and function in the emotional and physical health of the individual.

While crying may be a natural response to a hurt, for many of us it does not feel natural at all. Not all of us have been taught to feel comfortable with crying. In your childhood you may have been punished for crying rather than being rewarded. Most of us are unaware of the healing power of tears. Crying is the main action that helps you to release your suppressed emotions and heal. Although you may not be comfortable in admitting to crying, it is a natural response to hurt. To control or block your tears is to deny your body's natural method of releasing and healing. Although we know that tears release chemicals, no one knows what happens to those chemicals if you do not cry. We now know that crying is necessary for emotional healing. During my own process of catharsis and healing, I kept thinking that the tears I was releasing were somehow cleansing my body of the stresses that I had accumulated.

Many of you, however, are afraid of your tears. You may fear that if you start to cry, you will be unable to stop. I too felt a fear of losing control. However I reminded myself that for years I had exercised the discipline of keeping things under control and that I still had those skills. I also found that as the wave of emotion was approaching, it seemed much larger compared to the view I had of its size once it had passed! To give myself the courage to face it, I constantly reminded myself of the benefits that expression would bring.

Most of us need to re-learn that crying brings about healing. Fearful of tears, I began to learn and trust that crying actually soothes and brings about a reduction in stress. I discovered that when I was willing to let go and express my emotions, the stressful energy contained in them would dissipate and pass. The more I expressed my emotions and examined the underlying ideas, the less each day's events were clouded by past events that I had not resolved.

Crying is a natural process by which we can release the energy in your emotions. It restores your mind and body to a more natural balance. When you suppress your tears you end up using a great deal of energy to hold down or keep that energy at bay. You may feel as though you have stopped the tears, but what you have really done is pushed the tears and hurt into your subconscious. The feelings are not dealt with and the suppression ends up blocking your ability to feel joy and companionship.

With the release of chemicals through tears, your body heals emotionally and you become more emotionally healthy. Having resolved the emotional tension you tend to be less isolated, since you no longer need to keep others at a distance fearing that you will break down emotionally. Being able to tolerate emotions in others, you are able to express yourself more openly and to listen to others without the fear of old injuries being restimulated.

There are still many things to be learned about the various balances that occur in your body. It is certain though, that suppressing your emotions stops the natural healing process of your body. Repressing your emotions can lead to isolation, a reduction of clarity of thought, and reduced tolerance for emotions in others. Grief, for one, is a very isolating emotion. Fortunately, these symptoms are not permanent and you can be restored through emotional expression and the healing power of tears.

You may feel that you need to develop courage to face your feelings. Upon reflection you will realize that you have had the strength and courage all along. You survived the original event, and have had the strength to suppress your pain. You can learn to be more conscious of everything that is happening in the moment and not run from your emotions. You can heal the fragments of your life that need to be brought into the wholeness of your being and begin to feel alive again! When did you last cry? When did you last laugh? Think of a time you felt safe, when it was ok to cry. If you have never had this feeling, you have the power to create it now!

Expression and Self Esteem

As mentioned earlier, babies seem to have an unrepressed ability to express emotions and discharge. Recent studies have even shown that babies as young as twelve months can read and respond to actors' emotions on TV. The babies responded to facial expressions and were aware of negative emotions. However, depending on your upbringing or due to events in your life, you may have developed a conditioned response of ignoring your emotions and trying to avoid your pain.

In his book *The Six Pillars of Self Esteem*, Nathaniel Brandon says that to deny your emotions usually results in a loss of self-esteem. This occurs whether you are a child or an adult. Denying your emotions causes you to lose contact with your inner self and your ability to care for your soul. It is your soul that makes you human and you are most human when you find a deep connection with your soul. I have since learned that denying how I was feeling about my troubles obscured my sense of self, which I have now recovered!

In *Care of the Soul*, Thomas Moore writes, "Soul is not a thing, but a quality or a dimension of experiencing life and ourselves." Your soul can be defined as that which holds your values, beliefs, and center of being. In caring for your soul you must know how your soul expresses itself and you must be able to observe and be connected with it. Moore also writes, "We cannot care for the soul unless we are familiar with its ways." To be familiar with your soul involves fully experiencing life and observing your reactions to it.

Life is a process of encounters which are often viewed as either positive or negative. Often you try to avoid the negative issues and feelings in your life, but in doing so, you miss valuable lessons to be learned. Moore states: "When people observe the ways in which the soul is manifesting itself, they are enriched rather than impoverished." To listen to your soul, especially in times of trouble, brings great rewards. Facing the part of yourself that you fear the most is often what you must do to free yourself of pain and sadness. Being open to the pain of the soul brings awareness of yourself and helps you eventually form solutions to your problems. Solving those problems brings about an internal strength that you can carry forward with you. As Moore writes "When you regard the soul with an open mind, you begin to find the messages that lie within the illness, the corrections that can be found in remorse and other uncomfortable feelings, and the necessary changes requested by depression and anxiety."

It truly is a myth that you can completely control your thoughts and feelings. As you are reading this, please do not think of a pink elephant. What did you just visualize? A pink elephant! Even as I'm writing this, an image of a pink elephant came into my head. Ahhhhh! As I said, it is very difficult to control our thoughts! It is possible though, to tame or train your mind to respond more calmly, and this can be learned through meditation. Training, however, is different from controlling in that training provides a set of learned, acceptable behaviors while controlling attempts to force a condition onto an untrained mind. Certain Buddhist practices use the analogy of the mind consisting of twelve monkeys all attached by leashes to a pole. If the monkeys run free, then there is chaos, confusion and entanglement, but if you can teach the monkeys to sit still, then there is calm, serenity and order. While it is next to impossible to maintain total control over your mind, increasing your ability from a negligible degree of control to a slightly higher degree of discipline can greatly improve your daily living habits. The saying "Practice makes perfect" should be replaced with "Practice makes permanence!"

For a long time I believed that I could control my feelings. The price I paid was high. There are certain behaviors and things you can do for yourself to improve your emotional state, but this is different from accepting the thoughts and feelings that come into your consciousness. By attempting to selectively control your thoughts and emotions you block access to your soul. You need to let your soul be free to express itself. What you can control is your behavior around these emotions and thoughts.

Currently there are many techniques and seminars aimed at providing a quick fix for emotional problems. While some of these techniques seem to provide a reprieve, many are not long lasting, as the original problem has not been dealt with. In *The Power of Positive Thinking*, Norman Vincent Peale states, "It is important to discover why you have these feelings... That requires analysis and will take time. We must approach the maladies of our emotional life as a physician probes to find something wrong physically. This cannot be done immediately."

Peale importantly states, "An excellent and normal release from heartache is to give way to grief. In many cultures, the expression and showing of grief is considered to be embarrassing and is discouraged. It may be considered foolish to express yourself through the expression of tears or sobbing. This, however, is a violation of your natural mechanism for the release of emotional tension and pain. As Peale says, "This is a denial of the law of nature. It is natural to cry when pain or sorrow comes. It is a relief mechanism provided in the body by Almighty God and should be used." To restrain emotion, to suppress it, or to inhibit it is to rob yourself of your natural means for eliminating the pressure of life. To deny your emotions is similar to denying that you must eat and drink to nourish yourself. As with other needs, you must not indulge in them, but you must not deny them altogether. Peale states, "A good cry by either man or woman is a release from heartache."

I have personally warmed to the concept that life challenges are very much like a meal. We take in food, process it and discharge what we do not need, while at the same time, the body is nourished. Life challenges are similar, in that there is pain that you need to express through tears and other forms of expression, but there is also nourishment in new understanding and wisdom gained from your challenges.

In this chapter we have discussed the concepts of the physical body and its powerful ability to heal. It is also important to recognize that you must heal the physiology of emotions but also your "minds." When writing "minds" I am referring to the various aspects of mind as describe by Yogi Ramacharaka in his book Yogi Philosophies. Most reactions of the human race have been in response to the conditioning of instinctive mind -the mind that either fights or runs from a threat. Human beings possess mind powers that are greater than the animal world. We aslo possess an intellectual mind that is aware of itself as a person and aware of other people. This mind holds your belief system. The Yogis refer to even higher levels of mind, such as the spritual mind. Ramacharaka describes the spiritual mind as "becoming conscious of a higher 'Something Within,' which leads them up to higher and nobler thoughts, desires, aspirations, and deeds." Finally, Ramacharaka describes the highest level of mind as "the Real Self. Words cannot express it. Our minds fail to grasp it. It is the soul of the Soul. To understand it we must understand God, for Spirit is a drop from the Spirit Ocean." Your healing journey will take you through all the levels of mind! Tears are just the first step.

CRY (IF YOU WANT TO)

Cry if you want to I won't tell you not to
I won't try to cheer you up I'll just be here if you want me
It's no use in keeping a stiff upper lip
You can weep you can sleep you can loosen your grip
You can frown you can drown, and go down with the ship
You can cry if you want to

Don't even apologize for venting your pain
It's something that to me you don't need to explain
I don't need to know why. I don't think it's insane
You can cry if you want to

The windows are closed. The neighbors aren't home
If it's better with me than to do it alone
I can draw all the curtains and unplug the phone
You can cry if you want to

You can stare at the ceiling and tear at your hair
You can swallow your feelings and swagger and swear
You can throw things and show things and I wouldn't care
You can cry if you want to

I won't make fun of you I won't tell anyone
I won't analyze what you do or you should've done
I won't advise you to go and have fun
You can cry if you want to.

I can't make it all go away
I don't have any answers I've nothing to say
But I'm not going to lie to you and say it's okay
You can cry if you want to

Cry if you want to I won't tell you not to
I won't try to cheer you up
I'll just be here if you want me to be near you -Maybe I'll cry too!

Written by Casey Scott, Copyright 1993 SignalSongs/Tainjo Thang (ASCAP)
All Rights Reserved/Used by Permission

Part Two - Insight

6. Depression – Many Meanings, Many Causes

The Nature of Depression

Everyone gets depressed at some time or another. It is a fact of life. Although often labeled as an illness, depression can be a normal reaction to various events that occur in your life. Depression is something that hits almost all of us one time or another. Just as there are many types of losses, there are many causes for depression. It is important to stress the fact that depression can be natural response to these occurrences and it is normally a transient mental state that will be resolved. Those who experience long-term depression may find that their immune system is weakened. As a result, these people are less likely to be able to fight off infections and cancers. It is important then to try to heal depression so that health and immunity will be restored.

In surveying the discussion groups on the Internet, I found that one of the busiest newsgroups was the support group for depression. On my own website that provided information on a variety of mental health topics, depression was the most frequently accessed topic. In the newsgroup people exchanged information on medication, side effects, signs of depression, and things that facilitated the resolution of a depression. Many provided encouragement for others, and for some it was a chance to express themselves. The number of postings to this group gives an indication of the number of people who are affected at one time or another by depression. These individuals report lowered spirits, a loss of self-esteem, difficulty sleeping, and a difference in perspective. Other symptoms may include a loss of energy, weight loss or gain, changes in appetite, and physical complaints, without any medical basis.

Depression can be severe and challenging. Diagnosis is sometimes elusive. Andrew Solomon writes "Depression is a condition that is almost unimaginable to anyone who has not known it. A sequence of metaphors—vines, trees, cliffs, etc.—is the only way to talk about the experience. It's not an easy diagnosis because it depends on metaphors, and the metaphors one patient chooses are different from those selected by another patient."

The cost of depression is staggering. Counseling, therapy, medication, emotional struggles, and absenteeism from work all add up to huge financial costs, let alone the toll it takes on the people who experience depression. Psychologists and health professionals are now also aware of the concept of "presenteeism", where people are able to come to work and are present, but unable to fully function.

Types of Depression

Generally speaking, there are two types of depression that the fields of psychiatry and psychology try to treat. The first type is called an organic depression that usually is the result of an imbalance of chemicals in the brain. The second type of depression is called a reactive or situational depression that is usually a result of unresolved life experiences or an emotional trauma.

Some of you may have an organic depression that can be treated with medication, while some of you may have a non-organic or situational depression caused by personal traumas, losses, or unmet needs as described above. In some cases it may be a combination of organic and non-organic depression. Medications are often used to treat organic depression, while counseling and therapy, and self-help books like this one can help you to resolve a non-organic depression.

While there are two types of depression, the psychiatric medical community uses the guidelines of the Diagnostic and Statistical Manual of Mental Disorders as a tool for diagnosing depression. The nine symptoms listed in the manual are depressed mood, diminished pleasure, increased or decreased appetite, disturbed sleeping patterns, lack of co-ordination, fatigue, feelings of worthlessness, and diminished ability to concentrate. The manual suggests that for a diagnosis of depression, five or more of the symptoms should be present for more than two weeks. As we can see from the list, almost everyone will experience depression in his or her lifetime!

Regardless of whether you have an organic or situational depression, there is cause for concern in the practice of using medication for depression. Numerous articles have been published on the serious side effects of anti-depressants, as well as dangers in prescribing these medications to teens and children. While I would not advocate stopping medication, it is important to try to look at the life circumstances that may have led to the depression and to remember that for those without a serious medical depression, anti-depressants were originally meant to be considered as a short-term treatment combined with therapy. Most of the science around the anti-depressants focuses on the chemicals being transmitted and the alteration of the levels of these chemicals and hormones as the solution to depression. You have to wonder if it is the chemicals and hormones that create our thoughts, or if it is our thoughts and feelings that impact the level of these chemicals and hormones. What is important is that you seek help and understanding and allow yourself to explore the areas of your life that need healing. There is definitely value to having these medications available, as they can in the short run help stabilize and help one get back on one's feet. Antidepressants can be the kind of help that you may need for a short time while you regain a sense of being able to cope and help yourself.

The Metaphors of Depression

It is also important to understand the metaphors used to describe depression. I learned from my friend Sonya Pritzker that in Chinese culture, the symbol of two trees is used to represent depression. Sonya has written an excellent article titled *"The Role of Metaphor in Culture, Consciousness and Medicine."* We met while I was visiting a Buddhist temple where she was volunteering for a survey on depression. Her article describes how the symbol of two trees represents a forest. From within a thick forest, you can comprehend the sense of darkness, being unable to see a path, a canopy of growth blocking the light, and an inability to move freely because of the thick growth. Other metaphors she describes include falling down, darkness and lack of control.

Sonya writes "The concepts of darkness, lack of movement, and falling down can all be subsumed under the conceptual metaphor 'Depression is Down.' Being down is associated with sleep, or darkness, and when we are down, as in for sleep or rest, we are not moving. The journey that is life is restricted when we do not, or cannot, move." She goes on to say "Depression in the English language has many meanings. The American Heritage Dictionary (1992) lists nine definitions of depression, only one of which is the formal psychological definition. Another describes a similar condition of "sadness or despair." Others include "an area that is sunk below its surrounding; a hollow"; "a reduction in physiological vigor or activity"; and "a period of drastic decline in national or international economy", among others. Clearly, the metaphorical implications in these definitions point to the understanding in English-speaking culture of depression as a lack of activity, a state of being below or less than normal."

While we often think of depression as "feeling down" it can also manifest itself in a raised state of energy. Sonya writes "the clinical definition also includes symptoms one might not expect to see if metaphorical thinking were restricted to the notion of being 'down.' The symptoms are more restless, and include possible increase in appetite, insomnia, psychomotor agitation, and suicidal plans or thoughts. These symptoms point more towards the 'lack of control' metaphor."

Sonya makes a good point about the individual experience of depression as "The diagnostic guidelines…stipulate that an individual suffering from five or more of the above nine symptoms for a two week period or longer is clinically depressed. This makes it possible for each suffering individual to manifest differently, but within certain bounds. The conceptual metaphors implicated in the clinical definition are thus relatively flexible, allowing for the emotions associated with sadness, fear, and anxiety to manifest to varying degrees in depression."

Causes of Depression

Just as there are many definitions for depression, it seems that depression can result from a great number of factors. Any process of change (such as growing up) involves change and transition. Depression can occur as a result of a loss, a success, achieving a goal, a physical injury, a personal trauma, or simply as a result of a build up of daily events. Change of any type, be it geographical location, lifestyle, daily routine or contact with others can be a contributing factor in depression. Any loss of someone or something of value can be a catalyst for depression.

Other causes of depression are:
- a process of transition
- a job change
- poor thinking patterns
- lack of direction in life
- achieving adulthood
- discovering that life isn't measuring up to what you would like it to be
- unresolved grief
- a sense of helplessness
- an unfulfilling job
- beliefs you hold about yourself that keep limiting your self-esteem

One of the causes of depression in adult children is a sense of learned helplessness. You may have grown up in a family in which you did not have any power to effect change in your situation. For years it seemed as though you had to accept the decisions and behaviors of others, and that nothing you did mattered. This ongoing situation tends to instill a sense of helplessness later in life. One of the ways out of depression is to identify areas in which you can make changes. Fortunately, the helplessness is only a learned behavior. It can be replaced with the new attitude that you can make positive changes in your life.

Depression can also be caused by rumination. Often a feeling of sadness or hurt will be created by your personal belief systems, which may add to feelings of hurt from the past. Depression may also result from a lack of short-term goals. While self-analysis can be beneficial, self-absorption can cause you to lose your ability to also focus on others. There is an Irish proverb that says "You don't plow a field by turning it over in your mind!" While some evaluation is necessary, too much rumination can lead you into a spiral of self-absorption rather than being able to see the world around you.

Long-term depression can be the result of problems in a person's thinking and attitudes, while unresolved issues and trauma can prolong sadness resulting from the event. People who have avoided feelings or who are suffering from a significant loss may be characterized as depressed, yet it is grieving work that the individual may need to complete to resolve the sadness. In some cases, the events may be difficult to identify because the person has avoided their feelings and has not become appropriately and sufficiently upset by the events. A chronic feeling of sadness may also be indicative of the fact that certain areas of a person's life need changing. Some people may have an unsatisfying job or difficulties relating to others. Without resolution or positive change, the sadness will be an ongoing component of their lives. In the cases of earlier abuse, the depression may be the result of a wound to the individual's character or soul, which requires a process of grieving, self-acceptance and healing to resolve the depression.

From the above, we can conclude that the causes of depression are numerous. As well, there are some generalities about depression that should be examined. Depression has sometimes been described as anger turned inwards, but it is not fair to say that all depressions are the result of unexpressed anger. In labeling the depression as a disease, some may feel powerless to resolve the depression while they might be able to learn some behaviors that will naturally raise chemical levels in the brain. This area of research is so new that the effect on the brain of "healthy pleasures" such as singing, meditation, yoga, and physical exercise are not yet understood or measured.

The Value of Process

The process of life in itself often involves re-evaluating our beliefs and values. The process of developing these values may seem like a depression. Each transition or change involves letting go of something and accepting something new. In *The Secret Strength of Depression*, Dr. Frederich Flach writes "in order to move successfully from one phase to the next, a person must be able to experience depression in a direct and meaningful way." There was a period after completing my master's degree that I entered a very deep depression. I felt overwhelmed by the level of student debt I was experiencing, and the financial difficulties I was trying to resolve, while at the same time re-establishing my social life. Through the process of feeling and working through my depression, I learned how shaky my faith was in trusting that things would work out, and realized that despite feeling lonely, I had a number of friends who cared deeply about me. I also let go of some friendships that were not serving me. It became a time of cleaning house. At the time I was having a recurring dream of kittens being discovered in the basement, which had gone undetected for some period of time. As I moved through my depression and made sense of the fact that I had some new lessons to learn, the kittens became healthier and healthier in my dream each time I rediscovered them. While it took some time to work through this, I made great progress in learning that I needed to help myself.

One of the drawbacks to our current description of depression is that many professionals do not differentiate between depression and ongoing sadness as a result of unresolved grief or loss. The term depression is a wide, sweeping term used to describe a condition that has numerous causes. Just as the Eskimos have over thirty different words for types of snow; it would be helpful to expand the range of words to describe depression. Growing up in a cold northern climate, I know that there really are different types of snow: light flakes, heavy flakes, packed snow, wet, sticky, slushy, crunchy, and ice covered. Powdery snow is what the avid skiers love but it is usually only found at the highest peaks! Perhaps we can all learn to be more detailed in describing depression. Here are just a few words to help you be more specific. Which words might you use to describe the sensation of depression?

tired	lonely	isolated
burnt out	numb	lethargic
uninspired	fearful	uncertain
weary	tearful	stuck
hurt	let-down	disappointed

Although a time of depression is not an easy period for anyone, it can be a time of tremendous change and growth. As Dr. Flach writes, "to experience acute depression is an opportunity for a person not just to learn more about himself, but to become more whole than he was. Not only does depression afford a chance for insight, but 'falling apart' can accelerate the process of reordering one's life after a serious stress."

Although depression reduces vitality and makes it difficult to find solutions to problems, there are benefits to depression. Often, creative people will attribute the creation of their work to an episode of depression. Many individuals who have made significant life changes also attribute the changes they made to periods of depression. Often these people will emerge from a depression with a new and exciting view of life. Similar to the idea of the phoenix that crashes into the fire yet emerges as a beautiful new bird, a depression that is experienced and resolved allows us to rebound to new levels of understanding and meaning. Dr. Flach writes, "to be creative in any sense, a person must be able to relinquish old and fixed assumptions that block a fresh appraisal of a situation." Perhaps to be creative also involves being open to the experience of moving through a depression.

Perhaps as a society we need to challenge our view of mental health. Society has generally viewed the happy-go-lucky person as the well-adjusted person. Now we are gaining the understanding that episodes of depression are a natural part of life and growth. Perhaps the person who gets angry, cries, laughs or gets embarrassed, and who works through a depression, is the well-adjusted person. In an Internet posting on the topic of depression, an individual posed the question, "When will I be normal again?" Perhaps a better line of reasoning might be "I am depressed. I am normal. How long will this last?"

7. Hiding from the Real You!

The Masks You Wear

One technique that people use to maintain a degree of emotional safety is to wear an emotional mask. We end up becoming skilled actors or actresses in maintaining a front to others. Often people are seen as happy-go-lucky, yet they are hurting inside and too afraid to let others know what they are really thinking and feeling. In my childhood I became very skilled at hiding my hurt from others. It was a defense mechanism that saved me from additional shame and ridicule and that I carried into my adult life. In most cases, it is not because people wish to deceive anyone that they wear these masks, but simply because it is the best coping mechanism they have learned. As well, an emotional mask may also serve as a form of denial until the person is ready to face the issues that have brought about the emotional pain. While "denial" has often been thought of as a negative term, I truly believe that denial is simply a form of self-preservation since challenging one's beliefs and ideas can bring about confusion and instability in one's self-concept.

At times your masks were necessary to protect you and they may have been an appropriate defense at some time. These masks may no longer be effective tools for daily living and may now be harming or detracting from your enjoyment of life and sharing with others. To open up to another requires trust and courage, especially if you have been emotionally abused or humiliated by others who were in a position of authority or trust. To become an emotionally healthy person involves identifying your masks and beginning to come out from behind the mask with yourself and those you trust. Peeking out from behind the mask allows others to see you in a more open manner. The more you work at removing the mask, the more genuine you become. You are then able to form deeper connections with yourself and others. Which of the following masks do you use and which do you recognize as others' masks?

The Smiler

The smiler is a person who always seems to greet you with a happy face. They seem to be consistently up when you greet them, but their smile really masks their true feelings. When with closer friends, the smiler may let down their guard and confide some of their true feelings. With the appearance of an outsider, the mask will usually quickly reappear. While able to trust close friends, the smiler will maintain a front among most people. If asked how they are truly feeling, they might begin to honestly tell you, but would not likely be willing to face any pain they are feeling.

Polyanna-ism or Pronoid

Polyanna-ism refers to people who always seem extremely happy. They go around saying how wonderful all the rain is! Sometimes their excessively positive attitudes will begin to bother others. They never seem to get depressed and nothing seems to bother them. They may try to force their happiness onto others. In truth, they may be hurting deeply yet cannot show this side of themselves to others. Their behavior serves as a form of denial of the real pain that they cannot yet face.

Truly, it would be wonderful if you could maintain a life that would generate such a state of happiness, but life has its "ups and downs" and therefore most people, like yourself, have ups and downs too. There is a difference between a compensating positive outlook to avoid pain and a genuine positive outlook born out of a sense of freedom and choice. Life contains many issues that need to be worked on and resolved. Someone who is always up is not likely connected with their own feelings and issues. They are probably in a state of denial. The important question is whether their joy is genuine or a mask. Does this type of person have the ability to express and experience the wide range of emotions, or are they denying a side of their emotional spectrum and self?

As a form of denial, the pronoid will often mask pain by focusing on others. The pronoid will act in a manner that gives an impression of great concern for friends and co-workers. At times, however, when challenged emotionally, this mask of concern will show its cracks.

As an opposite of the paranoid, the pronoid often lives in a fantasy in which they overvalue themselves and overestimate their control of events in their lives. They may make statements about controlling their own destiny, and will attribute circumstantial occurrences to their well-developed sense of willpower.

In an article in the *Medical Ethics Journal*, psychologist Richard P. Benthal argues that the happiness syndrome is a mood disturbance. Dr. Benthal suggests that the pronoid is really out of touch with reality. The pronoid lives a tinted view in which, as Dr. Benthal states, "mere acquaintances are seen as close friends. Politeness and pleasantries are interpreted as deep friendships." The pronoid has difficulty expressing their true feelings about others and may be masking anger as well.

Mark Linden O'Meara

The Neutral/Flat Mask

An emotionally neutral person is someone who never seems to express any emotions at all. Their facial expression will remain mostly flat, with little smiling or expression of joy in their eyes. It is difficult to tell whether the emotionally neutral or flat person is up or down or anywhere in between, and rarely, if ever, does the neutral mask allow anger to be shown.

They have become very good at masking their emotions even if it is no longer intentional. This mask makes it difficult for them to experience closeness with others. A friend once told me that I was a repressed bundle of joy. I remember times when others in my family did not express joy and their faces seemed disconnected from their hearts. At the age of sixteen I got a phone call from my paper route supervisor informing me I had won a trip! I ran into the dining room and jumped up and down yelling "I won a trip to Florida! I won a trip to Florida!" I felt a sense of embarrassment when none of my brothers or even parents showed any reaction. I was greeted with absolute silence and absolutely no reaction or response. I learned at a subconscious level that showing joy was embarrassing and that there was no sharing of joy. These were their masks!

The Defensive Mask

Defensiveness is something you likely display when your beliefs or behavior are challenged. In some cases, you may even become defensive when someone tries to help you. While it usually results in frustration for the other party, a defensive mask serves the purpose of protecting you from hurt. The defensive person keeps others at a safe distance, thus preventing emotions and pain from surfacing. Often considered a form of denial, defensiveness is a way of communicating that the mask wearer is not ready to deal with the pain. To remove the mask requires a degree of trust and willingness to face some pain. Defensiveness often means "I don't want to get hurt."

The Victim Mask

The person wearing the victim mask is someone who often talks about his or her problems but does not achieve resolution of the emotional content. The victim may often seem sad most of the time and look and feel as though they are carrying the weight of the world on their shoulders. They try to have a good time but there always seems to be something dragging them down. They may demonstrate all the symptoms of depression, but be unwilling to admit that they are hurting or know why they feel down most of the time. They work hard at trying to feel happy but with all of the best intentions they just do not seem

76

to succeed at achieving much joy in their lives. Time and time again, their state seems to drop down into depression.

The victim will often blame others for misfortunes without truly looking at their emotional side and seeking to admit the depth of their emotion. Often the solution to the victim mask is to develop awareness of family roles, set boundaries and to realize that they have choices other than suffering or being a scapegoat.

The Busy Mask

One of the common techniques used to avoid feeling is keeping extremely busy. The busy mask wearers take on extra work and volunteer for causes that take up a great deal of time. They do not know how to relax and have difficulty slowing down from a hectic schedule that many people would have trouble keeping up with. If not busy with some task, they will find something to fill it with.

Although they give the impression that they really enjoy what they are doing, and perhaps they do, the busy mask is really a defense from facing themselves and their emotions. They are so busy that they do not afford themselves the time to be with themselves. They also likely fear time in which they have nothing to do. While it can be invigorating to be around this person, it can be next to impossible to relax with a busy type, as they will find some extra task to do.

The trap that the busy mask generates is that the person may burnout over time and may be forced to slow down. The busy mask usually results in a catch-twenty-two situation where it is painful to keep so busy, but slowing down also means facing emotional pain. The person wearing the busy mask will need to slow down gradually, giving up the need for frivolous tasks and new interests. Slowing down abruptly can be a tremendous shock. Slamming on the brakes on a car causes a skid and possibly an accident. A slower controlled stop is far more desirable. As with all illnesses and problems, prevention is the best cure!

The Intellectual/Rationalization Mask

A very important idea to consider is that emotions are not logical and that it is impossible to focus on thinking and on your emotions at the same time. By keeping all of your thoughts on an intellectual basis you can effectively avoid your emotional side and keep the emotions at bay. The cost of staying in your intellectual side is that your relationships suffer due to a lack of emotional content and connection. A person wearing the intellectual mask will be able to discuss ideas at length, but will have difficulty sharing feelings and at times may be intense in their discussion of ideas.

Mark Linden O'Meara

The intellectual mask may also be manifested in a rationalization of events. By thinking rather than feeling, the intellectual will rationalize events and behavior to the point that their feelings are dismissed. In both cases, however, the removal or dropping of the mask will bring back the associated feelings.

The Insensitive Mask

With all the television and movie violence and the negative things reported in the newspapers, it is very easy to become desensitized to the problems of others, and to begin to even be insensitive to oneself. It can become difficult to notice the good in the world when bombarded with negative stories and images. A minister at our local church suggested that the worst thing you can do before going to bed is to watch the news because of the negative things that would be planted in your mind before going to sleep! Imagine if someone told you about murders, car accidents and deaths over coffee. You'd probably have concerns for their mental health, as this would be a sign of suicidal tendencies. Yet for these stories to be reported to us on the radio when we wake up is considered "normal." We can become so accustomed to the negativity in the world that we become insensitive. I've also seen this mask in other people when they say things like "I had it hard, so it's their turn to feel what it's like" or "I put in my dues so they should too." All that it takes to remove this mask is to remind yourself of your humanity, and your common goal to make this world a better place than when you arrived in it. Two wrongs do not make a right.

The Fatigue Mask

Being tired most of the time can be the result of stress or a medical condition, but it can also be a method of avoiding life's issues. By staying in bed or by avoiding participation you can also avoid dealing with the issues of the day. Chronic sleeping in can often be a sign of emotional tension and depression.

The person with the fatigue mask can often drop the mask if some event truly interests them. Once that event passes they will likely revert to old habits of avoiding social activities in favor of what they may call rest. In fact, sleeping in late does not usually result in a feeling of being more rested but simply perpetuates a feeling of listlessness, hopelessness, and little accomplishment.

With the fatigue mask, you can shorten the number of active hours, which in turn reduces the number of hours that the individual is in contact with the subtleties of their pain. Again, be careful in judging yourself. You may be tired, which rest will cure, but too much rest is considered harmful.

The Joker/Clown Mask

Many of us have been around someone who knows all the latest jokes and can come up with a funny or witty line at a moment's notice. Joker masks can be fun to have around but this behavior turns into a mask when you use the jokes to keep people at a distance or to hide your pain. Especially with jokes, it is important to be balanced and appropriate. Can you tell a joke but also share something personal about yourself?

It is often much easier to be flippant than to show a deeper understanding and caring attitude. Humor is often used as a way of masking serious issues. In addition, the joker or clown so often pulls jokes that when they actually open up or disclose something, the disclosure may be taken for granted or discounted. This occurs simply because people are expecting a punch line.

To lose the joker mask you need to convince others of your serious side. It may involve some personal publicity work in trying to change others' image of yourself. As a person with a witty sense of humor who does stand up comedy from time to time, I like to share my new material. I can walk up to friends and without cracking a smile say something like "I went on a date last week. Turns out she was lactose intolerant. But that was better than my previous date who was just plain intolerant!" Of course people laugh, but they begin to expect a punch line each time I start a conversation. I've had to learn to say "here's my new joke." Like myself, the joker often finds that others welcome genuine and true friendship with a little bit of humor thrown in too.

The Caretaker/Gossiper

It would seem strange to classify these two masks together, but both are really of the same basis or foundation. The caretaker mask appears on some-one who spends the majority of their time looking after others rather than themselves. They show great concern for others while the gossiper will expend a great deal of energy talking about others. They may often focus on solving other people's problems rather than their own.

In both cases, the mask wearer focuses on others to avoid any attention on his or herself. They do not allow themselves the time to evaluate their own feelings and needs. Their focus on others is based on a need to avoid them-selves, coupled with a desire to help others. Many caretakers have defined their self-esteem through helping others rather than discovering their inherent reality and goodness.

The Listener

The listener is someone who devotes all of his or her time to listening to other people's problems, desires and goals. Unfortunately, although they may have needs and goals of their own, they hide from expressing these by giving all their attention to others. Although they would like to be listened to, they are fearful of exposing their own values and beliefs for fear of ridicule. In doing so, they have lost the ability to express their inner voice.

The Silent/Hiding Mask

By being silent about your own needs and feelings, you can often avoid confrontation with others. Those who experienced rejection and ridicule earlier in life when they expressed their needs and wants to others often wear the silent or hiding mask. They may have been punished for being assertive and therefore have learned to forego communicating their needs due to the fear of being rejected for making demands on others.

Ironically, another way of hiding is to draw attention to yourself as an authority, by coming up with better answers, or by being different. These attitudes or behaviors keep you from being "just one of the gang" and save you from the feelings you might experience if you feel you aren't fitting in.

In each case masks protect you from rejection, but you do not fully participate with others, nor are you communicative. While longing for closeness, the silent and hiding mask prevents you from developing the intimacy that you desire.

The New Age Healer Mask

In my years of involvement in counseling and various self help workshops, I have observed a condition that many new age people develop as an avoidance technique. As a public speaker and trainer I have observed that ironically, the best place to hide is at the centre of the stage. By doing this, you become the teacher, setting up an authoritarian, hierarchical relationship. I have come in contact with some new age people who possess a loving charm that helps them keep people at a distance. While I'm sure the intention of their loving charm is to be kind, the ability of these people to let you get close is rather limited. The focus of their interest is always on you as a client. The healer mask can be taken to extremes of persuasiveness. Healer mask types can remove their mask by showing that they can open up and build friendships rather than healer/client relationships. When at a post office to send one of my earlier manuscripts to a publisher for consideration, I began a conversation with a woman in line. After discussing my book she asked "Oh! Are you a healer?" I replied, "We are all healers – healers of our own soul, emotions, thoughts and behaviors."

Masks –Good or Bad?

Keep in mind that none of the above descriptions are meant to be judgmental. They are simply the result of habits you may have developed to hide your emotions and provide defense mechanisms to protect yourself. At one time these mechanisms may have been necessary and appropriate tools for self-defense. Unfortunately, these protection mechanisms may no longer be serving you. You are living under different circumstances and the threat may no longer be present, yet by habit you continue to use the protection mechanisms. You need to find a way to change your habits and achieve emotional health.

Many of you may wear one or more of the above masks at varying times. There are times when wearing a mask may be appropriate. Sometimes you will meet individuals whom you may not trust and therefore may prefer to keep certain things close to your heart and hidden. You may also find that certain areas of work require a friendly smile or demeanor. The key problem for many mask wearers is the inability to remove or lose the mask at times when sharing may be appropriate or when there really is no threat.

For many of you, your mask has become so much a part of our identity that you are unable to choose to remove the mask even when you might want to. Often you may miss opportunities of closeness because you are so accustomed to maintaining the mask. The mask can be helpful but it can work against you if your behavior and fear prevent you from removing it. If the latter is the case, then you need to accept and feel comfortable with your emotions. This is the key to removing the mask.

Removing your emotional mask allows others to understand and notice your needs. When you show you are sad or hurt, others can respond with help. If your mask is in place then others will not know that you are hurting and will not be aware that you need reassurance and help. By removing your mask, others will be able to share in your joy as well!

In order to remove masks, it is usually necessary to go out of your comfort zone. Joining a support group and actively participating by sharing at meetings can help build a sense of confidence in sharing your thoughts, ideas, and feelings. Activities such as public speaking classes, such as the Dale Carnegie course or Toastmasters can sharpen your sharing and presentation skills in a supportive learning environment. Learning to stretch yourself in terms of emotional expression can be accomplished by taking risks.

It is also helpful to imagine how far your own energy field extends from your body. The further we extend our own energy boundary, the more confident we can feel and the more visible. One of the most difficult courses I completed was a "stand up comedy" course. All classmates presented a six-minute comedy routine in a club at the end of our course. After completing the course, I found myself being more dynamic in my presentations and when around my friends - a benefit of going out of my comfort zone!

Mark Linden O'Meara

The Top Ways You Avoid Your Feelings

To keep your emotions at bay, there are a number of techniques that you may use to keep the pain away. Unfortunately, these techniques eventually catch up with you and/or block you from experiencing joy in your life. Emotional avoidance methods can be subtle and you may not be consciously aware of your methods of avoiding your feelings. Following is a list of some of the techniques used to avoid emotions and the reality of your life.

Keeping Busy

By taking on extra responsibilities, whether at work, in our families, or as a volunteer, you end up keeping yourself so busy that you simply do not have the time to feel. There is no balance in your life. You end up rushing around and being unable to slow down. Eventually you can burn out and then need to face the emotions you have been avoiding. Escaping from your emotions by keeping busy dampens the pain but does not allow you to heal.

Keeping the Focus on Others

By focusing on other people's problems you distract yourself from your own problems and avoid them. You may have a sense of value in helping others, but you are unable to take a close look at yourself. You may become defensive when someone tries to talk to you about your own problems.

Taking Drugs

Drugs (even prescription drugs) are often used to avoid feelings. Unfortunately, many have resorted to the overuse of medication to block feelings of sadness. To give a lift some may take hallucinogenic drugs to alter the perception of reality. You may get a false lift - a false sense of joy, but what goes up must come down, so you try to get the feeling again, and end up addicted to a drug and with your emotions unresolved. Facing pain can be difficult. In his book, *"Try Being Human,"* Alec Forbes writes, "Addiction would not occur if people took responsibility for their emotional states." This is not necessarily easy, but the goal is to learn and experience the wonderful range of human emotions rather than the limited, painful range you might be currently experiencing!

Drinking Alcohol

Alcohol can work as a suppressant. Having even an occasional drink or two can end up suppressing or numbing your emotions. When you start to feel pain, you reach for a drink to soothe and numb the pain, but the emotions are never actually resolved, only masked. Often after a few drinks you may think that you have achieved a greater sense of self and feel more centered. This is due to the fact that alcohol affects your judgment and on a very subtle level, you may be letting some defense down. Some of us may have wonderful sharing experiences under the influence, but the sharing ends once you sober up.

Maintaining Denial

The simplest way to avoid feeling is to maintain a wall of denial saying that "I'm not hurting" or "I'm not angry", even though all the evidence points to the fact that you have unresolved emotions. You may even be so good at denial that others actually believe that you are not hurting.

Maintaining Noise

To keep your mind occupied you might often turn on a television or radio just to fill the silence. Even when you are out in nature you may need some stimulus to keep your mind from feeling your emotions. At home you may have the TV or radio on even if you are not watching or even listening. You simply have it on to fill a feeling of emptiness. It becomes background noise. Even when you are out in the woods you may miss the beautiful sounds of nature by bringing a portable stereo. It is possible to achieve a sense of peace with nature. The forests are alive with meditative sounds. If you are running from your emotions it is difficult to sit still and enjoy the peace, so you create some artificial noise to fill the peacefulness. When you begin your healing, you may find that enjoying the sounds of nature will be healing and peaceful.

Smoking

Emotional depression has also been linked to a number of behavior patterns. Anti-depressants have helped smokers quit. Doctors have noted that smokers who can't quit are more likely to be depressed. Some studies have noted that cigarette smoking affects the chemicals in the brain related to depression.

Compulsive Behaviors

A recent treatment program for compulsive shopping was successful when the patients were treated for their depression rather than for their habit. As adults we seem to be able to develop numerous methods for dealing with depression that do not get to the root of the problem. In many cases, if the depression is treated, the compulsive behavior simply disappears.

Self Abuse

In recent years the medical profession has become aware of various methods of self-abuse other than drinking and taking drugs. These forms of self-abuse include sexual addictions, self-cutting and other behaviors such as hair pulling and physically hitting yourself. These behaviors are often used as a distraction from the emotional pain. The physical pain inflicted through these behaviors allows you to focus on something other than the emotional pain. Quite often a person is overwhelmed by emotion and uses this type of behavior for expressing emotion. This method is usually rooted in low self-esteem and an inability to express emotions in more constructive and appropriate ways. For this type of difficulty, it is important to find counseling and an appropriate support group. Learning new behaviors, such as reaching out, self-reassurance, or stress reducing techniques will help you to cope with distress and hopefully reduce the incidence of harmful coping mechanisms.

The Racing Mind and Obsessing

One way of avoiding emotions is to think obsessively about something or someone. Often you may find your mind racing, resulting in insomnia or an inability to focus on the task at hand. A racing mind is a protection device that your subconscious mind evokes to avoid feelings. If you are thinking all the time, then you will be experiencing yourself only on an intellectual level and will be blocking out the feelings that are the root of the problem. Simply acknowledging this and slowing down the mind to discover the feelings can often resolve this problem.

Computers and the Internet

One of the greatest inventions in the last few years has been the home computer and the Internet. The Internet has become a valuable resource to many people, and I do not want to undermine its value as a communication tool. Unfortunately, many people spend far too great a time focusing on the computer and its software rather than themselves and their relationships. Some may talk excessively about the hardware and software they are running, which is fine if both parties are truly interested in this subject, but many simply use the topic to avoid the discussion of issues, world problems, and their own emotions. With the creation of the Internet, many people spend hours on the chat and messenger services, web surfing and reading news. Some people have begun to recognize net surfing as another form of addiction. Some people spend hours on their computer, losing sense of cost, time and other responsibilities.

With hobbies or computers, being knowledgeable about a subject is both interesting to others and rewarding as a hobby if you have a sense of balance in your life. Not having this balance may indicate an obsession or an inability to focus on other areas of your life.

Comparing Yourself to Others

As a form of denial, an emotionally hurting person may try to deny their pain by noticing how others are worse off than themselves. You may take note of someone who, in your eyes, has had a worse time. You then remind yourself that things are better for you. This denial technique is a rational way to get you to think that the pain is inappropriate. But each of our circumstances is unique in some way. To expect two people to react exactly the same is not reasonable.

Your troubles and your reaction to them belong to you alone and you should not try to compare your troubles to others to try to make you feel better. Sometimes you may feel guilty for feeling pain or hurt, because your problems may seem insignificant to others. You also may not have been given permission, by yourself or by others, to feel badly. A counselor I was seeing while doing my undergraduate degree took care of this problem by saying "It does not matter how big the pile of poop is. The smaller pile smells just as bad!"

Dissociating

One way of avoiding emotions is to simply tune out what is going on around you. In cases of childhood trauma, dissociation is a common occurrence. Dissociation is now being recognized as a symptom of sexual or childhood abuse rather than a pathological state. Although present in psychiatric patients, it can also occur in the general population. By dissociating from yourself, you become more of a distant and numb observer, less present and less connected with yourself, thus avoiding the possibility of emotional pain or discomfort. The individual who is dissociated may be able to function at certain levels in social and work situations, but may be somewhat disconnected emotionally from day to day living.

8. Ouch! Things That Hurt!

"History has demonstrated that the most notable winners usually encountered heartbreaking obstacles before they triumphed"
- B.C. Forbes

In Buddhist teachings, the concept of joy is often described as the absence of suffering. Therefore, in order to achieve joy, you must develop an understanding of the concept of suffering and what causes it. Until you understand the nature of the problem corrective action will not be possible. The Buddhist teachings I have read define true joy as a permanent joy that permeates the soul. It is not the temporary joy that you experience as a result of distractions such as fulfilling a desire, or from drinking, drugs or sexual escapades. True joy is deeper. It resides in the soul and can be recreated. It is suffering that diminishes joy, yet joy can be reclaimed.

Also taught in Buddhism is the fact that suffering and dealing with loss is a fact of life. Each of us is born and it is inevitable that we will die. In between your birth and death, you will make friends and lose friends, you will set goals and you may achieve them. Other times you may fail. You will be involved in relationships and you will lose relationships, making way for new ones. You will have sickness and you will have health. You will have financially good times and difficult times as well. In *The Road Less Traveled*, Scott Peck suggests that it is important to accept that life is difficult.

Dealing with Loss

Losses are as much a part of life as are gains however it is usually easier for most of us to deal with the gains. Alexander Graham Bell said, "For every door that closes behind us, another door opens." Bell went on to say that often too much time is spent focusing on the closed door, and not enough time on the open one. This is true, however some of you never acknowledge the door that closed behind you as you began a new career, started a new relationship or move to another city, creating an un-grieved loss.

In *How to Survive the Loss of a Loved One*, authors Colgrove, Bloomfield and McWilliams describe various types of losses. There are inevitable losses (situations in which death or separation is imminent), temporary losses (absences from work, a lover going away for a period of time, a child going away to camp) and some not so obvious losses. There can also be losses related to missed opportunities and mini-losses that may accumulate during a day. Missed telephone calls, a missed connection or not hearing about something you wanted to attend until it is too late are examples of missed opportunities and mini-losses.

At some time or another you may have experienced multiple losses. When this occurs it is as though the stress of the events is not added, but multiplied. You may require the use of avoidance techniques until you are ready and capable of dealing with the event or events. A number of smaller or seemingly insignificant losses can bring about a depression, especially if they occur around the same time. Even a series of bad luck can bring about a depression or sense of loss. Whatever the loss, you need to allow yourself to feel the loss and go through the natural process of grieving and healing. Many women bond with their unborn children long before they are born and feel a great sense of loss after an abortion. Support groups are now offered for women who later in life, look back on an abortion with grief. Healing work needs to be done.

Quite often a loss may not become apparent until later in life. Realizing that you may have been deprived of a happy childhood can be considered a non-obvious loss. There is often no external event that triggers the loss, but an internal realization about the nature of your upbringing. This type of loss is just as real as other types of losses and needs to be felt, expressed and grieved.

Any change in your lifestyle can bring about a sense of loss even if the change ends up being for the better in the long run. Graduating, moving, changes in relationships, a different job are all stressful events. Again, the important principle you need to follow to keep yourself emotionally healthy is to feel and express the emotions that you develop regarding these events.

One of the most difficult and stressful losses to endure occurs when you are placed in a state of limbo. Is the relationship going to end? Am I going to lose my job? Is my health OK? Continually wondering about these and other questions can be more stressful than the event itself. Often when and if the event occurs, a sense of relief is felt because the feeling of not knowing is finally removed. Once the state of limbo ends you can then begin the process of healing and moving on.

In addition to feelings of physical and emotional pain, some of the symptoms of loss are:

anger	anxiety
emptiness	feelings of helplessness
mood swings	lack of concentration
despair	changes in energy

loneliness	reduced ambition
guilt	proneness to error
sleep disturbances	changes in sexual drive

The key thing to remember is that all or any of these symptoms are normal for anyone who has experienced a loss. Too often, these feelings are fought rather than expressed and experienced. If you have not had an obvious loss, yet you relate to a number of the above reactions, you might wish to examine your past for a not-so-obvious loss or a series of such losses. Some of the non-obvious losses can be a loss of an ideal or goal, achieving success, moving or similar changes. Learning new things about yourself can also be construed as a loss, especially when it involves a loss of innocence.

Keep in mind that your losses are personal and how you feel may be different than how others may feel. In providing support to the bereaved, counselors are often advised to refrain from saying "I know how you feel." The grieving person has no words to express the rainbow of feelings and thoughts that are occurring. It is not possible to match their feelings with our own.

Furthermore, it is important not to compare our losses to those of others. Often people will try to comfort us by saying that someone else may have had troubles that seem worse than ours. I remember being told that at least I had not lost my parents in childhood. This certainly did not help in my grief. In making such statements, others diminish your losses and in doing so, seemingly invalidate the feelings you are having.

Often, too, you may do the comparing of your concerns to those of others in order to deny your own feelings and how you have individually responded to or felt about a particular set of events. A great deal of pain comes from not accepting what is.

In all losses it is important to feel the loss, to admit that you have lost something and to allow the natural healing process to take place. Often your body has begun the healing process without your knowing it. Often you try to block this healing process because you do not understand it or because you do not understand the process of letting go. Colgrove, Bloomfield and McWilliams state that to feel pain after a loss is "normal, natural, proof that you are alive, and a sign that you are able to respond to life's experiences" and "to see pain not as hurting, but healing."

Day to Day Events

Day to day living is not without its minor inconveniences and troubles. A bad day occurs when you have a number of small mishaps. A missed connection or telephone call, poor timing, being splashed by a passing car, or even a minor dent in the car all add up to emotional stress in your life. It is necessary to acknowledge the troubles but not dwell on them. Daily life can be full of annoyances, and you need some outlet to release the emotional tension and stress created by these incidents. If you do not find these outlets for yourself you end up building a backlog of emotion that adds to your stress level. Eventually you may find that, similar to the phrase "the straw that broke the camel's back" at some point a seemingly insignificant event triggers a flow of emotion. Unfortunately this can be a rather unhealthy method of stress release because you do not have the ability to deal with each issue as it arises. You can reduce the level of stress sufficiently to be able to cope but you do not resolve the underlying issues.

Day to day stresses can be viewed as mini-losses that individually might not even be noticed or remembered a few days later, but the stress of the events takes its toll on your emotional health. After a build up of mini-losses you may find yourself crying unexpectedly or bursting in anger when you can "no longer take it." You may appear somewhat irrational in your behavior because another person viewing your reaction to an event does not know about the little events that have added up to create your discharge. If you maintain healthy emotional habits you will find ways in which you can reduce your emotional tension before you reach your breaking point.

Holidays and Christmas

For some, the Christmas period measures closeness, while for others it measures distance. It is a time of gathering and for some, a time of aloneness. It is a time of joy, for others a time of despair. I've experienced both. From my studies in counseling, and from talking to my friends and co-workers, I have learned that I was not alone in my difficulties. Our holiday rituals have a profound effect on people. Counseling intakes are highest after the Christmas holiday period. Sadly, suicide rates are highest at Christmas, and in the spring months, when the weather gets better but people don't. Christmas is a very stressful time for many. With healing and self-control, you can bring back the joy of holiday gatherings, finding safety in your self-control and self-acceptance. It's always great to have an escape plan though. I recommend having a friend to go visit so that you can take a break from the family setting should you need one!

Chronic Conditions

Having experienced the painful effects of a number of whiplash injuries combined with stress, I can easily identify with the difficulties of putting up with chronic pain from injuries. It was not until I took a course on living healthily with a chronic condition that I fully comprehended the impact that the condition was having on my emotional and mental health. I soon learned that chronic pain could lead to frustration and depression. In learning to take better care of myself and to be more proactive in my health management I was able to minimize the effects of my condition. Chronic fatigue or pain is a condition that many of us live with. We need to learn to differentiate between the physical pain and the mental pain. The physical pain often needs to be accepted, hopefully with some relief in sight. The mental anguish of wishing it were different or thoughts of anger and contempt and "why me" only exacerbate the suffering. With the suffering of the mind, mild pain becomes severe pain.

Fortunately there are support groups available that can help us deal with the mental health aspects of chronic pain. As you learn to acknowledge your difficulties and to reach out, you can find helpful support in your community. It helps to know that your problem is a common one. It ends isolation and also reminds you of your humanity.

Living, Loving and Learning

Living and sharing with others can bring great joy to your life, but in doing so you open yourself to the risk of losing someone for whom you care about. With the divorce rate hovering at the 50 percent level, there are great numbers of people who have lost their ideal of having a marriage that will last forever. There are many people who are angry and hurt about many things that may have gone wrong in a marriage or relationship. If these life challenges are not resolved, they will be carried into the next relationship or marriage, bringing a greater sensitivity to other issues.

You may often feel hurt by other people. Some people may do things intentionally, while others may simply be doing things not because they are mean people, but because they do not know better. Others may not have the skills to communicate without attacking. Often someone's behaviors or actions may not coincide with your goals, leaving you feeling frustrated and hurt.

All of us go through breakups and letdowns. You have your successes but you have your failures as well. The events occurring in your life will create emotions that need to be expressed and resolved. If you resolve the issues then you end up living, loving and forgiving, which brings about learning.

Rejection, Betrayal and Let Downs

Whether you are asking someone out on a date, for a job or for a raise, you feel a certain amount of vulnerability. I have heard that a simple answer for dealing with rejection is to say "Next!" Yet at times rejection is not so simple to deal with, particularly when we have to reconcile the loss of what we were promised versus how things have turned out. I don't know of any couple that did not mean what they said when they recited their wedding vows, yet many couples end up divorced, and even if you have not married, the love that was once there must be reconciled with the fact that a partner is leaving.

Rejection and betrayal leaves you feeling wounded, with feelings and thoughts that come faster than which you can respond. Initially you may even feel shattered. It is hard to accept that someone you love has chosen a different path that does not include you in their picture. Similarly you may have to face the fact that someone has lied to you, or had an affair, and you must reconcile the truth of their actions with what you did not believe possible. You need to acknowledge your deep feelings of disappointment. In your healing process you may come to understand that you don't have to take the issue personally, that it is more about the other person than it is about you.

I often hear of stories of the pain caused by the actions of roommates. I too have experienced very unpleasant situations with roommates who changed a great deal from when I first met them. While world peace is a noble cause, getting along with roommates is often a greater challenge. Many of us have roommate stories that left us feeling betrayed. People aren't often what they say they are.

Jealousy

Relationships come and go and so do friendships, but so many relationships and friendships fall victim to either your own or someone else's jealousy. When an ex-partner develops a new relationship, jealousy can destroy your current friendship. You may stop calling friends of the opposite sex because of your own jealous partner. Many of us have lost companionship due to the jealousy of other people's new partners. Insecurity and fear is the basis of jealousy. You must remind yourself that like excessive pride, hatred and anger, jealousy is one of the seven deadly sins. What a better world it would be if you could put aside your jealousy and, in true love for your partners and friends, allow friendships to continue to grow and foster extended family relationships and greater support in your life.

Bullying and Teasing

Bullying and teasing in school is now being recognized as a major contributor to problems later in life. Both leave a child or young adult with a low sense of worth and value as well as a lack of confidence in their social skills and their sense of acceptance. In my own personal work, I came across a number of men and women who had been teased and bullied. The scars lasted long into their adult life. It seems that although children can demonstrate a beautiful under-standing of how the world should be, they can also exhibit a cruelness that you rarely find in a person once they have reached adulthood. In my own healing from bullying and teasing, I learned that children need an outlet for their own anger and frustration, and that not standing up for myself, being physically weak, as well as lacking self-esteem, made me an easy target. I've learned not to take it personally, yet it has been quite a journey to get to this point. I realize that many children are unaware of the hurt they cause! One of the most successful bullying programs does not involve trying to rehabilitate the bully, but involves having a class 'adopt' a mother and young child. With "The Roots of Empathy" program, each week the mother would bring the young baby to the school and the children would interact and watch the growth in the child. As the school children bonded with the little baby, the incidence of bullying and teasing dropped significantly. As the children developed their sense of compassion and love, bullying seemed out of the question!

Heart and Soul Wounding

In our own emotional development there are many factors that either facili-tate emotional expression or encourage us to avoid it. The causes of your own emotional abandonment are numerous. Some of you were never taught to value your emotions. You may have had poor emotional role models and may have never been taught how to effectively communicate your feelings. Parenting not only involves putting food on the table, but also includes nurturing and paying attention to the emotional needs and concerns of children. Children need en-couragement to help them in their development, growth and decision-making. In some families, emotional expression, decision-making and expression of their thoughts may be de-valued and ridiculed, or you may even have been shamed for having emotions. In some cases you may have been hurt so deeply by the actions of others that you choose to avoid your emotions as a way of coping with your pain. Often you may refrain from expressing yourself when there is a lack of trust or fear that you will be ridiculed. These wounds often seem as though they reach deeply into your soul.

In all of the above cases, the shaming of your emotional side is an injury to your soul or heart. These injuries can run deep into the consciousness and affect your emotional state and comfort in expressing yourself until the issue is re-evaluated. Although you may not be able to recall a specific incident or trauma, an environment of constant shame, scolding or subtle put downs can lead to a demoralized spirit that will likely result in unresolved emotional trauma. This trauma will come to the forefront when later you discover that your treatment was unhealthy, unfair and undeserving, or possibly when you become involved in a relationship.

Another type of emotional abuse or scarring occurs when another person criticizes a child when the child is being creatively expressive. Children will freely express themselves through inquiring, wondering and will also artistically express themselves through dancing, singing or playfulness. Often children are robbed of their freedom to express themselves when they are shamed or ridiculed for their spontaneity. Excessive controlling will lead to a loss of connection with their creative side.

Actions that ridicule or shame your creative center or that shut down a child's expression of self is a crime against the soul and creativity of the child. The child is taught to suppress the expression of creativity - one of the greatest sources of human joy and expression. Fortunately though, the adult can still find within themselves his or her creative center, and learn to be comfortable in letting his or her creative aspects and talents shine again. Through emotional release and resolution, you can reconnect and rejuvenate your creative personality.

Reality Can Hurt!

Reality can be hard to take when the situation turns out differently than what you expected. Most people who are divorced, separated, or widowed never thought that this could happen to them. The shock of separation, starting over, or even just losing the innocence of childhood can be difficult. For many of us, it is a difficult lesson to learn that the only thing in life that seems constant is that it is changing.

Functional Atheism

I have often been troubled by the claims of some people that we create our own reality and that everything that happens to us is a result of our ability to attract things into our lives. The problem with this concept is that it feels great to have this belief system when things are going well. But when the tables turn, as they often do at various points in life, this belief system becomes a punishing frame of mind to live under. In his book *Leading from Within*, Parker Palmer defines functional atheism as "the belief that ultimate responsibility for everything rests with me." He states that this is "a belief held by people whose theology affirms a higher power."

It is ironic that people who go around saying "I guess it wasn't meant to be" also say "I create my own reality and universe." These beliefs seem to contradict each other, but not if they are utilized at various times to accept responsibility when things work out and to avoid responsibility when they don't. The problem with functional atheism is that it appears to be too general a belief that has been extrapolated to include more than was originally meant. It is true that you can learn to control your reactions, but sometimes things happen that are beyond your control. I can do all the positive thinking I want, but sun will always rise in the east and set in the west. There are other people in the world, and I can not control their choices or actions, nor can I control the weather.

When you adopt the belief of functional atheism and things don't work out, you can experience deep periods of guilt, shame and low self-esteem. Sometimes events happen that are beyond our control. Natural disasters, accidents, crimes and even decisions made by other people can often be outside our realm of control. There is great wisdom in the statement, "grant me the serenity to accept the things I can not change, the courage to change the things I can, and the wisdom to know the difference." The wisdom to know the difference is the key to living in a world of millions of people with different viewpoints, agendas, and outlooks on what is best.

Shame and Guilt

Being given or taking on inappropriate responsibility is another crime of the soul. Children inappropriately are given and accept responsibility for what has happened to them. Many adult children of alcoholics learn through 12 step programs that they were not responsible for the treatment they received as children. Without any other models, many of these children assumed that their environment and the treatment they were receiving were normal.

Realizing the falseness of the image of their family, and that their environment was not normal, leads the adult child to try to reconcile their past. This usually involves revisiting the past and resolving the fear and pain associated with their upbringing, and then allowing the development of healthier patterns of behavior in their current and future relationships.

Betrayal and Loss

You often have expectations that certain friends will stick by you and that you can expect their loyalty, but it is a fact of life that each of your friends will sometimes let you down. But sometimes a friend will make statements behind your back to take care of their own self-interest and protect them, which leaves you with a feeling that is deeper than disappointment. It leaves you with a sense of shock and a thought of "How could you?" mixed with anger and disappointment.

Sexuality and Orientation

While there are now laws that protect against discrimination on the basis of sexual orientation, there are still many pockets of negative treatment towards gays and lesbians. I remember the teasing I went through in my grade school class as some students thought it was fun to suggest I was gay though I was and am straight. This experience has taught me empathy for the difficulties others go through. I have heard people talk of parents disowning their gay kids, of selfishly thinking, "where did we go wrong" but also wonderful stories of acceptance. It seems the difficulties with parents usually occur when the parents expect their children to fulfill their dreams of grandparenthood and the TV show family lives of the sixties. Kahlil Gibran says, "Your children are not your children. They are the sons and daughters of Life's longing for itself… You may give them your love but not your thoughts, for they have their own thoughts. You may house their bodies but not their souls." The wisdom in these words means that parents need to raise their children without any expectations of their own, only with the best intentions for their child.

In terms of sexuality, I have read many articles and books on the earlier Hawaiian culture, which was much less restrictive and prudish when it comes to sexuality. Many of us were taught to hide our sexual organs out of shame and guilt. Yet the Hawaiian traditions required young girls and boys to cover their private parts out of recognition that these parts of the body were sacred. How many of us were ever taught that?

Becoming More Aware

Each of us builds constructs about how the world works, how people really are and how we fit into the world. Sometimes we grow into a new belief system gradually, but sometimes life hits us harder than we expect when we realize how people have really been behaving towards us. An overheard conversation, a realization of the lack of genuineness of some people becomes painful when you have to face up to the way people really are thinking about you. I remember a time when I had faced a lot of emotional pain. I had truly been dissociated and had been putting up a fake smile. When I worked through the pain and became present, I dropped the mask, but there was a great deal of pain as I realized that some acquaintances were sarcastically reflecting my mask back to me. There were many moments of awkwardness and embarrassment as these people realized that I was now aware of what they were doing. It was painful, but I reminded myself of my growth.

Keeping a Secret

Keeping a secret is difficult for anyone, but when the secret is something you fear others will reject you for, then the emotional stress is much higher. Keeping a secret about yourself from others can substantially compromise your immune system, according to a study at the University of California. We all have things we wish we had done differently, but the secrets that are most troublesome are the ones that are ever present in our minds on a daily basis, even if you have fabricated a story to cover your secret. The religious practice of confession has been a powerful healing tool to deal with these kinds of secrets. The power comes from sharing your deep fears and pain with a trusted witness. I remember the fear I experienced in grade eight as I changed schools due to being relentlessly teased. I was told to make sure no one knew what school I came from. I was in a state of fear most of the time that someone would find out about me. Taking this personally, I developed a shadow side to myself that needed care to resolve in my later years.

Crimes of Personal Invasion

Many people's homes are broken into each and every day. It is sad to realize the impact that this has on the victim's mental health. Knowing that someone has been in your personal space without your permission can leave you feeling angry and vulnerable. It is common to have disturbed sleep patterns and an increased sensitivity to unfamiliar noises for a long period after a burglary. I can remember clearly the day my van was broken into during my university years. Like many others, I awaken easily by noises on the street. There is a spectrum of emotions that you may go through when your personal property is taken, from anger to disgust but hopefully eventual forgiveness.

Long Periods of Unpredictability

While low levels of stress can be a positive motivator, high levels of stress can do harm to the mind and body, especially if the period of stress continues for a long period of time. One of the most difficult situations to deal with is unpredictability and a lack of control over things in your life. When the stress of trying to solve one problem after another continues and continues, the body remains in a heightened state of stress and the body seems to adapt albeit unhealthily to remaining at high stress levels. The stress producing hormones remain at elevated levels resulting in a sense of burnout and fatigue even after the stressful period has ended!

The Paradox of Perfectionism

While doing something well is a goal we all strive for, trying to do something perfectly often gets in the way of doing anything at all. While gifted performers show their talents with what appear to be perfect performances, the artists themselves often notice mistakes that are completely missed by the audience. When I played in a rock group, we would comment after a show about the mistakes made. As professionals, we would take pride in improving our craft, however most audience members did not have the skill or the perception to notice that any mistakes were made at all! Artists, writers, teachers or hobbyists often limit their ability to enjoy their efforts. At some point in time someone told you, or perhaps you yourself developed the belief that if something is not perfect it is of no value. This is not the real world truth of expression and creativity.

Perfectionism can range from thinking that what you've accomplished is never quite enough or procrastinating so that you never actually have to measure your accomplishments. It can be rooted in a fear of disapproval, failure, embarrassment from making mistakes, and from not living up to what you think you should be doing. Ironically, the ideal of trying to attain perfectionism can be quite harmful, even though it may be seen as a desirable trait. For gifted people, perfectionism is usually necessary to attain the extremely high level of performance and success. However, it is far better to have a sense of healthy striving than an all or nothing, compulsive and obsessive attitude of perfectionism. When you are unable to attain the high standards you set for yourself, anxiety and depression can set in. John Henshaw states "Don't let perfect get in the way of the good."

Other People's Rules and Decisions

Sometimes you are faced with the reality that there are other people in the world with different view points, different ways of going about things, and different styles of communicating. When you combine this with organizational rules and a legal framework that is slow to change or recognize mistakes, it is easy to get caught up in a challenging situation in which rules, that at one time made sense, simply don't in our situation, leaving us with frustration and sometimes disastrous financial situations. In these situations it is easy to become frustrated and to feel a sense of hopelessness, since challenging the rules can take a lot of time and energy. In the justice system, many people have been wrongly accused and convicted, stealing months or years of their lives while trying to fight to uphold their innocence. In the administration of government programs and tax laws, sometimes you find yourself in a unique situation where rules become unfair. It is sometimes necessary to accept that the rules won't be changed immediately and to try to move on and rebuild.

Unrequited Love

How many of you have at some time fallen in love, only to find that the person you have fallen for does not share the same feelings for you? Unrequited love can be disheartening as it challenges your sense of fate and self-worth, as you learn to live with the fact that someone else is chosen over you, even though you feel a strong bond with this person. You wonder whether to give up and move on, or hope for a change in the other person's heart. True heartache can occur when you place all your hopes on one person, yet a beautiful romance can blossom when the attraction and love is reciprocated. What inspiration this topic has been for the poets, writers, dreamers, songwriters, and romantics all through the ages!

Re-victimization

Sometimes our court system is not perfect. There have been concerns that the justice system focuses more on the offender than on the victim. This has changed recently with the introduction of victim impact statements, however to go through the court system to obtain justice often requires telling your story numerous times. Well intentioned officials may question why you did things and repeatedly question facts and figures, leaving you exhausted, feeling judged and your integrity questioned. Justice takes a lot of energy. This may happen outside the court system when pressing for fairness.

Vicarious Traumatization

It is commonly known in the health professions that observing or treating people who have experienced trauma can, over time, result in the traumatization of the caregivers themselves. This form of traumatization can also happen to the average person as we watch the horrific images of terrorism, war, and crime on the daily news and internet. It is only in recent history that so many troubling images are presented in our daily life as we go about our family activities and business. It is easy to become numb to these images, but on a subconsious level the images trigger thoughts and feelings that compromise our mental health and cause us to question our values, moral standards of society, and sense of safety.

Classifying Human Suffering

While a number of possible causes of suffering are listed above, it is impossible to describe all of the things in life that cause suffering. According to Buddhist texts, there are several ways to describe the categories of suffering.

The first category is something we have all experienced. By being born, you begin the pain of birth. I have not heard of any babies who were born laughing or singing. All are born crying as they leave the safety of the mother's womb to begin the journey called life.

The other categories are: age, death, sickness, separation from loved ones, undesirable confrontation with another person or thing, denial of your desires, and suffering due to the characteristics of the human body and mind.

This last category is one that you often need to work on the most. By understanding the nature of the mind and the characteristics of how to deal with challenges, you can learn to reduce your suffering and practice acceptance, forgiveness, compassion and kindness towards yourself and others. This is what ends suffering!

I have often witnessed how telling someone in a warm, focussed, and sincere manner that they are special, good and loved can reduce a person to tears. While this makes almost no logical sense, I believe such statements call forth the incongruence of our subconcious mind and what we are being told. Many people have a fragile sense of self-esteem. I notice that those who have healed their suffering and past pain can more readily accept words of love and encouragement.

For others, in their quest to end suffering and help others I have met many people who have expressed a desire to set up a healing retreat or healing centre. Keep in mind that a healing centre is not located in a remote place in the mountains, nor is it a place to retreat from the world, even though that may be beneficial at times. Your healing centre is in your place of work, your home, your friends and family's homes, the places you visit on a daily basis, and most importantly in your heart and mind. It is here that you will end suffering.

9. Abuse, Trauma and the Wounded Soul

Defining Abuse and Trauma

In terms of mental health, there is a strong link between some mental health disorders and childhood trauma. Many victims of trauma suffer from Borderline Personality Disorder, which is characterized by a pervasive pattern of instability of self-image, interpersonal relationships and mood, beginning in early childhood and present in a variety of contexts. Also included in the list of symptoms are recurrent feelings of emptiness and boredom, as well as self-mutilating behavior.

Pierre Janet suggested as early as 1889 that emotionally intense events are made traumatic when the integration of the experience is interfered with. Janet believed that these intense emotions cause a dissociation of memories from consciousness and result in the memories being stored as anxieties, panic, nightmares, and flashbacks. Janet observed that his patients had difficulty learning from their experience and seemed to focus a great deal of energy on keeping their emotions under control.

In *Therapy for Adults Molested as Children, Beyond Survival*, author J. Briere writes, "The diagnosis of Borderline Personality Disorder is a more recent phenomenon." It has been suggested that the label of Borderline Personality Disorder is most commonly placed on patients who exhibit the symptoms of severe post-sexual abuse trauma.

In a paper entitled *Childhood Trauma in Borderline Personality Disorder*, authors Herman, Perry and van der Kolk state that "the role of childhood trauma, including parental abuse, in the development of this disorder has received less systematic attention." In three small studies, the data suggested that in borderline patients, a history of childhood abuse might be common.

In other studies of borderline patients, up to 75 percent of the patients had experienced incest. In another study of psychiatric patients, it was found that eight of 12 patients diagnosed as borderline had a history of childhood abuse. A study by Brier found that 12 of 14 patients had experienced abuse before the age of 16.

Authors Herman, Perry and van der Kolk state, "The great majority of subjects with definite Borderline Personality Disorder gave histories of major childhood trauma; 71 percent had been sexually abused, and 62 percent had witnessed domestic violence." According to the study, borderline patients had suffered from abuse more often than others and also reported more types of trauma. These abuses and trauma often began in early childhood and were repetitive, resulting in high trauma scores.

In the cases of children who have been abused emotionally or psychologically, or who have witnessed abuse, there is likely to be a greater degree of mental health issues than those who have not. It is interesting to note that repeated abuse results in a higher total trauma score than for those with singular abusive experiences. This seems to validate the idea that prolonged emotional abuse can be as equally damaging as other childhood traumas. It is this emotional abuse that may leave you numb and unable to express your emotions later as an adult. The combined effect of numerous incidents of emotional abuse may lead to similar symptoms of repressed emotions, numbness and the irrational thinking that comes with unresolved issues and loss of your inherent nature.

Often it is not until later in life that you may realize the impact of your upbringing or realize that your family situation may have been abusive. As a child, you came to accept your environment simply because you knew of no other standard of behavior. You did not know that in other families, parents were and are supportive and nurturing. As a child you may have understood that you were in pain, but did not have the words or understanding to deal with the emotional injury until you become an adult. The fact that your needs as a child were rarely met may bring about emotional pain and habitual patterns in your adult life. Through emotional and healing work you can free yourself of these patterns and resolve the pain that has lingered below the surface of consciousness for so long.

In life it is not pain that causes insanity, but the lies we tell ourselves about the pain. These lies are often the only way you know of coping through the pain. Fortunately, you are able to heal by beginning to tell yourself the truth about your pain, accept it and let go of it.

Recognizing Abuse

Due to the lack of a standard to compare your own family life, you may not realize until later in life that your family upbringing or a relationship was not normal and that it was, in fact, abusive. Inadequate parents, controllers, hinderers, alcoholics, verbal abusers, physical abusers, and sexual abusers all perpetrate a crime on an innocent victim who often feels shame, blame and low self-esteem.

Following are the characteristics of abusive types that you may encounter. Keep in mind that many of these characteristics can be applied to spouses, employers, friends, and other members of the community as well, not just parents

THE INADEQUATE: Inadequate parents are those who are so focused on their own world that they can pay little attention to their children. The parents are often overly sensitive and cannot deal with any criticism. These parents often make excuses for themselves and hide their problems with statements such as "we're doing the best we can." Inadequate parents often lack listening skills and have not experienced their own emotional development.

CONTROLLERS: Controllers often experience a fear of letting go. They often believe that their children were created to serve them and that they own their children as possessions. The children are not allowed to develop their own set of standards or values and have difficulty exercising decision-making skills due to guilt and manipulation by the parents.

ADDICTS AND ALCOHOLICS: Alcoholics and addicts often make promises that are not kept. Denial of problems, mood swings, inconsistency, and blaming are all characteristics of an alcoholic home. Keep in mind that the drinking is only one of many symptoms of an alcoholic. Many parents could be considered to be dry alcoholics, who have given up the drinking but do not have the skills to nurture and assist in problem solving. Since addictions tend to follow family patterns, children of alcoholics tend to develop certain characteristics often referred to as para-alcoholism as a result of their conditions of upbringing. Para-alcoholics show the same style of distorted views and thinking, although they may not actually drink.

THE VERBAL ABUSERS: Verbally abusive parents often try to motivate children with disrespectful comments. They can be verbally direct, or their comments may be subtly abusive. Abusive statements may be in the form of comparisons to others or subtle put downs of choices of clothing, friends or interests. The parents exhibit a great degree of insensitivity and rob the children of autonomy and self-confidence. Challenging the parent often leads to denial and attempts by the parent to make the child feel guilty.

THE HINDERERS: The hinderer is someone who says or does things that hinder our development and maturity process. Hinderers do not provide the guidance you require to develop a sense of worth and autonomy. They also go further by saying things that erode your confidence and trust in your decision-making abilities. Hinderers instill self-doubt and discourage the development of your interests and thus your opportunities to socialize.

PHYSICAL ABUSERS: Physical abusers are those who use physical force to control or harm their children. The parent may often apologize for the striking, placing the child in an awkward and difficult situation of being expected to love and forgive an abuser. Physical abuse may also occur as threats, in which a domineering parent may behave in a manner that threatens the safety of the child. Physical abusers often have not learned the skills necessary to cope with their anger. Although they may express remorse, they do not have the skills to control their actions in times of anger.

SEXUAL ABUSERS: Sexual abuse has always been more prevalent than society would care to admit. The number of clients who reported sexual abuse astounded Sigmund Freud. Sexual abuse is not limited to unwanted touching or intercourse. Sexual abuse involves power and a lack of respect for a child's innocence. Abuse can be in the form of inappropriate comments, exposure or teasing. Abused children often experience numerous problems later in life that they may not attribute to the earlier abuse.

UNINVOLVED PARENTS: This parenting style involves providing for all the physical needs of the children and possibly being affectionate, but not being actively interested in the lives of their children. They are too focused on their own problems and self-absorbed to focus on helping the children through any difficulties. They may be completely unaware of problems their children are having. This leaves the children with no primary relationship in their lives unless they find a teacher or other mentor. The children will not have good role models for developing close relationships.

Other types of abuse include verbal abuse disguised as jokes; withholding approval or attention to gain power; being put down for having a different point of view; discounting your achievements or feelings; accusing and blaming; and denial of the fact that their actions hurt you.

Often an abuser will use various blocking techniques to avoid accountability for their actions. Examples of blocking are statements such as "it was only meant in fun", "I was only joking," or "you're too sensitive." These are statements that deny that abuse is occurring and puts the onus on the victim to change. Emotional wounding occurs when you are shamed, ridiculed, lack nurturance, or are humiliated.

I've learned that many people, while abusive, often have no concept of the harm they are doing at the time. In a video on sexual abuse and abusers, a perpetrator explained that he simply longed for connection with others and at the time had no idea that he was emotionally harming his victims. As he came to grips with the knowledge that he had deeply harmed others, he was overcome with grief, remorse and depression. He made a choice from then on to work on changing his behavior, and asked for forgiveness. Others may never admit to their actions or the impact they have had on others.

While not all of us have been abused, many of us are left with low self-esteem, an inability to make decisions, or a lack of clear self-identity with regards to our talents and traits. I believe this can be a result of a number of family and school environments that occurred as a result of a lack of parenting and nurturing skills. Following are two such parenting styles that can result in a lack of personal identity.

THE PROVIDERS: While children may be given a roof over their head, clothes to wear and food at the dinner table, parenting involves much more. Many parents are unaware of the needs of children with regard to the development of a healthy sense of self-esteem. Children of providers are raised without the encouragement, affection, sense of belonging and respect that all children need to develop a positive view of themselves as well as a positive outlook. While not directly abusive, a provider's lack of humanistic knowledge required to raise children with a sense of trust and safety leaves them with a lack of emotional connection with their parents and other family members.

THE DISCOURAGERS: Fear based parents tend to say no to everything. A fear of failure or of harm coming to the children results in an overprotective manner in which the children are discouraged from making decisions and taking risks. Part of growing up and assuming the role of adulthood involves learning to evaluate information and acting appropriately. The timing of a decision is important as well. If you do not pick the apple off the tree at the right time, it will either taste bitter because it is too early to pick, or will rot and eventually fall off the tree. Discouragement teaches children that their goals cannot be attained, or that they are not good enough, when in fact they may be able to form great friendships and community in pursuing their talents.

The Impact of Trauma

Psychologists are now learning about the impact traumatic events can have on the lives of people. Either as a victim of a crime or as a witness to a crime, people can be profoundly affected by an event that may only last a few seconds. A robbery, injustice or even an accident can leave us feeling shaken and upset. Often such events will trigger a personal re-evaluation. I recall a friend of mine was present when a bank was robbed. Although not physically harmed, she was quite shaken and almost in a state of shock.

Victims of robberies feel violated and often experience periods of fear and insomnia afterwards. Often, victims of sexual assault and rape will experience a complete change in their emotional chemistry. Victims often feel anger and resentment and experience a variety of behavioral issues as a result of a trauma. A sense of violation and loss of security and safety may permeate their daily lives.

In a Letter to the Editor of the Ottawa Citizen, Erica Saunders describes the pain and emotional trauma experienced as a victim of an attempted rape:

"I am a survivor of a violent rape attempt. I am usually a sweet, caring, sensitive person. These days I am totally the opposite. I am like a wild wounded animal. If there is a way to destroy a woman in fifteen minutes this is it. First you have to deal with policemen, then doctors, then yourself. In two weeks I lost 15 pounds. I still have problems with food. He touched me; I feel dirty; I take four to five showers a day. It was an unprovoked attack... I was robbed of my rights, left to deal with a rainbow of unwanted feelings."

Obviously, such traumas involve much more pain than the physical trauma. The emotional trauma can last for months and even years. Both psychiatrists and psychologists now understand the impact that rape or childhood sexual abuse has on adult lives. These victims may experience difficulty in relationships and in situations requiring trust, long after the event has occurred.

Traumatic Events and Delayed Reaction

In some cases the effects of the event may not be felt for months or years. This delayed reaction is actually quite common. In a book about Post Traumatic Stress Disorder (PTSD) called *Aftershock*, Andrew E. Slaby tells us that "Many of us have had aftershock experiences, going through the first stages of a crisis numb and in shock, only to wake up one morning a few days, weeks or even months later in tears, the full impact of what happened finally hitting home."

In many cases, a period of change, emotional pain, or loss can leave us with the same conditions and symptoms of PTSD. In cases of PTSD, the cause of the symptoms is the inability to process what has happened to us. As with any emotional trauma, you need to cognitively and emotionally process the event. In PTSD, failure to process the event results in the event being frozen in time, with a need to repeat your story. Often similar situations and events will trigger a heightened sense of emotion and fear, often referred to as re-stimulation. More often than not, at this time in the process, the telling of the story does not relieve the symptoms but heightens the intense feelings and behaviors.

According to the *Diagnostic and Statistical Manual of Mental Disorders* (DSM-IV) which is a psychiatrist's diagnostic tool, PTSD symptoms involve: efforts to avoid thoughts or feelings associated with the trauma; efforts to avoid activities or situations that arouse recollections of the trauma; inability to recall an important aspect of the trauma (psychogenic amnesia); marked diminished interest in significant activities; feeling of detachment or estrangement from others; restricted range of affect (unable to have feelings); sense of foreshortened future (i.e. does not expect to have a career, marriage, or children, or a long life).

PTSD may also involve difficulty falling or staying asleep; irritability or outbursts of anger; difficulty concentrating; hyper-vigilance; exaggerated startle response; physiologic reactivity upon exposure to events that symbolize or resemble an aspect of the traumatic event. With PTSD, some people may find themselves over responding to a sound, sight or smell that reminds them, even if only very subtly, of the event. Due to the heightened emotional sensitivity and anxiety, some turn to substance abuse or other forms of emotional denial. This is also true for many children who experience a troublesome or traumatic childhood.

Although the definition of PTSD was developed as a result of the problems of Vietnam War veterans, its implication is much wider. The former definition of trauma for PTSD is "an event that is outside the range of usual human experience and that would be markedly distressing to almost anyone, e.g. serious threat to one's life or physical integrity; serious threat or harm to one's children, spouse or other close relatives and friends; or seeing another person who has recently been, or is being, seriously injured or killed as the result of an accident or physical violence."

If we examine this definition we find that if a person experiences a number of stressful events at once, this could be considered outside of the range of usual human experience. This would be markedly distressing to almost anyone. It is quite likely that a period of intense stress could bring about PTSD symptoms. The PTSD criteria have now been changed. The new definition of trauma is "an event that was directly experienced, witnessed or learned about that threatened the victim's life or physical integrity." In addition, the requirement of being outside the range of human experience has been removed, as it was too restrictive. Also, a new category called acute stress disorder has been added, recognizing the fact that many people are adversely affected by overwhelmingly stressful events.

Studies have shown that 60 percent of persons with symptoms of mental disorder had suffered some sort of trauma two weeks before any illness appeared. In the months following a traumatic event, the risk of suicide is six times greater and the risk of depression is twice as great as prior to the event. Furthermore, PTSD has mostly been related to adults, but the symptoms of PTSD are often present in adults who experience abuse earlier in life. Children are considered to be very susceptible to PTSD since they have not yet developed the ability to express themselves in words, yet have developed the ability to remember feelings and sounds. Often the trauma will be stored as memory with no words to describe the trauma.

Since children do not have the understanding and rational capabilities to deal with traumatic events, the way they develop explanations of such events is very different from adults. If they are harmed, they will not likely have the words and understanding to articulate the hurt. Since psychogenic amnesia is one of the symptoms of PTSD, it is likely that children will bury away the memories until they are ready to understand and deal with them.

In addition, while children can be extremely perceptive, their ability to attribute events to their understanding of the world may be undeveloped and based on fantasy. To an adult, divorce or separation may seem an acceptable resolution to a problem. To a young child this may be seen as an extremely threatening and frightening event that shatters their sense of security and safety.

As an adult you may experience events that are outside the scope of your ability to deal with at the time. The concept of PTSD has implications for those who grew up in what seemed like a war zone. Although you may not be classified as having PTSD according to established clinical criteria, you may be exhibiting all or some of the symptoms due to the troubles you have experienced.

I believe that the determination of PTSD should not be a yes or no answer, but measured on a continuum or scale based on the individual's rating of the event and the subsequent impact of the event on the person's life.

In the year after graduating from my bachelors degre, I experienced a substantial number of health problems, change and losses. Although I was not a veteran from military service, I certainly felt that I was a veteran of my own personal war to survive those times. Those events were outside the scope of what one person might be expected to endure. Given that some people are stronger than others and therefore seem to struggle through a greater load, the definition of PTSD should be varied according to the individual's ability.

My own overwhelming events led to a process of redefinition of myself. Four years later, I found I had not dealt with the events, was emotionally numb and experiencing a number of problems. Revisiting the events, expressing the emotion and completing the processing of these and other events restored a sense of sanity and ability to relate with others and myself. I now consider these events to be part of my personal history, rather than unresolved issues that generate pain and emotional discomfort.

To resolve symptoms of PTSD, you need to re-visit the trauma and process the experience and feelings in safety. As with any emotional trauma it is helpful to find suitable professional help and assistance through friends and support groups.

10. Memories – Fact or Affliction?

Memory and Pride were fighting.
Memory said, "It was like that,"
And Pride said, "It couldn't have been!"
And Memory gave in...
                    - Nietzsche

Those who cannot remember the past are condemned to repeat it.
                    - George Santayana

A Forgotten Past

This statement by Nietzsche reflects the tug-of-war that your consciousness can play with regard to the recall of traumatic or distressing events or times in your life. I find Neitzsche's words also provide insight into the denial of those who are accused of abusing or of those who were present during situations in which unpleasantness occurred. With these people, it is pride that keeps them from admitting the true nature of their own experience. It is difficult for them to admit that things were a certain way.

For the survivor of abuse, amnesia often occurs. In my own case, I had forgotten numerous aspects of my own childhood. My own repression of painful memories was due to the simple logic of "out of sight, out of mind, out of memory, no more pain." But had I really forgotten, or simply repressed them? There is a distinction between the two. Due to the emotionally painful nature of the events, I was unable to bring those events and the associated affect into my present existence for to do so would have taxed my coping resources beyond my capabilities. In order to protect myself, my mind kept them in my subconscious. The price of doing so was a heightened state of anxiety and emotional numbness.

Voluntary attempts at recalling my childhood did not bring about any memories. It was the development of appropriate support and community, and the acceptance of my emotions in a safe place, that eventually brought about the recall of my memory. This recall occurred little by little, like flashbulb experiences, one at a time. As this occurred, my self understanding grew accordingly.

I have learned that my experience is not unique. Many adult children report that once they start on their path of emotional healing, they begin to remember events they had previously seemingly forgotten. In my own experience of healing I have met numerous people who have retrieved memories that were put away long ago.

It is also possible to forget the nuances of a situation as well. You may forget severely traumatizing events. You may also repress memories of how things were in a household or relationship. The tone of the environment may be repressed to avoid dealing with your emotional state at the time. For a long time I had forgotten how depressed my mother was when I was a teenager. Both my parents refused to admit they had problems. I had forgotten how my teenage environment had been contaminated with my parents' depression, helplessness, inability to cope, and a sense of extreme emotional sensitivity.

In Freud's earlier days as a psychotherapist, he developed the theory that conflict was the key to repression. The conflict may arise when the view you hold of yourself is different or incongruent with the truth of an event. Other conflicts, such as how you view a parent versus how you "should" view a parent, can result in memory conflict as the child or adult is torn between the two images. A person with a tyrannical parent may feel fear and anger towards the parent. This would conflict with the injunction that you should love your parents.

Prior to the work of Freud, two well known philosophers, Arthur Schopenhauer and Johann Herbart, wrote about our unwillingness to discuss or face unpleasant circumstances that harm our current interests and views of ourselves. Freud and Dr. Josef Breuer concluded that some people actively attempt to push memories that have deep emotional meaning and impact below the surface of their consciousness as a method of avoidance and sometimes of survival. Freud believed that repressed memories affect our behavior and emotions and in the end produced disorders.

Recent studies have indicated that we may possess two memory systems - one explicit and one implicit. Explicit memory deals with conceptual, factual and verbal information, as well as conscious and reflective awareness. The implicit memory deals with conditioned emotional response, skills and habits, sensor motor skills, and unconscious and non-reflective awareness. Under stress, the explicit system is impeded while the implicit system becomes more robust.

Emotional Memory

At the present time, we do not fully understand the role that emotions play in memory nor vice versa, although great progress is being made in this area. It is now thought that ninety percent of what we know about the brain has been learned only since the invention of the new Magnetic Resonance Imaging equipment in the nineteen nineties! There are some theories that suggest that memory may in fact be emotion. In 1995, Wendy E. Hovdestad and Connie M. Kristiansen of Carleton University studied over 200 female survivors of child sexual abuse. The study focused on the experiences, memory and recovery process. The findings of the study were consistent with other studies in that approximately half of survivors report some memory loss or disruption. Other studies have put this number between 59 and 64 percent. In this study, of the 51 women who reported recovered memories, over 62 percent reported that their memory returned during therapy.

The Carleton University study questioned the participants regarding which of 12 events had triggered the return of their memories. The study reported the following as the most prevalent triggers:

Before having any therapy:

An event similar to the original trauma	31.3%
Beginning an important relationship	30.1%
Watching a film or reading about sexual abuse	20.7%
Parenting	20.5%
A creative process	15.7%

While participants were in therapy:

A support group	47.6%
A creative process	41.7%
Watching/reading about abuse	36.6%
Beginning an important relationship	27.7%
An event similar to the trauma	22.9%
Stopping alcohol or drugs	15.9%
Ending a significant relationship	13.4%

In *Mind Meets Body: On the Nature of Recovered Memories of Trauma*, authors Hovdestad and Kristiansen write about compelling evidence that memory is multimodal. They state that we possess memory systems, one of which we are aware, the other operating without our awareness. Hovdestad and Kristiansen write that "Trauma causes alterations in the production and release of stress-responsive neurochemicals such as norepinephrine and the endogenous opiods, and extreme levels of these neurochemicals disrupt everyday explicit information processing. The implicit processing system, however, continues to function in the face of trauma."

The Recovered Memory Debate

There has been considerable controversy regarding the concept of recovered memories and Recovered Memory Therapy. It is important to note that there is a big distinction between the two. Recovered Memory Therapy is the name of a process of counseling developed by a group of people who believed that repressed memories were the cause of all psychological problems. In their approach to therapy there was considerable pressure for the client to discover hidden memories. In some of these cases the accusations that arose led to confessions, thus confirming the memories. In other cases, the abuse was denied, yet some convictions were obtained. Some of the memories were proven to be incorrect or simply challenged and labeled by lawyers as "False Memory Syndrome." This method of therapy has come under close scrutiny of licensing boards and as a result, strict guidelines and ethical considerations have been put in place by a number of professional associations. In discussing the concept and existence of suppressed and recovered memories, it is very important to discern between a) a type of controversial therapy and b) the established knowledge that as you begin to release your emotions, memories do often come to the surface.

Recent studies of amnesia and trauma victims have indicated that the emotional valence of an experience affects recall accuracy. Recurrent observations of traumatic memories indicate that these memories are stored differently than declarative memory, perhaps due to the extreme emotional arousal. In a study by Briere and Elliot, significant degrees of traumatic amnesia were reported for virtually all forms of trauma. Numerous studies have also shown that the age at which the abuse occurs as well as the frequency of the abuse are related to the occurrence of traumatic amnesia. Traumatic amnesia will more likely occur if the trauma took place at a younger age or if the event was prolonged.

In the concluding paragraphs of Dissociation and the Fragmentary Nature of Traumatic Memories, Van der Kolk and Fisler write:

"Recently we collaborated in a neuro-imaging symptom provocation study of some of the subjects who were part of the memory study reported here. When these subjects had their flashbacks in the laboratory, there was significantly increased activity in the areas in the right hemisphere that are associated with the processing of emotional experiences, as well as in the right visual association cortex. At the time there was significantly decreased activity in Broca's area, in the left hemisphere. These findings are in line with the results of this study: that traumatic "memories" consist of emotional and sensory states, with little verbal representation. In other work we have hypothesized that, under conditions of extreme stress, the hippocampally based memory categorization system fails, leaving memories to be stored as affective and perceptual states."

When you start to remember incidents from your past, why do you recall some memories but forget others? What are the processes and conditions that cause you to forget or put away memories and what brings them back? In *Unlocking the Secrets of Your Childhood Memories*, authors Dr. Kevin Leman and Randy Carlson suggest that the answer is simply that "People remember only those events from early childhood that are consistent with their present view of themselves and the world around them." The authors call this the law of creative consistency. "Without consistency", they write, "you'd be in deep trouble. It is your God-given ability to keep the present and past in balance so that you don't fall over the edge into frustration, depression or insanity."

What seems to be a compromise in the memory repression and recall debate is the concept of suppression. Repression is the unconscious exclusion of painful impulses, desires, fears and emotion. Suppression involves a conscious decision to avoid the things that are painful.

Newer studies on the topic of emotion and memory have clearly shown that concealing emotions hampers the memory of distressing situations. A study at the University of Washington found that when people try to avoid showing negative emotions, then their memory for the situation suffers. A key point to the study was that suppression greatly utilizes our resources and there are psychological costs affecting our mental health. While dealing with emotions can utilize our resources as well, the long-term outcome is better if the emotions are not suppressed. The task of working through difficult times has been rated equally with the task of suppression, but the health and growth you experience from expression does not occur when you suppress.

Facilitating Memory Recall

In the case of emotion and memory recall there are a number of factors that seem to facilitate the remembering of events. The first factor is the creating of a safe or comfortable environment. This may occur simply by beginning to accept the start of a healing process or by joining a support group. Secondly, memory recall usually occurs after the acknowledgment and recall of the emotion. The notion that memory reappearance will precede the emotion appears to be the reverse of what happens. Usually a cue of some sort will trigger the emotion and once the emotional expression is facilitated the memory surfaces and reveals itself.

In *Unchained Memories, True Tales of Traumatic Memories Lost and Found*, author Lenore Terr, M.D. writes that "In order for a repressed memory to return, there usually is a ground -that is a general emotional state and a cue." It is often this cue, that may be only a smell, taste, a simple reminder by way of a similar experience, or any cue from our senses. Terr suggests that vision is one of the strongest cues. Additionally, I believe that a visual cue, as seen through the mind's eye, can also act as a strong stimulus.

The nature of traumatic memories has been controversial as well as difficult to study. The recall of abuse often leads to confronting the abuser or realizing the true nature of individuals who have been close to us. Claims of abuse are often denied, however in some cases, full confessions and the alleged abusers have given apologies.

In times of recall, individuals like yourself may experience self-doubt about the memories. It is often important to remind yourself that although you may be experiencing self-doubt, you are also experiencing a great deal of affect, which likely has a basis in some event. If the emotion is processed, the nature of the event will be revealed to you when you are ready.

In recovering memories it is important to understand and accept the ability of your mind to protect you until you are ready to remember. A flood of memories could be overwhelming. Your mind is truly your ally in times of memory retrieval as I have heard many times from 12-step group members. It seems that the emotion and memory will bubble to the surface as you are ready to face and process these memories. Although the memories and emotion may feel overwhelming, your subconscious mind seems to instinctively know that you have developed sufficient resources and support to work through the trauma.

In one instance of recall my memories were triggered by a bloody nose. While trying to loosen a part underneath my van, my wrench slipped and struck me on the nose. As I crawled out from under the van, I found myself experiencing memories of being punched in the nose by the grade eight-class bully, who had at the time cornered me in a backyard and was threatening me. As the memory came back, so too did the feelings of rejection, anger and fear that were going through my mind at the time of the incident. Fortunately, at the time of recall, I knew enough about emotional processing to accept the feelings and release them.

Dealing with painful memories can consume a great deal of energy and personal resources. The key to retrieving these memories is the awareness and acceptance of what you are feeling.

Part Three - Growth

11. Learning the Language of Feelings

Part of self growth and developing self-knowledge involves learning to express the feelings, ideas and thoughts you are having. To describe how you are feeling is a challenge given the fact that language is imprecise, and at times it is difficult to translate body sensations into words.

While taking some Chinese lessons, I questioned my teacher about the expression of emotion in Chinese. I was told that there are four basic emotions and the rest are combinations of emotion or impressions we have of our self or others.

The four basic emotions are:

Bei	grief, sorrow, mourning
Le	joy, cheerfulness, optimism
Nu	anger, rage, fury, berating
Xi	value, compassion, happiness, love

Other feelings or states such as jealousy and envy are described as impressions we have as a result of our thoughts and beliefs about other people. Some psychologists suggest that your feelings come from your thoughts. Others believe that emotions come from a deeper experience. If we consider the four basic emotions as soul experience and other emotions as impressions from thoughts and beliefs, then we can reconcile the two theories. Recent research using Magnetic Resonance Imaging scans has shown that our emotional centre reacts much faster than your thinking process. Does this mean that the "thoughts into emotions" theorists are wrong? Not really! It means that we need a more complex model to describe what is going on. I believe that joyous feelings, grief, anger and happiness and love are soul or heart expressions, while other feelings may be triggered by thought processes. It is possible too that your soul feelings will impact your thoughts. In order to progress in your growth, regardless of the theory, you need to learn to express and communicate your feelings, both the soul and impression kinds.

In my travels to China I learned how precise the Chinese language is compared to the English language. It seems that many of the Chinese expression characters are actually a combination of words. For example the root word bei, which means sadness, can be combined with other characters to mean sad, sorrowful, melancholy, grieved, painfully sad, mixed feelings of joy and grief, compassion, bitter, miserable, sad and worried, grief over the death of a friend, grief and indignation, pessimistic and gloomy, overcome with grief, sad and choking with sobs.

The same goes for the word for happiness – xi, when combined with other words can mean outright glee, overjoyed, not feeling tired of it, buoyant, cheerful, fun, pleasure and contentment. I found that the Chinese language seemed far more robust that our English language.

There is also an important phrase "le ji sheng bei" which means "when joy reaches its height, sorrow comes in turn, extreme joy begets sorrow." These words of wisdom echo the familiar phrase what goes up must come down. Other phrases more completely described concepts rather than just feelings. A word describing bitterness referred to "going through years of suffering, to be full of misery but find no place to pour it out."

Imagine if we could all become more literate and complex in our describing of our feelings. I believe the best improvement in this area would be to try to describe the combination of feelings and the situation or movement that we are experiencing. This would help clarify and give deeper meaning to what you are feeling.

In reflecting on how you are feeling you can refine your description by describing not one but many feelings. Also describe the situation and what you are hoping for. For example instead of saying "I am hurt", try to go deeper. You could say "I am feeling sad and betrayed because I was let down when a promise was broken." This is far more precise and communicative than the words "I am hurt." Learn to be more descriptive!

Our Emotional Habit Inventory

In understanding your own emotional habits, you can look back to your own habits and comfort level in expressing yourself. In a book about adult children of alcoholics titled *It Could Never Happen to Me,* author Claudia Black provides a questionnaire that can help you to learn about your own history and current practices of emotional expression. By answering each question you can get a better understanding of your own emotional behavior inventory.

Answering these questions may take some reflecting and effort at remembering how things were. In addition, it is equally important to ask yourself how you would answer these questions, regarding your current behavior. Have you carried any of those behaviors into our adulthood? In answering these questions, I realized that in most cases I was crying silently even though no one was around. I realized that this was a carry over from my childhood. Many times as a child I cried myself to sleep, but silently so no one would know. By discovering this I gained a stronger sense of vocal expression, which improved my singing range and tonal quality.

How would you answer the questions below? Keep in mind that there is no right or wrong answer to these questions.

> When do you cry?
> Do you ever cry?
> Do you cry when alone?
> Do you cry hard or do you cry slowly and silently?
> Do you cry because people hurt your feelings?
> Do you cry for no apparent reason?
> Do others know when you cry?
> Do others see you cry?
> Do others hear you cry?
> Do you let others comfort you when you cry?
> Do you let others hold you?
> Do you let them just sit with you?
> What do you do to prevent yourself from crying?
> How is your pattern as an adult different from that of a child?
> What did you do with your tears as a child?
> Did you cry?
> Did others know you were crying?
> Did you let others comfort you when you were crying?

Although the above questionnaire deals with crying, you need to examine your habits regarding joy and laughter as well. In addition to repressing crying as a child or adult, often you tend to repress your joy as well. Many families do not share in the joy of others. Repressing emotions is similar to turning down the volume on a stereo. The full range of sound is lowered in volume. Unlike current stereos, which have numerous controls to shape the sound, you do not have the ability to selectively block out only certain emotions. If emotional repression is the norm in a family then it follows that joy and happiness will not be shared as well. The following questions can help you understand your past with respect to joy and happiness. Again, there is no right or wrong answer, but these questions will help you identify factors that can contribute to or distract from your current enjoyment of life.

1. Did you experience joy in your family?
2. Did others express laughter?
3. Did others share your joy?
4. Were you laughed at or ridiculed for laughing or being spontaneous?
5. Was depression a major factor in the day-to-day life of a family member?
6. Do you feel comfortable laughing and expressing emotion as an adult?
7. Were you taught to feel guilty for having fun?
8. Were you very quiet?
9. Were you spontaneous?
10. Were you expressive?
11. As an adult do you express your creativity in some way?
12. Are you creative in your work?
13. Can you easily have fun or be silly?
14. Are you easy-going?
15. How do you express anger?
16. What makes you sad?
17. How do you deal with sadness?
18. What makes you fearful?
19. How do you deal with fear?
20. What makes you happy?
21. What makes you laugh?

Fortunately, as a human being you are able to effect change in your personal habits and behavior in relationships once you become aware of your patterns and emotional hurt. Once you are aware, you can slowly change your attitudes and behavior, through your own emotional healing work, to encourage emotional expression in your children. You can change the way you behave in your own families. You can do things differently than the way your parents did. The first step is awareness.

So, What Am I Feeling?

If someone were to ask you "How are you feeling?" how would you answer? For many of us it may be difficult to accurately answer this question. In some cases you may never have actually been asked such a question. In a society where relationships are built upon communicating, the absence of an understanding of how you are feeling limits your ability to develop close relationships. How can you interact if you are unaware of your feelings? It is difficult to have self-knowledge if you are not in touch with your emotions.

So how do you feel? Here's a checklist to help identify emotions. Take a look at this list often; do a self-check; try to evaluate which emotions are present and which are not at a given moment. Which emotions have you experienced recently? Which emotions would you like to experience more often? Try combining words to try to express how you are feeling. There is no rule that you can only be feeling one emotion at a time!

How am I feeling?

Afraid	Aggressive	Agonized	Angry
Annoyed	Anxious	Apologetic	Arrogant
Bad	Bashful	Bewildered	Blissful
Bored	Cautious	Cheerful	Cold
Contented	Confident	Confused	Content
Curious	Defensive	Demure	Depressed
Detached	Determined	Disappointed	Disapproving
Discouraged	Disbelieving	Disgusted	Disillusioned
Disoriented	Doubtful	Ecstatic	Elated
Embarrassed	Empty	Enraged	Envious
Exasperated	Excited	Exhausted	Exuberant
Fearful	Frenzied	Frightened	Frustrated
Furious	Great	Grief	Guilty
Happy	Hassled	Helpless	Helpful
Hopeful	Hopeless	Horrified	Humbled
Hurt	Hysterical	Indifferent	Innocent
Insecure	Interested	Irritable	Irritated
Isolated	Jealous	Joyous	Liberated
Liked	Lonely	Loving	Mad
Meditative	Mischievous	Miserable	Morbid
Motivated	Negative	Numb	Offended
Optimistic	Outraged	Painful	Panicked
Paranoid	Pessimistic	Perplexed	Powerful
Powerless	Puzzled	Regretful	Relaxed
Relieved	Resentful	Restless	Sad
Satisfied	Scared	Sheepish	Shocked
Skeptical	Smug	Surprised	Sympathetic
Tender	Tense	Thoughtful	Undecided
Uneasy	Unhappy	Unsure	Valuable
Vulnerable	Withdrawn	Worthless	Worried

From the list above, check which ones you are feeling at this moment. Go through each word one at a time and think of a time or situation when the word describes how you once felt. Take the time to also imagine how each word makes you feel and how that word would feel in your body. Remember too, that sometimes you may have no words to describe how you feel. An emotion may be simply a sensation in your body. Many times I have encountered people who wish they could cry and they definitely believe it would be helpful and healing, yet no tears come. In my own healing process I experienced this a number of times. I learned that I had to be patient, that there was some lesson I needed to learn to unlock my pain. At times I had to be patient and trust that the protective nature of my sub-conscious would be wise enough to know when I was ready. I was never let down by this process!

At times however, when very busy, I would not make time to mediate and explore my emotions. The following process helped me in those times. Sitting quietly, I would scan my body for tension. I would ask myself "What am I feeling at this moment?

Try to use the concept of using multiple words and describing the situation, expectations and what you hoped for, and what could have been done differently to express yourself!

12. Discovering the Roots of Wisdom

Each of us gets hurt to varying degrees simply by living our lives. No one is immune to difficulties. How you deal with these emotional challenges greatly affects your future responses to similar events and challenges. I believe, as many others do, that a great deal of mental illness results from the inability to process emotions and the associated events.

One of the concepts taught in my computer business systems courses is the difference between data and information. Data are facts and figures, while information is the processing of the data into meaning, trends, and patterns. While on a subway in Beijing I was inspired to look further into this concept after noticing a young gentlemen seated across from me with the word "wisdom" on his t-shirt with a clear and precise definition. Wisdom is defined as the ability to discern or judge what is true, right or lasting. It is considered also to be insight, and the sum of learning through the ages, as well as a wise outlook, plan or course of action. Wisdom also is defined as the quality of being wise, knowledgeable and the capacity to make due use of it. It is also discernment and proper judgment. According to the writer Cowper "knowledge and wisdom, far from being one, have oft times no connection." Simply knowing facts, without understanding the underlying causes is not wisdom. Yet it is unlikely that you can develop wisdom without knowing the facts. It is important to discern between facts, which are measurable, and your opinions, which are assumptions based on what you have experienced. Many people often confuse the two. It is in this chapter that you can learn how painful events can shape your behavior, and how you can look at your behavior and develop insight and wisdom.

To experience emotions is only the data of your experience. To express and look at their inner meaning and the root cause develops knowledge. Each time you experience an event that triggers emotion, you have the choice of experiencing and processing the emotion or avoiding it. As you process the emotions, the energy dissipates and the event is converted to knowledge, information and part of your experience of living. If you do not emotionally process events and feelings, then you will become more sensitive to similar events and issues. Unresolved events become triggers. When you encounter a similar experience, the original emotion is triggered.

Recently, a Zen monk explained a model of emotional behavior to me. She told me that these ideas have been a fundamental of Zen practice for over 2500 years. The model shows us how our emotions and the way we think build habitual patterns of behavior and self-talk that appear in our conscious daily living. The model shows the levels of emotional integration: the event or condition; emotional expression or non-expression; self-talk, frozen needs, beliefs and attitudes; habits, patterns and behaviors; and consciousness.

Triggers

Most textbooks on learning describe the effects of stimulus and response. The same theories apply to our emotions as well. The theories of learning state that when two ideas are experienced together, the later presentation of one would trigger the recall of the other. Therefore if, in our own experience, a situation results in a certain response, similar situations will trigger similar responses.

I recently became aware of one of my own triggers and have begun to replace my previous behaviors with a more effective and rewarding pattern. In my family it took a great deal of courage to ask for the most basic things. Since the reaction of my mother would be inconsistent, approaching her usually resulted in a feeling of apprehension and fear. As learning theory would predict, I developed a fear of approaching people or bringing up my own needs.

Another phenomenon of conditioning is the concept of extinction. Extinction refers to an unlearning and progressive weakening of the response. Contrary to the belief that we must work hard at changing your behavior, extinction can occur rapidly when the unconditioned stimulus is removed and replaced with another. If the stimulus is repeated without the original response, the conditioned association undergoes a weakening. If a new behavior replaces the old one or you do not respond in the same manner, you will experience a change in your behavior or paired emotion.

For various reasons I learned to fear authority figures. I developed awareness of my conditioned response, and recognized that some authority figures could be nurturing and act as mentors. When I encounter an authority figure, I intercept my thoughts and intervene with a positive and re-affirming statement regarding authority figures. This leads to a reduction in my fear of authority figures and helps me let others begin to mentor me.

Just as conditioned responses trigger your feelings, so do your unresolved emotions. Similar situations will remind you of the paired feelings of the situation. Although you can work on changing your thoughts to avoid certain feelings, it is necessary to resolve the energy associated with the emotions so that the issue is resolved at a deeper level. Otherwise you will continually have to challenge your thoughts and responses.

Events and Conditions

Events and conditions in your daily life trigger your thoughts and feelings. The triggering event or condition is the first in a series of levels in the model. Day to day events, family conditions, stress, upsetting events, as well as the positive events will all lead to the next stage of this model sometimes without your awareness. Even if you do not intellectually acknowledge the event or condition, you notice that an event has occurred because of your emotional reaction. If you are consciously aware of your emotional response then you will more likely express your feelings. You may acknowledge the event on a very subtle level.

Often a reaction to an event or condition may not occur until years after the original event. You may gain the insight that a particular event affected you in ways you did not understand at the time. You may realize that the way you were treated was unfair or perhaps you may develop different standards. When you look back at an event you may feel anger or sadness, even though you may not have felt these emotions at the time of the event. This is quite common as you mature and begin to understand what kind of relationships you want in life, and as you begin to learn more about issues such as dependency, addictions or general dysfunction in relationships and friendships. After reading *Toxic Parents* by Dr. Susan Forward, I realized the nature of my parents' behavior. I then became angry with my parents because of the new understanding I had developed. I had not felt angry at the time that some of these events occurred. Of course, now having completed my healing in this area, I have forgiven them and have only love for my parents. I no longer have the emotional energy of anger regarding these issues, but a deeper understanding of myself and their own lives and issues.

Emotional Reaction

This stage occurs as your body and emotional center react with sadness, joy, anger, or other appropriate responses to an event or condition. In a positive emotional climate you will likely feel free and encouraged to express yourself. Alternately, in negative emotional climates you may feel it necessary to bottle the expression of emotion. Both emotional expression and avoidance lead to the next stage of the emotional model, but with different consequences.

Denial of the event or condition at this point does not halt the development of emotions, self-talk, attitudes, or behaviors. The event is simply pushed out of your conscious thinking, and results in subtle forms of anxiety, tension, stress, and sensitivity. You end up using energy to keep these thoughts of the event out of your current thinking patterns. This emotional blocking results in an accumulation of emotional "baggage." Later, because you have not dealt with the original issue, you become sensitive to similar events or conditions. These issues become trigger points that cause you to react not only to the current situation, but with the affect, attitudes and fears associated with the original and other similar incidents you have experienced.

In a nurturing environment you will be more likely to express your emotions. You will experience a sense of validation and being listened to. This helps you to develop positive self-talk, attitudes and self-esteem. In a non-nurturing environment you may learn to view your emotional expression and behavior as shameful and bad. The Buddhist approach to emotional numbness is that an individual is still feeling the emotions at a mind-body level. This blocking of the felt sense requires a substantial amount of energy. It is similar to keeping a car still by pressing on both the gas pedal and the brakes at the same time. The car does not move, but considerable energy is spent creating opposing forces. This energy could certainly be used in more purposeful ways!

Self Talk, Frozen Needs and Attitudes

From your own emotional reactions you move to a more conscious level of self-talk, frozen needs and attitudes. Once you begin to process your experience of an event and the emotion associated with it, you then begin to filter the event through your own experiences and beliefs. Through filtering and association you develop ideas and images of your self and others that become part of your way of thinking and eventually part of your behavior and attitudes.

Self talk is the little voice inside your head that churns over ideas and thoughts and advises you whether you can accomplish something or whether you should take risks. Your mind's voice is a part of your consciousness. Unfortunately, your ability to effectively reason is often limited by your emotional baggage or by emotional experiences that you have not resolved. Your voice may indicate fear or rejection, or a decision to avoid an issue. Often it is a voice that tells you of your own self worth. If you have often been harmed or abused and have not resolved these emotional issues, you will likely avoid getting close to others.

Often your self-talk can be very subtle and you may not be aware of its tone and effect. You may have a subtle feeling or symbol of yourself that is of low worth, or of someone who does not deserve love. If you have been nurtured or have accepted events in your life you will experience self-talk that celebrates your talents and has a firm belief in your worthiness.

Too often though, you experience events that challenge your self-esteem and sense of security. All of us share these human needs. They are needs such as food, shelter, companionship, a sense of belonging, and the need to express your caring for others. As humans, it is natural to seek the love and approval of others. If, on a repeated basis, you are denied the love or approval you need then you may develop what is called a frozen need. Frozen needs are unresolved wants or needs that were not met at some time in your life.

If at a time you were unable to be close to others, then you may develop a strong need for closeness. This becomes a pattern that permeates new and old friendships and usually results in a feeling that nothing is ever enough. This may occur with financial matters as well. If you experienced times of financial hardship, you may try to ensure that you gather as much as possible. The searching that you do in order to fulfill these frozen needs can lead you on a path of feeling somewhat empty at times, even though you may have attained a degree of closeness and financial success. Later on in your life you may often go about trying to fulfill these needs through relationships, addictions or by trying to obtain the validation you did not receive. You may also develop patterns of behavior that shield you from your pain or inadequacies.

Similar to frozen needs are the attitudes you develop as a result of your self-talk and the messages you may hear from others. Although you may be able to state some of your attitudes verbally, many attitudes are a felt sense that you can not put into words. As described in numerous texts on learning, attitudes each have a cognitive, affective and behavioral aspect. The cognitive aspect of an attitude often deals with consistency. You get what you expect and in some ways you expect what you get. The affective aspect refers to feelings associated with the attitude. Events that trigger feelings will lead to attitudes associated with those feelings. Simply working on your behavior or thoughts is not sufficient in effecting attitude change. In addition to challenging your thinking, it is necessary to examine and resolve your feelings regarding the attitude. I've heard many people say, "I know I'm a nice person, but I just don't feel it."

Habits, Patterns and Behaviors

Your behaviors are often based on expectations, attitudes and your previous responses in similar situations. Often you are unaware of your frozen needs and attitudes and therefore are not in control of your behavior. The development of awareness of your own attitudes, frozen needs and the emotions inherent in them is a major step in your healing process. What are your behavioral responses to the events and conditions you encounter in daily challenges? Are you open to constructive criticism? Are you afraid of expressing yourself? Can you express your love? Do you run from pain and attempt to seek solace in drugs, alcohol or other masking behaviors? Do you recognize that if you work through your pain, it will pass?

Clearly your beliefs about your ability to cope with pain will impact your response. If you are secure in your self worth and abilities, you are more likely to feel comfortable in expressing love and accepting criticism. If you are less secure, you are likely to be defensive and less open. As you have understood with frozen needs, your behavior will often be a reflection of your emotional state and learned behaviors. You may constantly seek to fulfill a particular need or you may choose relationships that seem to fulfill a need. Your habits and patterns of behavior are, more often than not, a manifestation of your unresolved emotions and attitudes. In many cases, unresolved issues will lead to addictions, compulsive behavior, anxieties, and running from closeness. You may be triggered and react strongly when encountering familiar issues. You may do things to cover up or rationalize your reaction, leading to further anxiety. In every irrational action there is usually one thread of rationality for the behavior.

These unprocessed experiences will help shape your behavior and actions. Furthermore, each incident, if not dealt with emotionally, will result in a loss of connection with your emotional self, increasing our capacity for irrational thinking and reactive behavior. Fortunately, if you begin to examine your emotional issues and start to work on them, it is possible to reconnect with your sense of rationality. The emotional energies that surround the self can be expressed and resolved, thus freeing you to be more creative, clear and aware. One by one, the strands of emotion that cover the self will be peeled away and will no longer be troublesome to you. They will simply become part of your experience and understanding.

I recently spoke with a man at a library while doing some readings on the residential schools that Native American and Canadian First Nations children were forced to attend after being removed from their families. As we talked, tears welled up in his eyes as he told me some of the things that he went through during his years as a child and teenager at a residential school. Only now was he beginning to understand the impact of the abuse he had experienced. He spoke of two failed marriages, low self-esteem and alcohol problems. Clearly he did not blame the abusers for the failed marriages, but he now had an understanding of the effect of the abuse on his self-esteem and emotional state, which resulted in behaviors that harmed his marriages. Since he had uncovered the underlying issue, he could now begin his healing process. He now had new options, choices and the possibility of doing things differently.

Understanding and acknowledging the impact of an event is a major step in the healing process. It can also be an act of self-acceptance and self-love to forgive yourself for a lower than desired performance in areas of your life. I had always felt ashamed of my poor academic performance in my last year of high school. I recognize now that I was grieving the loss of a classmate who died when he was hit by a car. I had not previously recognized the depth of the issues I was dealing with at the time and the impact it had on my performance.

In the introduction of this book, you may recall how I described myself prior to my healing work. I kept myself extremely busy, took on many projects and kept myself at a considerable distance from others. I could not slow down, nor could I let people assist me at times when I needed help. I was very independent, and unable to let other people know my true self. I believe that many of these issues were the result of not having processed the natural emotions that had occurred due to the losses I had experienced and the beliefs I developed about myself in the course of my upbringing. As I began to challenge these beliefs and to express and resolve the affect, my self-talk improved and I gradually learned new behaviors as a renewed sense of creativity and rationality appeared.

Relationships and Emotional Baggage

Relationships in themselves are processes of learning about each another. All relationships require effort and communication to resolve issues that arise. If one person in the relationship is much more aware of their emotions than the other, then an imbalance occurs in the relationship. All is not lost however; if you are willing to discover and express your feelings. Both can grow in their understanding of each other.

A genuine relationship is difficult if one or both partners in the relationship are unable to be genuine. Someone who seeks a genuine relationship will likely have trouble attracting or connecting with another genuine person simply because of the walls they have built up around their own emotions. These walls may have been erected long ago as a defense mechanism. The walls are still being maintained even though they no longer serve the person. The problem lies in the fact that the individual may not know how to tear down the walls.

Suppressing your emotions usually harms your relationships in the long run. When you suppress, you do not communicate with the other person nor do you resolve issues. These unresolved issues end up making you more sensitive and cloud the real issues in a relationship. Many of us have been raised to believe that blocking or ignoring a feeling or problem may cause it to go away. You may think you have dealt with the issue but in reality it has just been pushed below the surface. This may hinder your communication in the future.

Blocking your emotions is not a true solution for you. In the long run, you end up having day-to-day issues that trigger the emotions that you think you have dealt with. Unresolved and unexpressed emotions are like an unhealed wound. Until you take the time to let the wound heal, any attempts to use the injured part will only bring back the pain of the old wound or injury.

When you bottle up your emotions you may end up compromising your relationship with yourself and others. You may become depressed and communication with others may become difficult as it filters through the walls you have built up around your emotions. You may end up giving the impression that you want to be left alone even though it's the exact opposite that you want.

Regardless of the type of numbing mechanism you use (consciously or unconsciously), it usually takes a great deal of energy to suppress or avoid your emotions. Although you do not have a method of measuring that energy, you can see the effect on your life. You may not wake up refreshed in the morning. You may be listless and tire easily. You may also have less concentration and poorer memory skills. If you are the type that has stayed extremely busy, you may be afraid to slow down for fear of what you might feel or find.

Often the intense emotions you feel towards someone may be the result of underlying emotions that you may not be aware of. Your own intense emotions are like stained glass which cloud your own ability to see things objectively. In most relationships you experience day-to-day events that cause emotional responses. Your response, however, will be greatly determined by the deeper and subtle feelings you have for that person. If on a deeper level you are angry with someone, then your response to an event will more likely be anger. If you are passive, then this behavior only adds to the underlying tone of anger.

Because you have suppressed your emotions you have probably built emotional walls around yourself. This results in isolation that prohibits you from feeling and connecting with others. Anything that triggers deep emotions often results in a retaliatory stance to protect yourself from feeling deep-seated pain. I remember how at the age of eighteen, I spent two weeks staying at my girlfriends place while her mother was away. Her mother had asked that I stay there, because of her daughter's fear of staying alone. I had talked it over with my parents and was told that the decision was mine and that they would respect my decision. What happened after I stayed at my girlfriend's place was a completely different story. My mother erupted in anger and judgment. Clearly her religious views were in total conflict with her behavior. As I confronted her with the difference in her behavior and what she had told me she would do, she angrily told me that she did not love me, never did, and never would. Deeply hurt, I left the house. Fortunately my oldest brother heard the exchange and offered reassurance.

I have since learned that such a display of anger and hurtful behavior was not really the result of the present situation. It had taken my mother fifty-seven years to get to the place where she could be so angry and in such a state of poor mental health. In the subsequent years I learned of her loss of her mother at an early age, the loss of her first fiancée to war, the death of a twin, her subsequent miscarriages, and that she was living in a time when little help was available to her. With this deeper understanding of her troubles, it became easier to forgive, as I could understand the range of emotions and unresolved grief that she carried with her and that most of her behavior wasn't really about me. She was also dealing with the fact that her young son was now an adult making choices of his own. To her this felt like abandonment and separation and reacted strongly to her own internal backlog of feelings in an unhealthy way.

Any backlog of emotions can be a hindrance to a relationship, whereas emotional expression between two people who are comfortable with their own emotions will lead to a greater bond between partners. Perhaps it is time to make better use of your energy, to open up to others and let them help you!

Key Healing Concepts

At this point I would like to introduce some very key concepts that must be considered before reading the next chapters as the concepts discussed in this section will lay the foundation for change in your life, as they have in my life. Perhaps when I was going through the various healing changes I was not clearly aware of these concepts, but looking back they were all present and it is clear to me that the things I will discuss in this chapter were the fundamental principles that allowed me to make changes in my thinking, feeling and relationships. In writing this chapter, I have pulled theories and concepts from a number of sources. At the time of writing this chapter I kept hearing the same messages from a number of sources – from friends, from other activists I was working with on student loan issues, to theatre productions and the minister at the church I was attending. It seemed so clear that these ideas needed to be communicated in this section and that it is necessary to keep these concepts in the back of your mind as you read the rest of this book!

Be Wary of Opposites

One of the biggest traps in the healing process is to get caught up in "us" verses "them" thinking. It is so easy to think of yourself as the harmed individual and to lay blame and judge others who may have harmed you. While it may be true that you weren't treated properly, or perhaps don't like the way others behave, it is very important to practice compassion and try to see the good in others from the earliest point possible in your healing journey. Granted, this may be difficult, but I, like many others, can attest to the powerfully negative force of judgment of others that can get in the way of being kind and loving.

Rebbe Nachman says "The highest peace is the peace between opposites. If you remember this, the next time you meet someone who makes you uncomfortable, instead of heading for the nearest exit, you'll find ways for the two of you to get along."

If you really want to change others, become the change yourself. That means being non-judgmental and allowing others to be themselves. As the poet Rumi says "Many want love, few will be willing to become it." Leading by example and showing positive regard for others, rather than contempt, will do more to heal your relationships than any long deep talk about what troubles you!

Being Humble

As I look back on my own healing journey, I realize that there were many times that I experienced a sense of humbleness or as the Buddhists would say, I needed to practice humility. While the words are similar, this is very different from the sense of humiliation that I felt as a child and teenager, being teased and ridiculed. To be humble and practice a sense of humility means being open, receptive and in a state of putting aside pride. In this state you can see more clearly, and put aside your beliefs and your need to be right about something. In putting aside a need to be right, you can more clearly see the whole picture including other people's point of view. The other thing that can happen in a state of humbleness is that you begin to question your own world view and you may begin to realize that in all honesty, the things that you have been doing to solve a problem may not be working. I have heard many times that the true definition of insanity is "doing the same thing and expecting different results." As you open your heart and mind to new possibilities, you realize that how you got here is just as important as what you are doing now. You can be open to greater understanding and openness to new ideas by giving up your defense of your belief system, without seeing it as defeat or humiliation but humbleness towards a consciousness that is greater than what you have previously experienced!

Developing the Inner Observer

I know many people who have experienced very difficult times but came through it all. Although the stress levels that they experienced were extremely high, and they came very close to losing their sanity in these ordeals, the common thread that pulled them through was the ability to invoke an observer like quality that allowed them to see that they were deeply troubled and needed help. It is not necessary to get into deep trouble to utilize this powerful tool. In order to gain perspective on your difficulties, it is necessary to step back from the event and people involved in it and get some perspective. By doing this you can realize that the strong emotions you may be feeling are not necessarily the only aspect of the event, and you may be able to gain more insight by asking the questions of who, what, when, where and why.

In developing your ability to be an objective observer, you need to imagine that there is a camera filming the event from above. All characters can be seen in the film and you try to see the event unfolding, free of judgment, and feeling safe to see the truth and be more aware to set aside that which you fear.

By becoming an independent observer, you invoke honesty and clarity. It is important to observe any beliefs that have an edge of discomfort. This can often indicate a bias in the interpretation of the event or an opinion that you should probably question!

By becoming the observer, you can pull away layers of cloudiness and see the whole picture. The area I live in is often blanketed by fog in the morning. Yet I do know that above the fog is a beautiful blue sky. Just as the fog burns off, by examining the events that trouble us with better perspective, we can clear away clouds of confusion and incorrectly assumed beliefs. Sometimes just imagining that the problem is moving further and further away from you will give you greater clarity.

Being Innovative

It isn't surprising that most of us have an aversion to confusion. It is an unpleasant state of doubt and trying to understand our old beliefs while considering new ones. Confusion is necessary though if you want to move forward in your thinking, attitudes and feelings. By allowing confusion to be present, you open yourself to new ideas!

Moving into a new realm of being requires a degree of innovation. While the term "innovation" has usually been used solely in the business world, it is a key consideration in personal growth. Goran Ekvall did some pioneering work in the concept of innovation over twenty years ago. Based on his work, there are a number of categories that make up innovation. The first is how motivated you are for change. Secondly, you need some freedom to make change. How attached are you to personal and family attitudes? Can you make changes in your environment that have a chance of succeeding? The third concept involves how much time you can set aside for creativity and evaluating ideas and plans. I know I sometimes have had a habit of reacting impulsively, but now I make sure I take more time for evaluating and making decisions. I also have friends that I can bounce ideas around with and get suggestions. Another area of innovation involves safety. There are certain people I don't bother talking about issues with, but I do have a number of friends with whom I can speak my mind. This can be done with my friends in a playful and often humorous manner, which is another of Ekvall's requirements of being innovative. In order to be innovative, you need some kind of conflict and debate. It seems that it is conflict that moves us as human beings to act! Finally, innovation requires risk taking. You must be willing to take risks to solve problems.

Creating Creativity

I recently read an article that has been around since the nineteen sixties that is still very relevant today. Frank Barron was a pioneer in the area of understanding what factors facilitated creativity. One of the most important factors was a motivation to create meaning in one's life. The second was a sense of intuition or trusting one's inner judgment. In addition, creative people tend to like a challenge and are more likely to admit to others that they have troubles. A further characteristic is what is called ego strength or resiliency. Like innovation, a willingness to take risk is necessary. Fortunately these are all traits that you can develop in yourself and make choices about.

You have the power of imagination to visualize yourself doing these things and possessing these traits. That is the first step in developing them in you! While you may have learned some negative uses of your imagination, it is necessary to practice developing the positive value of your imagination. It becomes necessary to stop the heightening of suffering through imagination and to begin to use it wisely.

Would it surprise you to know that parents often react in fear of short-term loss rather than long-term benefits? When I think back to how I was raised, and listen to the stories of other adults, there seems to be a common thread of parents pressuring children to avoid risk. Yet don't we all know that some risk is necessary to challenge ourselves and to grow into our talents? Why is it that as adults we also avoid risk? It seems to be simply a human trait! Yet how much do you risk losing by not changing or trying new things? At the end of my life, I don't want to look back and say that I wished I had done things differently. I hope to say I am glad I took the path I did!

Opening the Johari Window

In the nineteen sixties, Joe Luft and Harry Ingram proposed the Johari Window model of self-knowledge and disclosure that has been taught in many psychology courses. The model consists of categorizing information about "everything about you" into the four categories of: known to self, not known to self, known to others, and not known to others. When things are known to self, and known to others, a person is considered to be "open." When things are known to others, but not known to us, we are considered "blind." When we know something but others don't, then information is hidden. When neither yourself nor others know something about yourself, then it is considered "unknown."

	Not Known to Others	Known to Others
Known to Self	Hidden or Private	Open
Not Known to Self	Unknown	Blind

Your process of personal growth involves trying to discover those things that you are blind to and unknown, and also in some cases to uncover your hidden talents. You also may wish to develop your ability to put things into the hidden category by setting boundaries. In personal relationship building you may need to learn to disclose more to yourself as well as others, and learn about other people's Johari Window.

I believe that the Johari Window model can be useful in understanding relationship dynamics. You can learn to identify the behaviors that occur when one person begins to see patterns that others do not wish to disclose, or are simply still blind too. Being the first person to notice a problem of alcoholism can threaten the stability of other people's knowledge of themselves. The denial will be strong because the concept is still hidden to them. There are numerous conflict dynamics involved, especially when one person increases their self-knowledge moving from hidden or unknown to disclosure with others. When you see what others don't want to see or vice versa, there is a threat resulting in conflict and irrational behavior. Part of your journey involves learning to accept that others may not wish to uncover their hidden information. You need to respect this, manage to continue a relationship with them, and continue on your journey of growth without developing resentment and frustration.

The Change Trinity

The last part of the recipe for change involves a collection of three sets of threes. They are easy to remember and hold the key to changing our emotions, thinking and behavior.

In order to heal emotions you need to "experience your emotions," "express your feelings," and "envision a healthier outcome."

With thinking, it is necessary to follow a similar pattern. "Think the old thought," "try a new thought," and "trust in a new possibility." Instead of repressing or trying to extinguish thoughts or emotion, try to let them be. Instead of letting your thoughts and feelings ramble, try to observe them. This is a powerful concept in Buddhism!

What often needs to change as well is your behavior. The first step in any change is to "be aware of your behavior." Sometimes you may be afraid to admit to yourself that you could be doing better, or that your behavior has gotten you into trouble! You can start to change your situation if you behave as if you had the emotional health and maturity that you desire in yourself. Again, "become your own observer" of what you are doing and what triggers certain behaviors will move you along the healing path. Finally, "Believe you can do better!"

"To know when one does not know is best. To think one knows when one does not know is a dire disease. Only he who recognizes this disease as a disease can cure himself of the disease"
- Lao Tzu

13. Mind over Matters

"For every problem, there is a solution that is simple, elegant, and wrong."   - H.L. Mencken

In a dinner conversation with some friends, the term "feral" came up. If you haven't heard the term feral before, it refers to something that was once tame, but has returned to the wild. The term is often used to describe cats that were domesticated, but then were left to fend for themselves in the wild. We discussed its meaning and thought of ways it could be incorporated into a sentence. I believe it has meaning in the area of Buddhism and hence healing.

The purpose of this chapter is to suggest ways that you can look at how your own mind has become wild with thoughts and beliefs that developed during your years of growing into adulthood. Like the feral cat, you once were an innocent being, with a clean slate to have ideas imprinted upon.

In taming the feral mind, it is necessary to notice if you are in the habit of practicing cynicism, negative attitudes, judgments or blindness to opportunity due to your negative experiences. These are the feral characteristics of many people like myself who needed to do some healing work.

While a feral animal does not have too great a prospect of returning to domestication, it is possible for you to undo the trappings of difficult times and challenges. Unlike the animals, you possess the ability to self observe, to gain objectivity, and to refrain from what at times feels instinctual. You have the ability to train your mind, to reshape your thoughts and build new constructs, beliefs, and behaviours.

In the business course I teach, we study a model of problem solving that follows the steps of identifying the problem, suggesting solutions, choosing a solution, implementing it, and evaluating and adjusting. Learn to follow this model, and more importantly learn how to determine what the real nature of the problem is. A couple I spoke to complained that they were always doing laundry. Their solution was to buy a bigger washing machine and dryer. After analysis, we realized that they were always doing laundry because they were running out of clothes! The solution, which worked out wonderfully, was to buy more clothes! Study the problem thoroughly. It may not be exactly what you think it is.

Discovering and Unlocking Beliefs

When examining an old hurt, it is as if that time and place in which you were hurt, is in the present. Although you may be physically removed from the time and place, when recalling the hurt you are mentally and emotionally at the same time and place of the past event. This is why it is painful to face your emotions. The fear of being hurt can be so strong as to cause you to avoid recalling the feelings of the situation.

In *Therapy for Adults Molested as Children - Beyond Survival,* John Briere writes: "Most papers and texts on the treatment of PTSD (Post Traumatic Stress Disorder) emphasize the need for adequate emotional discharge." Briere states that this emotional discharge is needed regardless of the type of trauma. Even though trauma often results in a tendency to avoid feelings that are similar to the event, facing the emotions and releasing is necessary for growth.

Recalling the event in present safety and with new insight and awareness, allows us to discharge the emotion in a manner that achieves resolution of the hurt. If you simply recall the event and feel the emotion without the change in symbolization and self-talk, then you only restimulate the hurt and healing does not occur.

Therapists often hear of client's fear of loss of control. Many people fear that if they start to cry, they'll cry forever. The idea is to relive the original incident in a situation that feels safe for the person, and to ensure that the person knows the pain can be escaped if it becomes unbearable. You have become skilled at using our intellect to avoid pain and you can use these skills at such times to your advantage if the pain is overwhelming. It is important to balance the pain of the original incident with the present sense of safety in re-examining the emotions and to emphasize that the person experiencing the pain can return to "present time." This can be accomplished by focusing on objects around the room or by answering various non-emotionally stimulating questions relating to the individual's present situation or daily life.

To resolve pain you need to become your own observer and participant in your pain. In present safety you can experience the original pain, fear and threat to yourself and begin to understand its true nature. T.J. Scheff writes, "When the balance of attention is achieved, the client is both participant in, and observer of, his own distress. Under these conditions, the repressed emotion ceases to be too overwhelming to countenance; the client becomes sufficiently aware of it to feel it and to discharge it." When re-experiencing a hurt, you will feel the pain, fear and danger of the original incident. You must remind yourself that although the experience from the past is very real, the present is safe, and you are physically removed from the original danger.

Mark Linden O'Meara

In identifying the beliefs that are trapped in the emotional content, it is also necessary to identify the internal conflict that is causing the anxiety. Usually the conflict is a result of two partially opposing aspects or beliefs. According to Gestalt therapy, resolving the conflict involves the softening of the self towards the unaccepted belief. This involves being willing to look at the issues that are troubling you. It is a willingness to look inside and to allow the feelings and to be felt and acknowledged.

When you do this, a point of balance is maintained and you become as much of an observer as a participant, otherwise a re-stimulation occurs rather than a healing experience. By being your own observer, you can become more aware of the true nature of the event, your self-talk, and beliefs that you hold about the event. You can then objectively examine the content and nature of the beliefs and whether they are in fact true. With present safety, the assistance of a counselor or a support group and your own improved judgment and self-value, you can better judge if these attitudes, beliefs, self-talk, and messages that you were given or created ever were or are still rational.

More often than not, you will discover irrationality or improperly laid guilt or responsibility. In other instances you may discover that you made a promise to never be hurt again, never be poor again, or never be ridiculed. Through the discovery of the underlying cause of your pain you can learn to practice acceptance of yourself and others. You will learn that you did the best you could at the time. You can then adjust your attitudes and beliefs accordingly. Learning theorists agree that it is easier to replace a negative habit or belief than to try to eliminate it. From this comes the acceptance that it is easier to change yourself by substituting a positive belief.

If you believed that you were unworthy and then learn otherwise, if you believed you were bad or brought on the hurt and then realize otherwise, at such moments you release and heal. You learn that, now, in the present, there is a contradiction between the original situation and the truth of the situation. Your newer, healthier belief contradicts your previous belief, causing you to release and let go. With new beliefs about the situation and yourself, you will heal emotionally.

The content and nature of some of these new beliefs and attitudes are numerous. Here are a few examples:
- You learn that you are now safe.
- You learn that you have power and can do things differently.
- You discover that you didn't deserve the treatment you received.
- You learn that you were and are lovable.
- You discover that you can now make other choices.

- You learn that you can remove yourself from the situation if it were to re-occur.
- You learn that you are competent.
- You recognize that you were in a no-win situation.
- You learn that you are capable of having a happy life.
- You learn that you weren't responsible for what happened.
- You learn that what happened wasn't fair.
- You can see the situation in a different light and perspective.
- You can accept that others make mistakes.
- You can accept that you did the best you could with your knowledge at the time.
- You can accept that you do not need to be perfect.
- You learn that you are not useless, that you have value without having to earn it.
- You can accept that life is not perfect and at times is unfair.
- It wasn't about you – you don't need to take it personally.
- You don't have to be alone.

Prior to sitting down and writing this section, I realized that I had great resistance and anger regarding the concept that in the end it comes down to your thinking. Over the years many people had told me "You have to change your thinking" or "It's all in your thoughts." The concept of positive thinking seemed very distasteful to me. Even in my training as a counselor, I found a great deal of resentment and dissatisfaction with the theories that only dealt with thinking. As I began to wonder why, I realized that it seemed to reduce my issues down to a simple statement that minimized the complexity of the issues. On top of this, these theories seemed to ignore a very important part of my personality – my emotions.

In reconciling the notion that thinking is very important, I recognized another truth that held the key to resolving my issues regarding thinking. If we look at our world, everything is made up of atoms. Yet to simply state that everything in our world is just a collection of atoms ignores the complex relationships between and among atoms. The plants, metals and relations between all of the things around us are very complex. The same holds true for our thoughts. At a basic level, it is our thoughts that make up our personality, but there is much more going on in the complex relationships of memory, body sensations, tension, laughter, joy and love.

In your healing process it is often necessary to challenge your beliefs about certain events. Often you need to re-evaluate these events and experience a process of learning regarding them. Although these events were in the past, the emotions associated with them are being felt in the present. While you are focusing on those feelings in the present, you may also need to focus on your current thinking patterns and belief system.

Although you may have established beliefs and patterns, we as humans are intelligent enough to learn and develop new beliefs once we receive new information or insight. Often, the discharge of emotion will result in a greater clarity of thinking that will allow you to examine your belief systems and behaviors.

Some beliefs you hold may not even be apparent to you, simply because they are inferred rather than explicitly expressed. Often well meaning parents will make statements such as "if you do not do well at x, you will never be or have y." X could represent school, homework, table manners, being quiet, or any other behavior that they want from us. Y could represent any result that they wish, such as going on to college, having friends, a successful marriage, or job. What "Y" represents is their model of success, which in all likelihood, will be accepted as your measure of success, perhaps unconsciously, as something you should obtain.

Statements made to you in such a manner result in an implied "should." For example, a friend told me how his father often scolded him as a child and teenager by telling him that if he did not stop a particular behavior that was annoying to him, he would lose all his friends. A statement such as this says a number of things. My friend felt that he had been told that his friends did not value other qualities in him and would give up on him simply because of one or two minor weaknesses. In addition, there were other messages that were internalized from these parental behaviors. What he recently realized is that he had developed a belief about success, that he should always have a considerable number of friends, otherwise he would feel unsuccessful. He placed an unconscious burden on himself to satisfy this implied should. By coming to recognize this implied belief, he was able to resolve these feelings and feel a greater sense of self-acceptance and comfort with being alone.

The realization and understanding described above is a cognitive realization. These realizations are just as important to your healing process as is emotional expression. These changes in your cognition or thinking lead to changes in your emotional state. Changes in behavior can also have similar impact on your emotional state. To change your behavior, you often need to gain an understanding of your moods. This involves measurement and diagnosis of your moods. In *The Feeling Good Handbook*, Dr. David Burns outlines a process of measurement and diagnosis of moods, and identifies distortions in thinking. He then provides practical solutions involving the modification of our thinking for these problem areas. According to Burns, most people make cognitive errors in the areas of perfectionism, approval, "shoulds", overgeneralizations, the cause of past events and your ability to shape your current situation. One other area is the ability to imagine catastrophic consequences of your actions, fearing the worst, although the worst case rarely occurs!

Another important aspect of healing is the linking of insights with feelings. Insights are essentially useless if they are without attachment to our feelings. If the insights are purely intellectual then they have no effect on our emotions. It is through the combination of insight and feelings that you achieve healing and growth.

Altogether, healing involves developing a new cognitive map of yourself and of the world in which you live. It involves challenging your cognition, your behavior and your emotions. You may learn a great deal about human nature, about yourself and about others. You may discover new aspects of yourself, new creativity, and new talents. You will grow in understanding and self-knowledge.

The Stages of Challenging a Belief

While writing these pages I attended a talk on the nature of reality, which I found very interesting, not because of the subject, but because of the subjective nature of reality itself. One of the key points the moderator made was no single reality is ever totally provable, nor is it possible to have a single worldview with more than one person in the world. It is interesting to note that in the history of humanity, there have been numerous realities that have been now proven foolish, but were sacred beliefs in their time – such as the earth is flat, the sun and stars revolve around the earth, and a good bloodletting will help cure a disease!

While the incorrectness of these beliefs is now obvious to us, there are many beliefs we hold today that were not considered possible or reasonable only a few decades ago. For example, until the nineteen seventies, employment ads were divided into two columns- male help wanted and female help wanted. Such a policy would violate today's laws. While these changes are accepted now, the effort required to challenge these policies and get them changed was enormous. Using these changes as a guide for your own personal beliefs, you can see that there is a process during which beliefs get changed. I would suggest the following stages as a framework for developing new beliefs:
- an intuitive sense, opening up, a flash of insight
- feeling threatened
- confusion and ambiguity
- envisioning a new idea or way of acting
- application of the belief

- testing of the belief
- acceptance and affirmation of the belief
- re-testing the belief
- affirmation that the old belief was incorrect but served its purpose

In order to develop new beliefs you need to gain perspective and objectivity. When you are in the middle of a large city, you only see the skyscrapers surrounding you. However, when you can rise above the skyscraper, you will see the pattern of city blocks, roads, and the overall picture of a city. Moving even further back, you can sense the map of the state and continent. The same concept holds true with your problems of self-development. Your difficulties often lie in being able to get an objective perspective. Perspective does not come to us instantaneously but comes with a sense of irritation that something is amiss. Irritation and confusion are usually necessary before insight. Allow the confusion to exist. In your personal life, you need to examine which beliefs you hold that perhaps need to be let go, whether they are societal, family or personal beliefs. Be willing to question the validity of your beliefs! This is the sign of true intelligence!

Attributions and Subtext

One of the critical aspects in my healing process was to examine my own attributions. Attributions are reasons you develop to explain why people do and say things. From being a child to living as an adult we all make assumptions as to why people do things. Often these assumptions are incorrect. From my own childhood, I remember making assumptions about why my parents did certain things. When I was in grade four, my father had major surgery to treat cancer. The surgery changed his facial features. I remember the weeks in the hospital and how I missed him. On the day he came home, we were told to stay in the kitchen. I had missed him so much and wanted to convey this to him so I broke the rules and went into the living room to welcome him. Both my mother and father got angry with me. I assumed that my father did not want to see me, and my first encounter with him in weeks was painful and I felt very hurt. Through the logic of a child, I assumed he did not love me. Looking back on how the surgery disfigured him and talking it over with him in later years, he told me how happy he was to be home, how he had missed us, but since we were so young, he did not want to scare us with the stitches and swelling on the side of his face. It now all makes perfect sense. Of course, my parents were not adept at ascertaining my needs, but I could certainly see that my attributions and assumptions were incorrect. This led to my healing of this incident and others.

As I examined my attributions in various situations, I began to see how much my father deeply loved me and how he was humanly limited in his ability to show his love. I recently came across some research that showed that some fathers stated that they were less responsive to children on days with more job stress and more irritable on days with greater social stress. The children on the other hand could not discern a difference between the stress levels!

In learning to identify your assumptions and attributions it is helpful to turn to a concept in the field of acting. In every scene there is what is called the subtext. Subtext is what happens below the surface. It is not the words said, or the actions completed, but the intention, goals, thoughts, feelings and body language of the people playing out a scene. It is often not what is said, but how it was said, or even what is not said. Even more important is how you interpreted what was said. In drama, the script is written to convey certain motivations and tension between the characters. When writing a script the author has a clear understanding of what is to be communicated. In our own lives, this is not true! Can you really know the true intention of others? It is so easy to err in making assumptions as to why people do things!

Here are some questions that help understand the underlying subtext in a situation

1. I expected him or her to…
2. I believe his or her intentions were to…
3. I think he or she acted in such a way because….
4. I felt ….
5. I wanted him or her to….
6. I acted in such a way because….
7. The underlying conflict of the situation is…
8. I think he or she wants….
9. In this situation I need…..

Try to stand back from a situation and understand how your mind works. Self-help groups can be very supportive and insightful, as you get to observe and learn how others think and work through issues. In this sense, new ways of thinking and looking at assumptions are modeled for us.

Try to understand what judgments you are making about other peoples' intentions, motives, feelings, and reasons why they do things? It is important to note that in each situation, others are making assumptions and attributions as well. It may appear to us that they are doing irrational things but at some level there is a string or rationality in their mind for what they are doing! What judgments are you making about yourself? What feelings do you have that you are or are not expressing? What would you like to occur? How would it change how you feel about yourself and the other person? How would it feel to accept that they couldn't give this to you, not because they don't want to, but because they do not have it to give?

Increasing Your Self-Knowledge

In learning about you, there are some helpful tools available to understand our personality traits. While it is beyond the scope of this book to explain all the theory on personality types, there are a few basic concepts that can be helpful.

To increase your self-knowledge, take the time to evaluate yourself in a non-judgmental but honest manner. I have found the following questions to be very helpful in learning about my strengths and weaknesses!

1. What positive ideas do you have for yourself?
2. What negative ideas do you have about yourself?
3. What negative messages were you given about yourself?
4. What positives did people tell you about?
5. How do you talk to yourself when with people you know?
6. What do you say to yourself when someone seems disinterested?
7. Complete the following sentence: I'm _____!

The above questions help uncover your inner dialogue. You can discover what you are really saying to yourself about your soul. To use the questionnaire requires a sense of gentleness, personal caring and honesty! Do this out of love for yourself, not out of criticism! It can be a key to unlocking the door to self-love.

Seeking Counseling

In earlier years there may have been a time when you thought that the pain would never end. As a child you may not have the ability, simply due to your age or circumstances, to reach out to someone or to find a safe place from your troubles. At times as an adult you may not have had the tools, support, help, or knowledge to reach out and go through the healing process. The pain may have seemed endless.

As an adult you can make choices and find help. There are numerous 12-step groups (such as Al-Anon, Adult Children Anonymous, Alcoholics Anonymous or Emotions Anonymous) that can provide support and help in your healing process. There are counselors trained to help and guide you through this process. Keep in mind also that, although you may feel as though you are the only one with this problem, there are others who have experienced similar problems, have healed and are willing to help. Go to a 12-step group and see for yourself. You can learn that emotional pain can be resolved and that you can find joy - even if it is for the first time!

There is no shame in seeking assistance, but there is power in having a witness. Seeking out a counselor can greatly help your healing process. At times you need some guidance or someone to listen who is objective and can reflect your feelings back to you in a way that no friend can. Personally, I have at many times sought help; even though I am an author of this self help book. The fear of reaching out kept me stuck for many years. I find that it has been important to see a counselor who is at least two steps ahead of yourself in their own healing work or to talk to someone who has experienced and healed the issues you are facing. Experience is a great teacher!

Discovering Your Attitudes

Although we have built a strong case for emotional expression, it is a fact that emotional expression by itself is not enough to bring about healing. If you are to resolve patterns and heal emotionally, you need to examine your attitudes, behavior and self-talk as well as express yourself emotionally. True healing occurs when you work on your behavior, emotions and thinking. Fortunately, the three are intricately related and therefore working on one will have positive effects on the others. Too often one of the three will be compromised due to the stress you are experiencing. Just as a drinking habit may numb your emotions and negative thoughts will affect your moods, so too will positive thoughts and emotional expression lead to improved behaviors.

When examining and evaluating your beliefs, you must do so without judgment and self-criticism of yourself. You need to create an inventory of your actions and feelings in a moral and honest manner. You need to look at the values and beliefs you hold in the situation and determine if those values are appropriate. Often you have wholly swallowed the values of the role models around you. In particular, this happens in childhood, when you have yet to develop your own distinct identity, values and belief systems. As a child you may have felt powerless to change the rules. Even if you had a voice, sometimes you were outnumbered. I once heard a minister define democracy as "three foxes and a chicken getting together to decide what's for dinner." Even if you protested, you may not have had the power to change things. Later in life you need to examine these beliefs to determine their validity in your own life and the way the world works. You need to evaluate the values, messages, beliefs, self-talk, shoulds, level of responsibility, and perhaps how much power you did or didn't have at the time.

New Behavior!

Often you try to resolve a behavior pattern by trying to develop new habits and by trying to counteract the behavior itself. A more appropriate and likely more effective method to alleviate the behavior pattern would be to go to the root or foundation of the problem by re-examining the event, emotional expression and images that result in the pattern. This type of self-examination will bring about a longer lasting solution to the problem than the short-term attempts at changing habits to bring about behavior modification. Both methods will cause change in behavior, but examining the root issues will bring about a resolution of the emotional distress and more lasting result.

Since a surprising proportion of your behavior can be the result of emotional distress, alleviating the emotion can result in the removal of the distressful behavior. Once the emotional distress is dealt with, you no longer have to resort to obsessive or compulsive behavior in an attempt to block the emotions. You may no longer need to reach for a drink, drug or other addictive substance to escape from your pain. You may begin to experience closeness as you become more open and genuine. You can take off your emotional masks without fear. You will also likely have a greater capacity for rational thinking once you release and resolve your emotional distress. Habitual patterns of behavior that were a symptom of your distress are removed from your daily life because you have resolved the deeper problem.

Since emotions affect your behavior, the question should be asked, "Do behaviors affect emotions?" Clearly they do. Current research has indicated that certain behaviors increase the level of serotonin in the brain. Since depressed people tend to have lowered serotonin levels, certain behaviors can help alleviate depression. In *The Healthy Pleasures*, authors Robert Ornstein Ph.D. and David Sobel M.D. describe a number of pleasures that are within our reach everyday that can add to our enjoyment and fulfillment. These pleasures may involve such things as investing in yourself, developing a pursuit of happiness, telling yourself a good story, and developing a healthy pleasure reward points system for yourself. Other behaviors such as meditation, art therapy, and singing have been known to reduce levels of depression.

Often the expression of emotion leads to new behaviors, and new behaviors lead to better emotional states as well as more rational thinking. All three are linked together. Changing one affects the other, which in turn produces other changes. Pick the easier things to change, and you'll notice results! A recent study in California has shown that changes in behavior and cognitive therapy can bring about changes in the chemicals in the brain, including the structure that is implicated in Obsessive Compulsive Disorder.

In the process of studying the cognitive-behavioral model of counseling theories, therapists-to-be learn that this theory proposes that if you control what you are thinking and doing, then the feelings and physiology will follow. The analogy used is that of a car: the thinking and doing are the front wheels that steer the car, while the feelings and physiology follow right behind.

While these concepts are valid, it is important to note that feelings of sadness and depression can come from more than one source. Feelings of sadness and depression can be generated from your own thoughts and behavior. A negative attitude will lead you to depression. Behavior that isolates us can also lead to depression.

But another source of sadness and depression occurs when you are emotionally hurt or experience a loss. These feelings are not the result of your thinking or behavior, but a natural reaction to a life event. Grieving needs to be completed to resolve these feelings. Emotional expression may be required to resolve feelings of sadness, anger or resentment concerning a loss or trauma.

In treating depression and emotional hurt it is necessary to recognize that there are two different sources of emotional pain, both requiring different treatments. In cases of trauma, it may be necessary to re-examine and mentally revisit the incident to resolve the feelings. Simply trying to feel better by changing your thinking may work for some but not all.

If, however, you combine emotional expression and changing your thinking and behavior, then the results can often be astounding in terms of healing, growth and personal development.

> The thought manifests as the word,
> The word manifests as the deed
> The deed develops into habit,
> And habit hardens into character
> So watch the thought and its ways with care
> And let it spring forth from love,
> Born out of concern for all beings
> —The Buddha

14. Getting Un-Stuck

No problem can be solved from the same consciousness that created it.   -Albert Einstein

In your healing journey there will often be times when you get stuck. In these times you do not see solutions and you seem to repeat patterns of behavior. Sometimes a lesson or test reappears, yet you make the same mistakes or simply don't know what to do. At times it may be your own behavior or attitudes that get you stuck. You fall into a trap or hole. To become unstuck means to learn to recognize the holes you fall into and to acknowledge them and eventually learn to walk around them. Some of these holes and traps are:

fear	helplessness	guilt	anger
despair	powerlessness	fear of failure	insecurity
isolation	loss of control	panic	depression

Often these feelings or states arise because you do not understand what your body is telling you about your feelings. You may lack knowledge or feel overwhelmed by the signals. You may fear being wrong or being rejected for showing your emotions. You may also be playing old tapes of a past situation in which you may have been helpless or powerless. Again, you need to achieve a sense of balance that tells you that in the present you do have choices and that you can act differently than you have in the past.

Are you living in the past instead of the present? Are you going over events again and again without any resolution? If so, then you must change your thinking patterns and address your feelings on the issues. As you become more aware of your feelings and your history you begin to comprehend how things were around you. You have a number of options to choose from in the way you will proceed. You can choose to go over your past and remind yourself how tough it was, or you can address the feelings and realize that you survived and that you can and will heal from those events.

You need to put the past behind you and hold hope for a better, healthier future. To do this you may need to face some emotions, accept the past and change your thinking that occurs in the present. If you do so, then you will likely find happiness or the types of relationships you are looking for. The bible states that what you ask for, you shall receive. If you ask for more pain you will find it. You may even give it to yourself by beating yourself up over past events and things you wish you had done differently. The other choice is to accept what was and to choose a better path and a better way - now available to you because of the work you have done! If you look for happiness, new friends, support and kindness, then these things will come to you!

You need to recognize that you have options and that you are no longer powerless or helpless. When you recognize these qualities of your new present situation, your fear and despair disappear. You can learn that emotional release and healing can bring an end to the isolation that occurs when emotions are accumulated. Remember that crying due to the pain of hopelessness and despair is different from crying for the purpose of healing.

The Self Pity Trap

Often when you are sad or grieving it is easy to fall into a trap of self-pity. Self-pity involves feeling overly sad for yourself as a victim. If you are finding yourself developing a "poor me" attitude, then you may need to look into your pattern of being helpless and without power. In your emotional healing you need to remember that you are not helpless and that you can change your situation. Your goal is to heal and be free of lingering sadness rather than remain a slave to it. You need to realize that you are much more than the pain you carry around and that you are much more than your emotional state. Although you may have carried your pain around for a long time, you need to entertain the idea that it is possible to rise out from it and to experience a more joyful state of being. Your emotional state is not necessarily part of your personality. It is something that can be resolved and released to reveal a more creative and energetic you!

Temporary self-pity does have its value in our healing process. Identifying that you are feeling pity for yourself can help you discover that there is some hurt to be resolved or simply that you need to acknowledge that you are feeling sad or unhappy about something. To deny the sadness is to deny your feelings, but to remain in the pity can be a trap that will block your emotional healing. True, it can be part of healing to feel sad, but when this becomes an excuse for the way you are, then you are not healing but hiding. You are avoiding going further along in your healing process.

Imagine a triangle with feeling, pity, and denial each in a corner. In your healing process you may move from corner to corner of the triangle, however your most healing times can occur when you are operating at the center of the triangle. Denial plays its role in healing by allowing you to deal only with what you can handle. Overwhelming yourself can be harmful and can place a great deal of stress on your mind and body. Pity and sadness allow your mind to acknowledge your sadness and that you have been hurt, but you must eventually move closer to the center position of detachment.

Detachment is a term often used in 12-step groups describing a sense of objectivity from others and your problems. Detachment means that you can objectively see the problem in its true light, without the clouds of emotional patterns that have sabotaged your objective thinking. For example, you may have given your power to others or allowed others to be your unofficial parents. As a result you end up reliving your roles with your parents with these people, thus clouding your understanding of your needs and desires of these people.

Detachment also means being able to differentiate your problems from other people's problems. Through detachment you learn not to suffer from the reactions and actions of other people. You begin to develop your sense of self-esteem measured by your own set of judgments and values as well as a strong belief in yourself. You learn to accept that it is not possible to have everyone like you. By developing a sense of balance between feeling, self-pity, and denial, you can learn about yourself, acknowledge your own feelings, and see issues in a realistic and objective manner.

Holding On

Many of us unsuspectingly become stuck in the last stage of emotional release. Many of us get to the expression stage and genuinely work on expressing ourselves. To complete the process you need to be willing to let go of the emotional energy. You need to be willing to exist with the issue at hand being completed and gone from your life. Sometimes a particular emotion has been around you so long that it feels as though it is part of you. To let it go may mean rediscovering yourself and finding out who you might be, without the emotion that has defined your behavior for such a long time. You may not be happy with the emotions you are experiencing but you may feel comfortable having them around. They become a possession with which you are unwilling to part.

Too often you may refer to anger or other emotions with the word "my" in front of it. You end up claiming ownership of your anger. Instead of saying "this anger," you say "my anger" or "my sadness." You end up holding it close to your chest and are afraid of letting it go completely. Letting go of an emotion means risk. It means that you will be moving on to the next issue in your life. This may frighten you to some degree and as a result you cling to your current emotional state. The cost of not going all the way with your emotional expression is that you hang on to the emotion and it can then be easily re-stimulated. Imagine trying to launch a toy boat in a pond with a small string attached to it and tied to the shore. The boat will head off but it will never be able to sail freely or continue on its journey. Emotions are the same in that you must be willing to completely let go of them; otherwise you end up in a state of emotional tension that never quite fully resolves itself.

In order to successfully release the energy associated with your emotions, you must be willing to go completely through the process of release. To simply become aware of the emotion and feel it is not enough. You need to be able to completely express it, and then fully let it go and dissipate. You must be willing to let the emotion leave you and give up any benefit you obtained from having it. If you do not give up the benefit of your emotional state, its expression becomes parasitic. It has served its purpose, but it is now being used to make someone else wrong, to punish another person or even yourself. Your attitude must be changed otherwise your continued expression without resolution ends up harming yourself and others. It is especially easy to get in touch with anger or sadness, to feel part of it and then back off, without resolving it.

When you do this you simply re-traumatize yourself as well as the people around you. You trick yourself into thinking that you are doing well by experiencing the emotions. To achieve emotional health you must go further. You must be willing to completely express the emotion and completely let it go. You must get in touch with the feelings, feel them, learn what incorrect beliefs you hold, and let the emotions leave you. Your goal is growth and acceptance of what is. If you hold on to old beliefs and feelings, then you become addicted to your view of the triggering situation and use the emotions as an excuse for your way of being. You learn to speak the truth without drawing a battle line.

Increasing Your Awareness

In order to solve problems it is often helpful to examine and expand your scope and awareness of the problem. Often you become stuck because you fail to see other options. Just as though your problem were confined to a small room, you end up breathing only stale air that surrounds the problem. You need to bring some fresh air in or, as the saying goes, "shed some light" on the problem. This can be achieved by searching for new ideas as well as expanding your range of solutions. It is possible that you may decide to stop resisting your problem. It takes much more effort to resist something than to actually do something about it.

It is often helpful to step back and look at others who were involved in the original problem. I always felt responsible for an incident that happened walking to school in grade one. Two of my brothers and I walked to school with another friend from the neighborhood. As we got a few blocks from home, my friend refused to continue to school. We were physically trying to drag him, knowing no other option at the time. A car pulled up and the man yelled, "Leave that boy alone!" He looked like one of the boarders at my friend's house, so we continued on to school and left him behind.

My friend did not show up to school for a couple of hours. When he did he had scratches on his face and he was screaming and crying. He had been kidnapped. I don't know if he had been sexually abused. The police were called and an investigation began. My brother told me that it was my fault for leaving him. I felt tremendous guilt. In hindsight, it was not my fault that this man did the things he did. It was not my responsibility to get this friend to school, and it was a normal reaction to respond with fear toward this man. Furthermore, there were two or three other people with me who also took no action other than to continue on to school.

Here is a further example. A friend of mine told me how at an early age, he asked his mother why his brother looked different than the rest of his family. His mother responded that his brother was adopted. As a child of five, he was in awe that his parents would take in a child and provide a home. He told his brother how neat he thought it was to be adopted. All hell broke loose. His parents hadn't told his brother that he was adopted. Both children were traumatized by the incident. Reviewing the incident, his parents should not have told him without telling his brother first. They were adults and should not have expected a five year old to keep such an important secret, which it shouldn't have been in the first place. Nor did they convey that it was extremely important to keep this information to himself until they had a chance to talk to his brother.

By objectively looking at the situation you can realize that the expectations placed on the children in these incidents were unreasonable and unfair. It was inappropriate to blame them for the outcome of these events. While you may not have ever been involved in incidents of kidnapping and revealing an adoption, you can look back on incidents with a greater understanding of the roles that others played in situations. By realizing that others had responsibilities as adults, you can more easily understand the situation and let go of misplaced responsibility!

Finding others with a similar problem can also help identify other possible solutions. You may try changing your patterns of behavior or simply decide that you no longer need to be a victim, because being a victim often precludes you from accepting responsibility for yourself. You can more closely examine the responsibilities and roles that others had in the situation. There may also be an opportunity to look inside and discover what your own feelings and beliefs are and whether these beliefs are rational. You may also begin to look at your expectations. If you can imagine your problem as being within the context of a larger plan, you may be able to look at it more objectively and seek outside help.

Reaching a Crisis Point

Although it would be nice to think that humans constantly strive to solve their problems on their own initiative, it is often a crisis that precipitates an increase in understanding. I have often joked with friends that many of the lessons I have learned were affectionately called an 'AFGE' — Another Friggin' Growth Experience. It has often been noted in the Alcoholics Anonymous and other 12-step programs, that reaching a crisis point, or 'hitting bottom' is crucial to the troubled person's recovery and subsequent elimination of the addictive behavior. In the case of career choices, many career decisions are made due to a career crisis such as a loss of job or health. In both cases clients often later regard the crisis as a positive event that dramatically changed their lives.

With the case of hitting bottom, many recovering alcoholics will say that the signs of their problem were there all along and that it took a very loud and clear message for them to get that they had a problem. Sometimes you think that admitting you need help is a sign of failure. You may feel a sense of failure if you cannot solve things on your own. Like many others, I have come to realize that trying to do it all on my own can itself be a failure – a failure to accept the help and knowledge of others To admit you need help can take a lot of courage. It's not a failure but really a victory! Look at yourself and assess where you are. Can you do this alone or could you make use of the resources that hundreds of thousands of people have used and are using now? I have grown from being independent (dependant only on myself) to being interdependent (dependant on myself and others). This builds community!

It is a sign of growth and of your ability to trust when you reach out to others. It's not easy at times, and at times doing so may be well outside of your comfort zone. But, because you took the step forward and did something different, it really is a victory! It is the start of healing, the start towards achieving some serenity.

A crisis point may result from the building of tension and emotional stress that becomes unbearable due to a financial, relationship, or health crisis. It also may occur as the result of recalling incidents that were long forgotten. It seems that many individuals attempt to ignore a crisis, often leading to behavioral problems and emotional distress.

Mark Linden O'Meara

Since crises often appear to bring about long-term positive change, I believe it is important to recognize that the events that occur in your life seemingly happen for a purpose — to nudge you along to your next level of understanding. In earlier times I would have run from my problems and feelings, denied them or told myself I was silly for having the feelings, but now I recognize that the feelings are natural and normal. I also know now that it is far healthier to feel them and release them than to stuff them down like I used to do.

Modifying Defeatist Behaviors

In your healing process you often become aware of various self-defeating behaviors or habits that limit your ability to develop a sense of self-esteem. The development of self-esteem is a crucial component in identifying many of the contradictions and falsehoods that you have erroneously believed about harmful events. Identifying the true nature of the perpetrators and increasing your self worth brings about release and healing. Self-esteem is a sense of self that develops in small portions, like building blocks, on top of each other. Building a stronger foundation of self-esteem allows you to see the contradictions of hurtful events.

Too often you may sabotage or undermine your own self-esteem with behaviors that stem from your attempts to get deserved love and attention. Too often you may do one or more of the following:

- addictively seek approval
- allow others to determine our worth
- addictively and dependently seek love
- set unreasonable goals and expectations for yourself and others
- avoid setting boundaries
- give away personal power
- minimize the positives
- exaggerate your experiences to make them seem more impressive
- engage in black and white or all or nothing thinking
- generalize your experience using words such as always, everybody or nobody,
- using the word "should" too often (referred to as "shoulding on yourself")
- expect perfection from others and yourself

All of the above behaviors can diminish your sense of self-esteem and can prevent you from developing a spiritual and emotional backbone. Developing a backbone is done by keeping your personal power and setting boundaries with

154

others so that you can choose when you wish to let someone be involved with yourself. The key to a backbone is the ability to make choices and follow through with them.

Often when you are confronting your own issues you end up confronting behavior in others; moreover, you may need to decide what your own standards of acceptable behavior are. You can then use this yardstick to measure how you are being treated in relationships. Confronting the inappropriate behavior of others can be a challenging prospect and often requires that you go out of your comfort zone. When challenged to do so, you may feel intimidated and fearful and unable to focus on the whole situation. When you face such a situation, you can increase your chances of success by feeling your breath and your feet on the floor, and by seeing the person and focusing on the space around him or her. If you do this you can maintain your sense of strength and accomplish the boundary setting you wish to achieve.

In order to achieve healing, it is necessary to bring an end to the behaviors that are contributing to your own sadness. Constantly going over an event without re-examining the context will only serve to re stimulate hurt and sadness. Similarly, negative thinking can be a habit that is contributing to your sadness. If this is the case, then you need to counter your negative thoughts with positive ones. Recognize what you can change and what you can't. .Sometimes the only thing you can change is your thoughts, as the past can not be changed, but you can change how you look at it!

Taking the time at the end of the day to note three positive things that happened, no matter how small, will help you to learn how to notice the positives. You may have trouble noticing the positives simply because you have been overly proficient at noticing the negatives without developing the skill of noticing and giving weight to the positives. If you do not come up with any positives, then this is an indication of how undeveloped your skill is in this area.

If you practice noticing the positives, in time you will become more positive. If you fight the idea of stating positives, then perhaps this is an indication of anger that needs to be resolved. Noticing the positives does not mean denying the hurt or the negatives in your life; it simply means giving weight to both and attempting to achieve a better balance of recognition of the negative and positive things going on in your day-to-day life.

Believing in Purpose

At one point I realized that most of the people who came into my life arrived merely by coincidence, and that most of the things I had done that I really was proud of usually came about by a strange set of circumstances. I developed a sense that there was something special and orchestrated regarding the seemingly coincidental occurrences in my life. There are many times that I have met the person I needed to meet to help resolve issues "just by chance." Or is it just by chance? This pattern of events is called synchronicity. Synchronicity is not a person place or thing, but it is a field of energy that seems to direct you or arrange a certain set of circumstances for the thing that you need to happen to help you move along and grow. Synchronicity is not something you can go looking for. It will find you. It is easy to confuse it with circumstances when you go looking for it. While in China a friend was having difficulties with her computer. As she mentioned that she needed a repair person, I noticed an advertisement for such a service. "That's synchronistic!" we both echoed. She took down the number and called, but the repair person never showed up and her computer was still broken two weeks later. It turns out it was synchronistic, but only in the sense that it pointed out that with hindsight, you can more clearly see the positive and synchronistic event. Going around looking for synchronicity is like looking to find money on the ground. It happens when you aren't looking! Synchronicity can also happen without your knowing about the consequences or results. It is truly magical.

I keep marveling at all the things I take for granted. The complexity of my body, the beauty of nature, the thousands of stars in the night sky. in the country away from the lights of the city, the complexity of the human mind and all the creatures that inhabit this planet. Was this all random? When I tied the concept of synchronicity and the beauty of what has been created around me, I developed my sense of God - the beauty of creation and the continual work of synchronicity in my life.

In healing, an important concept to consider is a willingness to believe in a supreme intelligence or higher power. This higher power can be whatever you want it to be. A higher power is something you define for yourself. Some of us may have discarded our earlier images of a God, while some of us may not even believe in a God. What you need to believe in, however, is that there is some force in this universe that is greater than you are and that it will protect you, help you with your issues and bring you what you need to go through the process of healing. Some of us may have a difficult time with religion, but you can develop a healthy sense of spirituality.

Many spiritual people I encounter believe in a direct link to God, that God does not punish, nor is God to be feared and that God will help us along the way. Although your experiences may be painful, there are lessons to be learned in all of your troubles. After the publication of my first book, I experienced severe financial difficulties and faced bankruptcy. If you are reading this book now, it is because through that painful experience, I was able to let go of my difficultires and continue writing. I re-wrote my book after learning many more valuable lessons. I am now providing much more valuable additional information to help people heal. While it was a very difficult time, the key to moving on was seeing the good in a very difficult situation.

As you begin to unlock your pain you learn that you can trust that your environment will provide you with the people, events, materials, and awareness that you need to heal. Some call this synchronicity or serendipity, while others call it coincidence. The common factor is that if you are committed to healing then your environment will bring you what you need as you are ready.

While some of us may be reluctant to accept the notion of a higher power or God, the key idea here is to be willing. Willingness will let you be open to the possibility that the right things will happen at the right time to help you along your path to emotional health. According to Steven Covey, author of *The Seven Habits of Highly Successful People*, most successful people believe that events happen for a purpose. When you are in the healing process, events in our lives will likely help you to better understand yourself and to resolve your issues. The right relationship will come along, losses may occur, or changes in your life will happen. They will especially occur if you are willing to believe that there is a greater purpose or a higher power helping you in your quest for spiritual health.

During the times when I was at my lowest, there was always some special little event or person that appeared to help when I needed help. One afternoon I was feeling quite low, yet decided to go out and buy some posters to brighten up my apartment. As I was driving back from the store I pulled up to a red light at an intersection. While waiting for the light to change, a family crossed the street. A little boy looked at me and saw that I was not very happy. He waved to me, smiled, and mouthed the words "It's OK!" My higher power had done its work through this child. The boy's message carried me for weeks.

I have always received what I needed to continue the process of healing. I did not always get exactly what I asked for, but I did get what I needed. I remember being very frustrated with an employer. While confiding to my friend Diane about my troubles, she jokingly said, "Mark, the solution to your problems is to get laid. I'm going to say a prayer to this Higher Power that you get laid." The next day I called Diane back with the surprising news that I indeed had gotten laid...off! I joked that she should be a little more specific with her prayers next time! A common saying in 12-step groups is "be careful what you ask for, you might just get it, but it may not be exactly what you had in mind!" Although the loss of employment was not an enjoyable experience, it was the push I needed to change careers. In a way, it was exactly what I needed and it happened at the most appropriate time.

In your healing process, you can trust that things will happen to you when you are ready. Although you may feel tested and strained at times, you are given only what you can handle. Your mind plays a very important role in subconsciously deciding what you are ready to deal with and letting you know when you are ready. If something happens or if you gain knowledge about something, it is because you are ready.

In my journey I have read many books, some of which I came across quite coincidentally. One such books was "We Pray thee Lord" by Roy Wallace Thomas. After having a coffee with a friend in a nearby town, I had a strong intuitive feeling to go into a small sceond hand store. I was already driving to the ferry terminal to catch my ferry ride and was concerned about time. I drove for a few blocks and realized that I was having one of those moments where I was not listening to my intuition and would be wondering what I had missed. I turned the car around and went back where I found Thomas' book. I opened it and found the following about "scientific hunches" as researched by a Professor Baker back in the nineteen thirties. Thomas describes Baker's work:

"The scientific hunch [is a] unifying or clarifying idea which springs into conciousness suddenly as a solution to a problem in which we are intensely interested. In typical cases, it follows a long period of study, but comes into consciousness at a time when we are not consciously working on the problem. A hunch springs from a wide knowledge of facts, but is essentially a leap of the imagination in that it goes beyong a mere necessary conclusion which any reasonable man must draw from the data at hand. It is a process of creative thought. The general conditions under which these scientific revelations appear were indicated as good health, relaxation, freedom from worry and from interuption. Many mentioned some form of exercise or manual employment such as shaving, dressing, motoring, gardening, fishing., golfing, walking, playing solitaire, listening to music.... Baker found that hunches come to most scientists in that borderland of consciousness just preceeding sleep or when the mind is fresh upon awakening or when the mind is occupied with some other matter. Thus the hunch appears when the mental conditions are ripest for the subconscious or deep self to yield its contribution."

If you feel stuck at some time, try setting up the above conditions for insight - gain knowledge, then let go, and see what your higher self brings you!

Part Four - Healing

15. Release and Let Go!

To remain whole be twisted.
To become straight, let yourself be bent.
To become full, be hollow
Be tattered that you may be renewed
Those that have little may get more.
- Lao Tzu

The Process of Releasing

When you are ready, your mind will allow you to gradually begin feeling the emotions that have been suppressed. Your mind is your own powerful ally and it will protect you from emotions that you are not yet ready to face. Sometimes you need to learn a few lessons, build sufficient strength or gain certain skills before you are ready to deal with your issues. Your subconscious mind is smart enough to know when you are ready.

When ready, you will likely begin to experience brief or fleeting moments of sadness, anger or fear. This is likely a signal that you are ready to start to feel again and that there is some unresolved emotion to deal with. As quickly as the emotion surfaces in the early stages of release, it may just as quickly disappear. Your mind at this time is probably telling you that there is something to be worked on. The first feelings may come to you like a wave then disappear.

A reasonable reaction might be to try to hide or to run from these feelings. If you can understand that getting in touch with these feelings and releasing them will bring you greater benefits in the long run, then you will not fall into your old habits of hiding from them. The emotions you touch on may seem intense and frightening to you. You may want to focus on the fact that it must take a tremendous amount of energy to keep these emotions below the conscious level. Think of all the energy that is being used to hold these feelings in place and how that energy could be put to better use!

At this time it is important that you do not dismiss or reject your feelings. It is important that you validate your feelings and take ownership of them. You must remind yourself that, given your situation and events, which occurred in your life and how you dealt with them, your feelings are reasonable and appropriate.

160

First awareness of emotions may involve a state of confusion. As you become aware of emotions you may feel as though you are receiving a number of jumbled signals. Slowly you will begin to understand those signals and identify what these emotions are and learn to articulate what you are feeling.

It is important to note that there is a significant difference between logical understanding of an event and experiential understanding. In other words, there is a great difference between talking about your emotions and expressing them. You may logically understand and rationalize events, reactions and other peoples' actions, but to experientially understand means to emotionally accept and let go of the event and feeling so that your inherent nature is no longer affected by the issue. Facing your emotional issues will allow you to integrate events into your life and bring you closer to others.

In the early stages of awareness you may also begin to remember certain events in your life that you had long forgotten. These events, like your emotions, may have been kept out of your consciousness due to the painful nature of the events or, as mentioned earlier, the conditions under which the events occurred. It can be quite common to find that memories from your childhood, previously forgotten, can come back with their associated emotions. If you do find yourself remembering events or incidents, it is because you are ready to deal with these aspects of your life that you may not have previously dealt with.

Awareness of your emotions can come to you in your dreams as well as through events in your daily life. Typically, dreams in which there is water coming up from a sewer, or a river overflowing, indicate that your emotions are a source of concern. On some occasions you may dream of painful or sad situations that seem so real and emotional that you wake up angry or crying. You may also find yourself waking to find no trace of tears and wonder why. As mentioned, your mind is a powerful ally and although your dreams may seem disturbing they can help you to better understand yourself and gain more awareness. Dreams are often a message from your subconscious in the form of symbols, to tell you something you need to hear or to know about.

Although the first stages of awareness can be somewhat overwhelming, you need to remind yourself that it is possible to work through these issues and heal from them so that they will no longer have so much power over you and your relationships. If you are beginning to feel, this is because you are ready. You may find it encouraging to trust a higher power to help you through and to provide you with what you need to release and heal!

Often you need to revisit events that happened in the past, yet there is often a tendency for other people to say "It happened 3 years ago, why don't you let it go?" You may say to yourself "That happened years ago, so why is it still bothering me?" Many times you may have heard the words of wisdom to "let it go." For some people these words of wisdom may be possible, as they have developed the ability to let go. For others it may only be a form of denial to say "It's over, get on with it" In either case, the fact that you are hurting is being missed.

If you listen to your heart and acknowledge your hurt, your response might change to "Yes, it happened three years ago and I'm learning to let go, but I haven't let go before so I'm just learning how to do it. It may take some time, but I'm working on it." Some say time is the greatest healer, but that depends totally on what you do during that time. If you were numb and did not know how to express your emotions and heal then your hurt will continue until you learn the process of letting go. Their advice is true. You must let go, but more importantly you must learn how to let go.

In your life you are bound to be hurt at sometime. It seems to be a fact of life. There are very few people, if any, who can say they have never been hurt. Each hurt is like a wound that needs to heal. Sometimes you may encounter a hurt that is deep. It is not a scratch that will heal in a few days. It is a deep hurt that stays with you for a while. It is a deep pain - a rip or tear in your soul. If you do not allow this tear to heal, your soul will not be able to give what it has to offer. You will be walking around wounded and it will affect your relationships in ways that you cannot imagine.

You need to heal the wound, to give your soul the time it needs to heal and to rebuild itself. Your soul will come out well and strong in the end. Acknowledge the wound. Acknowledge the hurt and the pain. Let it go, release it and allow the healing to occur. Doing so will open you up to so many opportunities.

First Awareness

As you become aware that your emotions are surfacing, you may help yourself to feel them by focusing on the area of your body that seems to hold the depth of the emotions. If you wish to release your pain you can help to get in touch with it if you focus on the part of our body that represents your emotional center. When you are in touch with grief you usually feel tension in the chest and throat. When you get in touch with deep pain and release it, you may feel a connection with a deep aspect of your own personality located in the region of the heart or in the chest cavity. This can be considered one of the chakras or energy centers that are discussed in many Eastern religions and meditation philosophies. Emotions manifest themselves in various areas of the body and the best way to become aware of them is to learn to be aware of what is going on in the body.

Beginning to Feel Again

I like to use the analogy that suppressed painful emotions are like meat that has gone bad but has been put away in the freezer. When suppressing your emotions, they don't seem to cause any bother until you start to get in touch with the feelings. Then you begin to feel the hurt and the pain. Like the bad meat in the freezer, it doesn't smell until you begin to let it thaw. When you thaw them out they have to be dealt with. But you can deal with them. When they are frozen, you don't seem to have to deal with them but they take up space in your compartment. Soon the compartment gets full and you can't put any more in! You can start to heal and get into better emotional health by emptying your frozen emotional freezer.

Beginning to feel again involves a number of steps and concepts for you to grasp. First, it is simply not possible to flick a switch and begin to feel again. You cannot simply begin to experience feelings generated in the present. When re-establishing your emotions you usually must face the past emotions that you have not dealt with. In other words, you cannot ignore the past when it comes to beginning to feel again.

If you were able to flick a mental switch and turn on your feelings to the full level, you would be overwhelmed and not know what to do. Fortunately, the mind is smart enough to recognize when you can or cannot handle the emotions. It will protect you from what you are not yet ready to deal with and therefore protect you from harm.

When you begin to feel again, you are beginning a gradual process. Your mind will allow you to feel what you are ready to feel. The mind will have its own agenda and as a result you must be content with getting in touch with feelings as they arise. At times I have heard of therapists or individuals attempting to schedule a time to feel their emotions. Judging from what I have experienced and what others have expressed to me, suppressed emotions will come to the forefront when you are ready. They are usually triggered by some event such as a scene in a movie, recalling a past event that you had forgotten or events that occur in our dreams. Often your dreams can have a high emotional content, and when going through a catharsis it is not uncommon to wake up from a dream sobbing.

Many people have expressed that getting in touch with emotions is similar to peeling an onion. Getting in touch with your feelings involves peeling away one layer at a time. You peel away a layer to find another. Eventually you get down to the core of the onion or the core of your emotions. By this time you usually have a greater understanding of yourself and have achieved a greater sense of emotional health.

Mark Linden O'Meara

Admitting you are numb and that you are hurting is a major and crucial step in your getting better. Beginning to feel again requires surrendering and accepting that you are hurting. Even though you may not be feeling all the pain and may not be in touch with your feelings, you are in touch with the fact that your state of mind is one of unhappiness and stress. You recognize your previous behavior of running from your emotions.

For many of you, admitting you are hurting may seem like defeat or a failure since you have fought so hard and for such a long time to win this emotional battle. As many recovered people can attest, it is really a victory to admit that you are hurting. It is a crucial step in finally recognizing something about yourself that you may have been denying for a long time. It is a courageous step and your first victory in achieving emotional health!

At the same time that you surrender your fight against your emotions, you must develop a commitment to release your suppressed emotions and to heal. At first you may be frightened by the prospect of turning on our emotions and releasing them. However, as your work progresses you will experience benefit from releasing your emotions and begin to comprehend the benefits of your work. If you are not committed to releasing your emotions and healing, it will be easy to slip into old patterns again. Sometimes this will occur, but if you are truly committed to your own healing process then, upon the realization that you are repeating old patterns, you will begin to work on establishing new, healthier ways of resolving your past feelings.

In your healing process it is important to give yourself permission to feel. You must reassure yourself that allowing the feelings to surface is OK and will actually benefit you. It is like gradually turning on a tap. The water comes out slowly at first, but you have control of the rate of flow. If something touches you or moves you, you should let yourself feel it. If someone compliments you and you feel sadness, allow yourself to feel it. If something or someone brings out some anger in you, you should let yourself feel the anger and the hurt behind it. For a long time you may have been in the habit of stuffing your feelings down whenever they appear. You must learn to feel the feelings and let the energy dissipate. Allow yourself the time and focus to get in touch with what is coming up for you.

At all times it is also very important to accept whatever you are feeling, be it anger, sadness, joy, guilt, or any emotion whether it seems appropriate or not. You may have felt shame for feeling certain ways in the past, or have been ridiculed for crying when young. In some cases expressing joy may also have been considered inappropriate. In some families, numbness and avoidance of expression extends from anger to sadness, to happiness and to joy as well. It is important that you are not judgmental of your emotional states.

164

Much of psychotherapy has sought to extinguish feelings and symptoms, yet my own personal experience has shown that acknowledging what I am feeling without trying to remove it has led to the dissipation and disappearance of the feelings. It is like a campfire. You can allow the fire to burn, but it eventually will burn out if you do not put more wood on the fire. Extinguishing emotions has a similar effect of putting water on the fire. The flames and light get smothered and a lot of smoke occurs. Thinking negative thoughts, feeling victimized and being resentful puts more wood on the fire. Yet given the right conditions, the wood can dry out and the fire started again. Letting the emotions be and expressing them is like letting the fire burn until it consumes itself. The event that triggered the emotion from then on has no power over you, nor can it be resurrected unless you metaphorically put wood on the fire by reliving the event and giving it power.

It is equally important not to try to rationalize your feelings. If you are feeling a certain emotion or combination of emotions it is OK - even if you cannot explain why you are feeling a certain way. Trying to understand or rationalize why you are feeling a certain way usually gets in the way of being in touch with your feelings and expressing them. Feelings do not need to be explained. They exist - sometimes illogically. Feelings are feelings. They exist on their own without rationalizations. They just are.

When unresolved emotions surface, you may not know exactly why they are surfacing or what event in your life caused the original feelings. It is a myth that when you get in touch with some unresolved feelings, your memory of the event will arise at the same time. This may occur, but it is not always the case. Upon further release, however, you may find yourself remembering things you had long forgotten. The important thing to keep in mind is that the feelings are there and need to be released, regardless of whether you know what caused them in the first place. Many times I went through periods of release not knowing why I was experiencing the feelings I was having at the time. Even without knowing their source, I worked on releasing these feelings. I successfully resolved them and moved myself closer to emotional health.

The Emotional Life Cycle

Releasing your unresolved emotions involves passing through a number of stages in order to completely release the emotional energy that you have trapped inside yourself. Furthermore, these stages may be repeated a number of times in the process of freeing your emotions and healing. Often you may not be aware of what originally triggered the emotion. What you may only know is that you are hurting for some unknown reason. You need to move through these moods and feelings and simply allow them to surface and be felt.

The process of healing is also a repetitive process. It involves becoming aware of certain feelings and releasing them, then becoming aware of other feelings and releasing them as well, and so on until you become emotionally clear. You can get in touch with your unresolved emotions one layer at a time. When you achieve release, you essentially peel away a layer of the unresolved emotions. You can then move on to the next layer of emotion and become aware of it when you are ready. This process can take some time, but if you are committed to your emotional health and put some effort into changing our ways to achieve a release you can begin to realize the benefits relatively quickly.

Earlier in this book I suggested that emotions are processes of energy. The idea of emotional processes can be further enhanced by the idea that an emotion has a natural life cycle of energy that, if fully expressed, results in the dissipation of the emotional energy. Emotions, if allowed to take their course, will come and go of their own accord. The reality about an emotion is that if you acknowledge and express the emotions, then the emotional energy will fade over time unless it is re-stimulated. Most of us however, block the emotional process at one of the four steps in its life or energy cycle.

The first step that brings about emotion is the event itself. The event may bring about sadness or joy or perhaps one of the many other emotions. To start the emotional process you need to acknowledge that the event occurred. This means letting go of the denial process you may have maintained. If you have a habit of denying that you have been hurt or do not give much weight to the positive things that happen in your life, you shut the emotional process down at that point. Your body may, however, react by moving into a subtle state of awareness involving increased muscle tension and other symptoms. Denying the actual event can often lead to a state of disassociation from reality to a point at which you may not remember certain events. With patients who have experienced Post Traumatic Stress Disorder, symptoms of psychogenic amnesia are quite common as the mind blocks painful memories from consciousness.

The next stage that you would normally move into is one of awareness of a feeling. Again, feelings are a whole body/mind experience so the emotion may be experienced in any part of the body as a gut feeling, muscle tension or facial expression. With the body experience also comes a conscious tone to the emotion such as a change in mood. Again, if the emotional experience is acknowledged and allowed to flow freely, then the stage of expression can occur. Should you try to avoid the awareness by altering your state or using some of the avoidance techniques mentioned earlier, you will likely end up with physical symptoms or a reduction in your ability to think rationally. As mentioned earlier, you will become more sensitive to similar issues and be less willing to tolerate emotional expression in others.

The expression stage can take many forms depending on personal preferences and methods of expressing yourself. In this stage there is no one way of expressing an emotion, and no right or perfect way either. Emotional expression is deeply personal and is really an expression of your soul. A few techniques and methods of emotional expression, outlined in a later chapter, will help you to discover your own personal style of expression. Again, many people stop the emotional cycle by shutting down and "swallowing" their emotion. Tears are blocked, anger is pushed down and even joy is restrained due to being self-conscious. All of these actions lead to the same symptoms of emotional blocking listed in the previous step. In this step however, since you have awareness, you are doing a greater deal of harm to your self-esteem because you are denying your own emotional existence. Nathaniel Brandon wrote that denying your emotions is one of the main causes of low self-esteem. When you deny an emotion you end up committing a crime against your own soul by disowning yourself.

In the early stages of healing, an emotional catharsis may leave you with a great deal of energy or alternately you may feel exhausted. The energy that you may experience is like an unconstrained spring. Think of a spring that has been compressed. It is being held down just as your emotions were. Release the spring and the energy in the spring causes it to stretch and recoil until it reaches its natural position. A release of emotions can have the same effect on you. You may experience variations in energy and mood fluctuations in a manner similar to the spring being released.

At this time you may feel exhilarated, as the energy you have been using for suppressing is made available to you for other purposes. You may find yourself requiring less sleep. You may want to change things in your life. You may seem to be on an emotional roller coaster at times. As you progress through your healing process the amplitude of the waves usually decreases. You will eventually find yourself in a more natural state where your mood varies to certain degrees but not as widely as in your early stages of healing.

I believe that it is at this time in the healing process, when variations in mood occur, that many people get labeled as manic-depressive. Manic-depressives are people who have a depressive disorder, and experience wide mood swings. Unfortunately many people consider such a diagnosis a sign of a condition that will last their entire lifetime. While a person who has experienced a substantial loss may experience mood swings, it is important to note that in the process of releasing pent up energy the mood swings may in fact be a natural process of beginning to recognize and deal with your emotions. As the emotions are expressed, the mood swings should decrease over time.

Returning to a more natural state may take some time. You will discover a new baseline for your consciousness. Until you settle down to your new emotional state, it is better to put off any major decisions or lifestyle changes until you come to terms with your release and gain an understanding of how you feel after the catharsis. Releasing emotion is very demanding and requires energy. Although you may not have exerted yourself physically, emotional expression can leave you exhausted. The healing process can take a great deal of energy from your body. You may have little or no energy for a period following a release. I often found that a day or two of rest was very helpful. I would find a place to relax, do some reading or curl up with my pet. This period was a time for rejuvenation and consolidation. Go to a park, read a book, watch a sunset, or do some other calming activity. Allow your soul and heart wounds to heal!

A New Emotional Baseline

Completely releasing an emotion may be frightening for you simply because you may have never done this before. You may have never experienced the release associated with grieving a loss and the healing. A scar may remain but the wound can heal. Releasing and letting go of a long held emotion can bring about a sense of unfamiliarity. Maintaining a daily routine of the same feelings provides a sense of security and avoidance of change even though the emotions do not serve you. To let go of familiarity opens up new possibilities and awareness. You may find yourself wondering who you really are without all of your emotional baggage.

When you have a depression that has been with you a long time you may actually feel somewhat uncomfortable with it gone. You may have to establish a new emotional baseline for yourself. Although this may seem somewhat frightening, the long-term benefits are what you need to focus on. Releasing your unresolved emotions places you in a state of transition. When the pain is gone, you can be more open. Others may feel more open and communicative with you, which may be unfamiliar to you. In addition, you will have given up a part of yourself that was around for so long, and therefore comfortable. Your depression may have actually seemed to be one of the only consistent things in your life, although not a very positive one.

By releasing your deep rooted feelings you may find yourself adjusting to a state of consciousness that seems unfamiliar. Part of the depression may have lifted and you begin to feel differently about yourself and somewhat unfamiliar with your new level of consciousness. At this time you can reduce your fear and insecurity by reminding yourself that you are in a state of transition and a new beginning. Your life situation and emotions will eventually settle, leaving you healed and better prepared to solve problems and feel joy in your life.

If you have released a great deal of emotion, you may have finally expressed something that you have carried around for ages. The expression and resolution of these long-held feelings has been a subtle part of your consciousness. With these subtle background feelings now resolved and gone, your consciousness can feel different and unfamiliar. You may even feel as though you have amputated a part of your consciousness and that your sense of self feels different. You may need to get to know yourself without your depression or anger. If you have become accustomed to depression, feelings of joy may be unfamiliar to you. Welcome them!

16. Going Deeper

Stop, Look, Listen

In the rural areas near where I grew up, there were train crossings without the barriers that would stop traffic if a train were approaching. Drivers were expected to stop before the tracks and use their own judgment as to whether it was safe to cross. These tracks were usually marked with a sign that said "Stop, Look, Listen." These same words can be used as a process of identifying your own feelings.

The first instruction is to stop. This may mean taking some time to put aside what you are doing and to remove your distractions. To stop what you are doing means to suspend your thoughts and to focus on yourself for a moment. It only takes a few seconds to do this anytime or anywhere. You can do it in the silent interval of a conversation or between responses. Quite often the focus of counseling is to assist the client in stopping for a few moments at a time and looking inside.

The next step is to look at what is going on inside you. This may mean focusing in on a vague unfelt sense of tension or anxiety in your body, a sense of lightness in the case of joy, or heaviness in the case of sadness or grief. While you may not be able to identify the emotion at first, you can identify that you are feeling something. At this time, simply listen to your body non-judgmentally and accept that clarity may come later. In the case of repressed memories there may not be an understanding of why the emotions are occurring. Perhaps there will be no words attached to the feelings.

The third key word of the sign is to listen. Slow down, look inside, notice tension and listen to what sensations you are experiencing. You may be experiencing a combination of feelings. That is OK. Be willing to accept some discomfort and feel what is present. Give the emotions space and room to be present. This will help in the processing of the emotions and subsequent memory recall or increased awareness. Just as a doctor becomes quiet and uses a stethoscope to listen to a patient's heart, so too must you quiet the things around you, focus and listen to what is going on inside. Doing this allows you to obtain the information you need to gain the awareness required to create a shift in your feelings, behaviors and thoughts.

For many of us, facing feelings is frightening even though we may realize that it is necessary for healing. In your goal of expression and resolution, you can learn to face the feelings with a new sense of discovering new perspectives and new options. You can also discover that, although the pain is being felt in the present, the incident that caused the pain is in the past and that you are removed from it and can experience safety. This sense of safety was not available to you at the time of the emotional injury.

Awareness through Breath

All forms of meditation use breathing as a technique to enhance relaxation and self-awareness. In your emotional work, you can use breathing as a tool of emotional discovery. In *The Mirror of the Body*, authors Kaye and Matchan describe breathing as follows. "There are two kinds of breathing: The automatic, unconscious breathing performed by all living organisms, and the conscious, controlled breathing we can choose to do for a specific purpose." The second type of breathing can be used for two purposes as well. Conscious breathing can be used to induce relaxation or it can be used to increase awareness and aid in the release of emotional tension.

Besides exchanging oxygen and carbon dioxide, breathing also induces a reflex action that nourishes the body. Breathing, which is intricately connected with your nervous system, can be used as a tool in meditation to bring in energy and to remove and release negativity and tension.

Since emotional or nervous tension usually results in a greater degree of muscular tension, the flow of energy and breathing is often restricted. Breathing, although done without any real effort on our part, involves a process of contracting and releasing many muscles. Shallow breathing may be the result of the emotional tension. Taking deep, abdominal breaths can almost always induce an instantaneous sense of relaxation. Accordingly, abdominal breathing can induce changes in brain wave patterns, resulting in a feeling of relaxation. Breathing balances, relaxes, and restores the body and mind. As Thomas Gaines states in his book *Vitalic Breathing*, "the act of breathing spreads the life-force through the body."

Knowing that the breath is a source of vitality, you can also identify the breath as a source of focusing and centering yourself. By relaxing through breath work, you can begin to relieve the tension and become more aware of emotions causing the tension.

While I have learned about deep abdominal breathing through yoga and singing lessons, it is through a book called "The Science of Breath" by Yogi Ramacharaka, that I truly learned to breath properly. This book talks about lower, middle and high breathing that we should all learn to do. This method of breathing forms that basis of further breathing exercises. I quote directly from this hundred year old text:

The Yogi Breath

The Yogis classify Respiration into our general methods, viz. (1) High Breathing. (2) Mid Breathing. (3) Low Breathing. (4) Yogi Complete Breathing.

(1) HIGH BREATHING.
This form of breathing is known to the Western world as Clavicular Breathing, or Collar-bone Breathing. One breathing in this way elevates the ribs and raises the collar bone and shoulders, at the same time drawing in the abdomen and pushing its contents up against the diaphragm, which in turn is raised. The upper part of the chest and lungs, which is the smallest, is used, and consequently but a minimum amount of air enters the lungs. In addition to this, the diaphragm being raised, there can be no expansion in that direction. A study of the anatomy of the chest will convince any student that in this way a maximum amount of effort is used to obtain a minimum amount of benefit. High Breathing is probably the worst form of breathing known to man and requires the greatest expenditure of energy with the smallest amount of benefit.

(2) MID BREATHING.
This method of respiration is known to Western students as Rib Breathing, or Intercostal Breathing, and while less objectionable than High Breathing, is far inferior to either Low Breathing or to the Yogi Complete Breath. In Mid Breathing the diaphragm is pushed upward, and the abdomen drawn in. The ribs are raised somewhat, and the chest is partially expanded. It is quite common among men who have made no study of the subject. As there are two better methods known, we give it only passing notice, and that principally to call your attention to its shortcomings.

(3) LOW BREATHING.
This form of respiration is far better than either of the two preceding forms, and of recent years many Western writers have extolled its merits, and have exploited it under the names of "Abdominal Breathing," "Deep Breathing," "Diaphragmic Breathing," etc., etc., and much good has been accomplished by the attention of the public having been directed to the subject, and many having been induced to substitute it for the inferior and injurious methods above alluded to. Many "systems" of breathing have been built around Low Breath-

ing, and students have paid high prices to learn the new systems. But, as we have said, much good has resulted, and after all the students who paid high prices to learn revamped old systems undoubtedly got their money's worth if they were induced to discard the old methods of High Breathing and Low Breathing.

Although many Western authorities write and speak of this method as the best known form of breathing, the Yogis know it to be but a part of a system which they have used for centuries and which they know as "The Complete Breath." It must be admitted, however, that one must be acquainted with the principles of Low Breathing before he can grasp the idea of Complete Breathing.

The Complete Breath

The trouble with all methods of breathing, other than "Yogi Complete Breathing" is that in none of these methods do the lungs become filled with air- at the best only a portion of the lung space is filled, even in Low Breathing. High Breathing fills only the upper portion of the lungs. Mid Breathing fills only the middle and a portion of the upper parts. Low Breathing fills only the lower and middle parts. It is evident that any method that fills the entire lung space must be far preferable to those filling only certain parts. Any method which will fill the entire lung space must be of the greatest value to Man in the way of allowing him to absorb the greatest quantity of oxygen and to store away the greatest amount of prana. The Complete Breath is known to the Yogis to be the best method of respiration known to science.

1) Stand or sit erect.

2) Breathing through the nostrils, inhale steadily, first filling the lower part of the lungs, which is accomplished by bringing into play the diaphragm, which descending exerts a gentle pressure on the abdominal organs, pushing forward the front walls of the abdomen.

3) Then fill the middle part of the lungs, pushing out the lower ribs, breast-bone and chest. Then fill the higher portion of the lungs, protruding the upper chest, thus lifting the chest, including the upper six or sever. pairs of ribs. In the final movement, the lower part of the abdomen will be slightly drawn in, which movement gives the lungs a support and also helps to fill the highest part of the lungs.

At first reading it may appear that this breath consists of three distinct movements. This, however, is not the correct idea. The inhalation is continuous, the entire chest cavity from the lowered diaphragm to the highest point of the chest in the region of the collarbone, being expanded with a uniform movement. Avoid a jerky series of inhalations, and strive to attain a steady continuous action. Practice will soon overcome the tendency to divide the inhalation into three movements, and will result in a uniform continuous breath. You will be able to complete the inhalation in a couple of seconds after a little practice.

(4) Retain the breath a few seconds.

(5) Exhale quite slowly, holding the chest in a firm position, and drawing the abdomen in a little and lifting it upward slowly as the air leaves the lungs. When the air is entirely exhaled, relax the chest and abdomen.

A little practice will render this part of the exercise easy, and the movement once acquired will be afterwards performed almost automatically. It will be seen that by this method of breathing all parts of the respiratory apparatus is brought into action, and all parts of the lungs, including the most remote air cells, are exercised. The chest cavity is expanded in all directions. You will also notice that the Complete Breath is really a combination of Low, Mid and High Breaths, succeeding each other rapidly in the order given, in such a manner as to form one uniform, continuous, complete breath.

The Chakra Connection

While I have kept most of the material in this book within the realm of modern day psychology and personal insight, I find at this point the need to delve into what seems mystical at the present time.

I have often been a skeptic when it comes to energy healers and the like, simply because I have met many who claimed to move energy, but few have had any effect on me. I found that when the time was right, and I was willing to do the work and take ownership and responsibility for myself, the perfect guide would appear to help me. It was at a very painful time late in my healing process that the most profound changes occurred. With the news that a love interest had no romantic interest in me, and subsequent disappointment a very deep powerful dream occurred in which I felt tremendous sadness, but avoided showing this to my parents. In the dream I confronted them with the fact that they had taken no interest in my daily life and had no idea of the things I was going through. As I awoke sobbing, a great deal of pain and rawness existed in my chest area.

I was deeply sad and in pain, but in surrendering to my pain, I experienced a profound healing over the space of about 5 days. It was during that time that I realized that something very deep and powerful was missing from my manuscript for this book that you are now reading. During that 5-day period I took very good care of myself, getting massages and giving my energy to the healing process. I chose to see a counselor who could help me move through the emotion, rather than just talk around it. I was in great pain, but knew that I was moving through a powerful transformation.

Coming out the other end, I managed to release very deep emotional and muscle pain as well as profound sadness and grief over not being listened to and my lack of friends and family connection over the years. As I moved through the pain, the muscle tension released and my throat and chest area became more flexible and free. Breathing became easier, and the asthma I had experienced seemed to diminish.

I had experienced deep release before, but there was something special about this release. I believe I got through to deep core issue, and in healing this issue found that my relationships, friendships and acquaintances changed around me. It was a body and emotional shift that produced dramatic, deep results.

As I mentioned, I felt that something was missing from this book and the answer came quickly. I needed to be able to describe how to be in one's body, and to develop a method of scanning the body, and relate how I became more physically present in my own process. Thus came the wisdom of chakras – the energy centers of the body, mind and spirit. Many different theories abound about colors of chakras and sound that should be used for the chakras, but in my own healing it was the developing of my ability to sense the chakras rather than using some external influence that brought about healing. Furthermore, the ability to sense more than one chakra at a time brought a greater sense of being present. To be fully healed means to be able to sense what is blocked and unblock it. For my particular energy, my chest area and throat were badly blocked, as confirmed by a speech and throat specialist who examined my vocal cords with the aid of a small camera. The vocal chords were fine, but the muscles in my neck were tight and constricted. My area of healing need was in the throat and chest, which correspond with communication and heart-felt love, both giving and receiving.

Most energy models identify seven basic chakras. The first chakra is the seat of the soul, located half way between the anus and the genital area. This chakra helps you feel grounded and connected to the earth. The next chakra is in the genital area and deals with your pleasure, ecstasy and reproduction. Just below the belly button is the third chakra, which has to do with your center of power. The next higher chakra is the heart chakra which is in the center of your chest. This area deals with love, openness, self-esteem and compassion. The throat chakra is close to the thyroid gland and vocal chords, the openness of this chakra reflects your ability to communicate. The second to last chakra is slightly above the midpoint between the eyebrows and is also referred to as the third eye. It represents your wisdom and insight. The crown chakra is considered the highest-level chakra and it connects you divinely.

Another important area of the body to be aware of is the solar plexus. This is considered to be a "spiritual" mind of the body. According to Yogic philosophies and studies, this is an area of the body that psychically, if not physically, is a powerful nerve centre. It is located just back of the pit of the stomach, extending on either side of the spinal column. Whether or not you believe in chakras or energy, I can attest to the sense of emotional awareness that is often centered in this area. It seems the more aware you are of this energy area, the more likely you will be present in your body. According to the Yogic philosophy, the solar plexus radiates energy to all parts of the body. This energy is called "prana" or life force.

Try to be aware of these various points of your body and the sense of energy around them. Try breathing into and exhaling from each chakra and open to give and receive healing energy!

Developing Body Awareness

One of the best ways to get in touch with an emotion is to relax yourself and take note of where in your body you are experiencing the feeling and tension. Taking a deep breath will allow you to relax and become more aware of the tension in your body. Are you feeling a sensation in your stomach, neck, shoulders, back, or face? Are your facial muscles tight? Do you feel relaxed? Do you feel an urge to do something or to work on something? By spending some time with yourself and focusing on your body sensations, you can begin a meditative process of unlocking your emotions. Only by slowing down and becoming aware of your body sensations do you begin to connect with your emotions.

One way to scan for emotion is to breathe into the various parts of the body and sense tension. Breathing in and focusing on the chakras one at a time will allow you to gauge how connected you are to your body. Now I will give a little bit of advice here that most people need to adhere to when dealing with muscle tension. Just because your neck is hurting doesn't mean that the problem is in your neck. The body is a very intricate mechanism that does not lend towards isolating individual parts. Proof of this can be found by lying down, placing a hand below your belly button and lifting your head. You should find that your abdomen muscles contract. Another example of how things are linked together is the fact that the muscles that attach to the jaw actually wind all the way down the neck and to the lower back! It is important to view the body as a whole not as a collection of individual muscles. Tension in one area can cause contortions and pain in another area. As you become more aware, you will be wise to the subtleness of your body.

In discussing the chakras, it is helpful to become more aware of each chakra, but also try to be aware of more than one at a time. A deep sense of centeredness, self-worth and compassion arises when are aware of all of your chakras at once. I also recommend trying to sense the chakras through ones eyes. Looking out into the world through your eyes, you connect each of the chakras to your vision. To do so requires being fully present and in your body. It takes practice!

Five Stages of Deep Release

With the challenges I have faced, I have worked through a great deal of pain. The benefit is that I no longer carry this pain and I am no longer as deeply triggered by similar events. Having successfully worked through numerous issues, I can say with confidence that the following stages were necessary each time I needed to work through an emotional and mental difficulty. Some of the lessons I went through to be able to write this section challenged me to the core of my existence, but the rewards of coming through the other side were plentiful and continue to this day.

Biting the Bullet

The term "bite the bullet" comes from the days of medical practice when anesthetic had not yet been invented. If a doctor needed to perform an operation on a patient, the patient was given a few drinks to loosen them up. They were then told to bite on something very hard, usually a bullet, to distract their mind from the pain. In today's terminology it means to accept that what you must go through will be painful, and there is no way to avoid it.

The same is true of your emotional pain if you want to let it go and be healed from it. You must accept that you need to face the pain rather than avoid it. Sometimes there are difficult things to face, but at times it often takes more energy to avoid it than to start moving through it. We all fear the unknown, but resent being stuck. Biting the bullet and facing the pain allows you to get un-stuck and begin the process of healing, even though the first steps involve pain.

Exquisite Pain

I use the term exquisite to describe the emotional pain you are working through because the feeling of this pain is life changing. You are not feeling the pain out of self-pity or to seek comfort in familiar feelings. You are feeling the pain with the intention of burning through it, of letting it consume itself, so that you may eventually be free of it. I have found when I try to get a sense of what that event feels like in my body rather than simply visualizing a painful event in the mind's eye, it becomes more real.

Burning through pain is a noble cause as the Buddhists state that the burning through of pain to get to the other side of it is the way of burning through the karma that you have been given. The pain is exquisite when you can envision the transformational effects of your healing work.

Surrender

In order to fully feel your pain it is necessary to surrender to it, to fully embrace it, to fully feel it, without denial of its strength, without pulling away from it when it gets overwhelming. You may feel as though you won't live through such an intense pain, but if you can take care of yourself through affirmations about your worth, goodness and desire to heal, you can surrender, knowing that you can bring yourself through it. You can experience the fear of change yet also be aware of the joy of your new birth. You may be fearful of surrendering. You must face your pain fearlessly.

The Death of Pain

In the depths of pain the time comes when after surrender and a feeling of being forsaken you can let the pain die. There comes a point of stillness in the pain that includes intensity with purpose. You have felt the depths of despair, loneliness and hurt, and have surrendered to these feelings, but you have not surrendered your will to live, only the will for this pain to continue. You become willing to exist without this pain that has been a faithful but unwelcome companion. You realize it can no longer serve you, but you have been afraid to let it go. As humans, we strive to keep everything alive. Your pain is no different, but this does not help you. You need to let go, to allow the pain to die, and in doing so, part of you dies with the death of the pain. It frees you to move on, but since you are often afraid of change, you are usually afraid to let your pain die. We are a stubborn lot sometimes. Be willing to let the pain die, and see who you will become without the pain. Miracles can happen from completing this process. I know, and you know, because I survived my pain to write this book!

Completion and Awakening

When your pain dies you may feel exhausted and out of sorts, but this usually is an exhaustion of relief, and a re-integration period occurs during which you gain great insight. During this time it is necessary to ground yourself to the earth so that you can rebuild on a solid awareness and sense of your new self that is emerging. Insight will come, and their will be changes in how you respond to people and they to you. Your body image will change as will your sense of relatedness with others. You begin a journey of new hope and let go of the issue that was troubling you. With this issue gone from your persona, you can see other people in a different light, perhaps without the anger, and with a little more compassion. Your values may change and your respect for yourself and others will grow. You will also be able to acknowledge your own courage to face your pain and discover the depth of your resourcefulness. Your body chemistry will adjust to the newly found energy. In some Christian circles this process of feeling pain, the surrender to it, experiencing its death and the awakening is the metaphor of the crucifixion of Jesus Christ. Perhaps this is the most powerful healing metaphor you will come to know.

17. Renewal – Better than Before!

The Aspects of Healing

In describing the meaning of healing, it is necessary to examine a number of aspects of your life. Catharsis alone may bring relief; however, if beliefs are not changed, does healing really occur? Similarly, if you alter your beliefs but persist in unhealthy behaviors, you cannot truly claim that you have completed your healing work. Therefore, a definition of healing is complex. Let's examine the major aspects of healing.

First, healing involves the removal of lingering emotional hurt through resolution of the pain. How you do this may be personal and unique to your own situation, beliefs and circumstances. It involves identifying and processing unresolved events so that the emotional content becomes information and our personal history.

Furthermore, healing involves resolving the "shoulds" and "musts" that you tell yourself and that others have placed on you. If you are living by someone else's standards and expectations, you are not truly living your own life. You need to recognize these expectations, some of which may be only indirectly implied. When you start to live by your own rules of consideration for yourself and others, you will be able to define what your own expectations are. You will achieve a greater sense of self and self-fulfillment. You need to challenge other people's beliefs that you have swallowed without evaluation. Do you wish to own and maintain a particular belief? You need to integrate the parts of yourself that were disowned or cut off to please others. Often this was done simply to survive in a threatening environment.

A memory I recalled through healing work was that as a young child, I used to love to dance and sing for my parents. I would run from the living room to the kitchen and dance for them, having queued up my favorite record. One day my mother shouted at me "stop being so ridiculous and silly." I ran back to the living room stifling my tears. From that day on I stopped dancing and the process of shutting down my creativity began. Through my healing work I have reconnected with my singing voice and joined a choir. I now play guitar and have taken voice lessons, and recorded a CD, discovering that it is never too late to enjoy the talents I have. Another aspect of my healing process, particularly with my music, involved reducing self-criticism and the tendency to be hard on myself.

Healing also involves the acceptance of responsibility for your choices and accepting that you may not have been responsible or deserving of what happened to you. Healing is also about setting boundaries and developing the self-respect you deserve but may not have received. Often victims of abuse will feel a sense of shame or guilt. An abuser perpetrated the sense of shame, but over time the victim may internalize these messages. It is necessary to challenge these unfounded beliefs and feelings and learn to consider that you are lovable and did not deserve what occurred. You need to challenge your self-talk and respond with more positive and loving messages to yourself.

As with your self-talk, healing involves challenging your behavior and learning new responses. In the case of addictions, you may need to learn how to reach for help or assistance, and to share and express your feelings in new ways, rather than numbing them with your addictive behavior. This can be a frightening prospect, but a rewarding action when you learn that you can manage your feelings in more productive ways.

Healing also involves revisiting old issues, challenges and traumas, and resolving them. It also involves the acceptance and integration of feelings and memories. New feelings may emerge from this process as well as memories long forgotten. Healing may also involve learning to let others help and learning to trust again. Healing is diligently nursing yourself back to health with new behaviors, thoughts, feelings and actions.

Some changes may be profound. You may choose to associate with a more positive group of people, to become more assertive, or to diminish certain behaviors. In cases of addictions, you may decide to call someone for support, or go to a 12-step meeting, rather than repeat the addictive behavior.

Instead of repeating a behavior, you can try a new behavior. This more often than not brings about new and different results, moving you towards greater emotional maturity and self-understanding. By changing your behavior you end up changing your feelings. Conversely, by changing your feelings you end up changing your behavior. Additionally, changing your behavior can change your thinking, and changing your thinking also changes how you feel. In other words, your thinking, feeling and behavior are inter-related. In your healing process it is necessary to work on all three, but a change in one area will often lead to changes in other areas. It is a complex process that begins with small changes in the way you manage yourself.

Finding Your Voice

So many of us have, at times, been truly victimized. You did not ask for what you got, and although you may have tried to change things, you were unsuccessful due to the enormity of the problem. Learned helplessness is a recognized pattern that develops when a person is unable to effect solutions to a problematic situation. For many children, the ability to implement solutions to their problems is hampered and restricted by the behavior of the adults and the organizations around them. As a result, many adults carry around a belief that they cannot help themselves. They do not recognize that they can find their own voice and personal ability to change some aspects of their lives. People who have been victimized sometimes remain in the role of victims. Some go as far as having a vested interest in being sad and being victimized, thereby becoming the perpetrators of their own unhappiness.

Reclaiming your life and finding your own voice and autonomy can lead to a more fulfilling life and increased joy and happiness. To do this you need to become more comfortable with your interests and values. Are you fearful of others finding out what kind of books and music you read and listen to? Are you afraid to decorate and put up posters that will show others what you believe in? Perhaps creating your own bookshelf that shows others who you are can be a helpful conversation starter. You can begin to let others know of your talents and interests. You can also become an initiator rather than always waiting around for someone else to start something! Doing so can help you develop a sense of competency.

Creating New Emotions, New Behavior

A major insight is to realize that you are much more than just your thoughts and feelings. An image that comes to mind is a statue of the lady of justice, who in her hand holds a scale, and a sword, balancing the needs of justice and the power of her decision. We often notice the scales and the sword, but not the blindfolded woman holding the scale. We try to balance our emotion and thinking, but we can lose sight of the fact that the person is present, rather than just being the balancing action of the scale and the decision power. When your sense of a greater self becomes strong, you will discover that you can have a sense of mastery of your thoughts and feelings. You will develop a greater sense of choice, and what is often referred to as the ability to regulate your emotions. While it seems like a paradox that after all this emotional work to stop controlling your emotions, you end up learning to do just that, but this time it is through choice and the exercise of free will. You learn to make choices as to how you will react. In a sense, you are no longer reactive, but proactive.

You are the driver rather than being driven by your emotions. In your healing process, you develop emotional competence, a sense of being that allows you to see your own emotional state and the state of others. You learn to read others emotions, learn about your own needs as well as theirs, and to adapt your behavior to make a situation work for both of you. You can also discern when your outer world does not match your inner world and reconcile them appropriately through healing and emotional work! You also learn that you do not have to fear change. The sooner you step through the door to change, the sooner you reach a passage that leads to a new arena of creativity. You learn to trust the process of life!

Developing a Healthy Lifestyle

As mentioned earlier, healing work is not complete unless you put into practice what you have learned. Often this involves separating from an unhealthy life, beginning to experience a healthier life and eventually living a healthy life. What are the aspects of a healthy life? I believe the answer to this question lies in a research project by Dr. Rod McCormick at the University of British Columbia. Dr. McCormick interviewed 50 Native American adults to identify critical incidents concerning the facilitation of healing. Over 400 incidents were then categorized. I believe these categories, referred to as "healing facilitators", are representative of the aspects of leading a healthy lifestyle and are also actions you can take to move towards a healthy lifestyle.

The categories identified (in random order) were as follows:
1. Establishing a social connection.
2. Anchoring oneself in tradition.
3. Exercise.
4. Self Care.
5. Involvement in challenging activities.
6. Expressing oneself.
7. Obtaining help/support from others.
8. Participation in ceremony.
9. Setting goals.
10. Helping others.
11. Gaining an understanding of the problem.
12. Establishing a spiritual connection.
13. Learning from a role model.
14. Establishing a connection with nature.

In reviewing the list, it is clear that these behaviors and actions are all positive steps that can help establish a positive, healthy lifestyle. In my own experience, I believe it is necessary to maintain a sense of balance and effort in each of the above categories. It is interesting to note that most of the above take place when you are involved in a 12-step program or other similar support group!

Facing the Truth

One of the prime rules of healing is that healing cannot occur if you are mired in denial of the truth of the hurtful event. Denial serves a purpose in protecting you from the pain when you are not ready to deal with it, but often you end up using denial without being aware of its consequences. Denial often prevents healing.

In examining any event you must be willing to accept the truth about it. For example, you may have to accept that you were laid off, that you felt rejected, lonely or isolated, or let down by yourself or others. You may simply have to acknowledge that indeed you were hurt.

Healing is a process of telling yourself the truth. You may have felt pain, shame, fear, loss, or helplessness, or you may have felt anger. You need to face these truths and realities of the situation in order to allow healing to take place. Often you may have to own up to secrets that you have hidden from yourself and others. Often it is your secrets that cause you the most pain. You may not need to reveal them to others but you need to at least be truthful with yourself. A big part of healing is self-forgiveness.

"There came a time when the risk to remain tight in the bud was more painful than the risk it took to blossom!" - Anais Nin

18. Resolving Anger and Resentment

The Nature of Anger

In writing this chapter, I must first admit that I had a very deep change of heart in the way I believe people can heal from anger. Over the years I had heard of many methods of releasing anger, and I tried many of them. Most of them were exercises that involved punching a pillow, screaming, or some similar expression of anger energy. I found that over time, none of them really worked, as later I still found myself being angry. These may have been short term solutions to deal with energy, but in the long term I still found myself being angry. Fortunately with some Buddhist teachings, some insight, and a combination of challenging experiences, I learned to heal my troubles, and therefore reduce my anger. I've learned that anger isn't the problem. My thinking, habits, and my views of other people and myself were what needed work. I will share these insights with you. I hope they help you.

Clearly, anger is one of the most destructive emotions that you can experience, whether it is occurring internally, or if you are the recipient of someone else's anger. There are also some misconceptions regarding anger that I hope to clear up in the coming pages. As I mentioned, there have been a number of suggestions over the years that venting anger is helpful however newer thought on the topic, with the guidance of Buddhist leaders, suggests that solely venting anger tends to train people to maintain their anger. Furthermore, venting exercises such as screaming and yelling can do damage to your vocal chords. In the coming pages I'll describe some myths about anger as well as provide personal examples of how I worked through and resolved my anger.

I believe that the term anger is often used incorrectly to describe a range of emotions and states such as resentment, aggression and even rage. While anger can often lead to aggression, it is possible to experience anger and resolve it without communicating it and without becoming aggressive. I have also learned that rage appears to be fear based in that rage usually results from an overwhelming sense of being unable to control your situation or unable to effect any change. Researchers have found that perpetrators of violence usually do so when experiencing a strong fear of losing control. Rage can be burning beneath the surface, erupting when control is threatened. Rage is a state in which someone is out of control, yet is trying to establish control in an ineffective manner. Studies suggest that people who are filled with rage are also filled with shame, or a deep-seated resentment regarding oppression and silencing. Resentment, on the other hand is a slow burning anger of choice and a self-fed poison that eats away at your soul. Resentment does considerably more harm to the person doing the resenting than to the one being resented. Refraining from anger requires a great deal of repressive control and may be maintained unconsciously.

I would also like to differentiate between three possible states that can occur. Two of them deal with timing. If an event has already occurred and you have not practiced self control, you may find yourself already angry. In this case, your body's chemical mechanisms have already produced numerous hormones and muscle reactions, These need to be calmed and taken care of and the energy reduced in a healthy way. The second state is when you are truly angry, but won't admit it to yourself. This can be a severely draining state as the energy is present, but not acknowledged and deeply repressed in muscle tension. Your body has already reacted but the mind refuses to acknowledge it, leaving your soul in poor health and low spirit. The third state occurs when you are fully aware and in control of yourself and an anger provoking incident occurs. In this situation, you can practice various exercises and self control to not get angry. This is the power of prevention.

I am now of the firm belief that getting angry is not a resource that you or I should draw on repeatedly. It is a state where we are often dangerously out of control. To get angry is to be human, but not necessarily humane. Through simple chance and synchronicity I met a great martial arts and Qigong teacher who helped me to understand the true meaning of martial arts, anger, self-control and compassion. I asked him "How do you deal with anger?" His reply was very insightful.

"The people around the world don't get the real meaning of martial arts. It is not to attack or to kick other people. It is just to kick and attack our own anger. With Qi Gong you learn how to attack and control your anger. When you get up in the morning you listen to some calming music and do some practical and corrective Qi Gong exercise so you can kill the negative energy or the negative thinking that maybe you are going to do a bad thing. So when you do some Qi Gong you can have internal balance, self confidence and self control which leads you to be flexible in your life and strong with yourself. When you are in some hard situation with others in your life you can control yourself so that if someone gives you bad energy, you can give back goodness."

Of all the emotions, anger seems to be the one that you can easily feed and build upon. Like adding wood to a fire, your thoughts can easily increase the heat and intensity of your anger to the point that you are in a rage. I have always found it important to develop an awareness of when I am feeding my own anger, and to recognize and become more rational and accepting at these times. I've become aware that when angry, I change to very shallow breathing. Recognizing this and taking deep, slow, calming breaths helps me relax and reduce my anger and frustration. Instead of working myself up, I recognize my level of anger and ask myself what I need and what I am expecting from the other people in the situation.

There are some valuable lessons to be learned from some of the world's great religious leaders. In researching this book I searched the bible for references to emotion or anger. The one phrase that came up over and over again was that Jesus "was slow to anger." There is great wisdom in these few words. From Buddhist teachings I have learned a great deal about anger. In Making Your Mind an Ocean, Ven. Thupten Yeshe writes:

"I encourage people not to express their anger, not to let it out. Instead, I have people try to understand why they get angry, what causes it and how it arises. When you realize these things, instead of manifesting externally, your anger digests itself. In the West, some people believe that you get rid of anger by expressing it, that you finish it by letting it out. Actually, in this case what happens is that you leave an imprint in your mind to get angry again. The effect is just the opposite of what they believe. It looks like your anger has escaped, but in fact you're just collecting more anger in your mind. The imprints that anger leaves on your consciousness simply reinforce your tendency to respond to situations with more anger. But not allowing it to come out doesn't mean that you are suppressing it, bottling it up. That's also dangerous. You have to learn to investigate the deeper nature of anger, aggression, anxiety or whatever it is that troubles you. When you look into the deeper nature of negative energy you'll see that it's really quite insubstantial, that it's only mind. As your mental expression changes, the negative energy disappears, digested by the wisdom that understands the nature of hatred, anger, aggression and so forth."

I have come to the conclusion that while some say that anger should be expressed, it is often your needs that require a voice. When anger is calmly expressed as needs and requests for change, meaningful communication can occur. Communicating your needs is important but if you do so in anger it is likely that the other person will become defensive and retaliate. Then you may find yourself in a more difficult situation. The other options are to let go of the issue, change your expectations, forgive, practice mindfulness, or simply walk away from the situation.

Often you may trick yourself into thinking that the only way you can resolve your anger is to receive an apology. While an apology often helps, if the person you are expressing your needs to does not listen or does not adjust their behavior, then you end up remaining angry and possibly getting angrier unless you look at your unmet needs. You will also end up with a greater degree of anger if the other person retaliates rather than listens, unless you have cultivated the ability to accept others limitations and to practice compassion.

Resolving anger often requires that you develop new insights or change your own expectations of the other person or organization. Resolving anger may require that you adjust your own behavior. A further consideration is that your anger may be out of proportion to the actual event due to unresolved issues. Often you may transfer anger towards a person when they remind you of someone else with whom you are angry. This type of transference occurs with other feelings as well, but more frequently occurs with anger. In a situation like this, you need to step back and observe your own issues. You need to gain insight as to why you are really angry with this person or if the anger seems unreasonable. We must be careful though, because the concept of anger transference can be used to avoid accountability.

Very few people realize that their needs may be expressed without shouting or yelling. Once you start to yell and shout, the other person becomes defensive and effectively stops listening. Think of a time when someone has yelled at you. Do you listen carefully to each word he or she is saying? No, your listening skills are turned off almost immediately when someone yells at you. A need or desired behavior expressed in a firm confident tone will usually get the message across much more effectively. When needs are communicated without yelling, the other person will not be as defensive and be more likely to hear what you are trying to communicate.

By speaking in a firm, confident and self-respecting tone you end up emphasizing what you are trying to get across and the other person is more likely to listen. Once voice levels start to rise, the other person usually responds in the same manner until you are in a shouting match in which no one wins. By keeping your voice firm and not matching someone else's yelling you can effectively communicate your thoughts and feelings.

Once you have expressed your needs, you will usually uncover the hurt that created the anger in the first place. This hurt will usually manifest itself as sadness that can be released through acceptance, writing and crying. Remember that anger does not need to be acted on. It only needs to be acknowledged and to have its energy dissipated through changes in your thinking and expectations.

CCWC- Undoing the Anger Habit

In my travels to Asia, one of the startling differences was the behavior of drivers in traffic. At the time I was in Beijing, the traffic rules were very different from North America. A friend said to me "I hear that in North America, you have to obey the lines on the road" as we crossed diagonally on foot across a 4 lane street! This was one apparent difference, but notably was the lack of any expression of anger, as drivers intertwined in four lanes of traffic on a road with only three lanes painted on the road. I noticed a deep politeness and consideration among co-workers as well. At times, while riding my bicycle, a car would come within inches of me and my bike. From my North American driving upbringing this would raise the hair on my back, the first tendency was to shout at the driver. When I did this they looked at me quizzically. I spoke to my friend Sonya about this and suggested that it seemed that the Asian people were far more aware of the distance between each other, whether in their cars, on bicycles or on foot. She corrected me and educated me on the cultural differences, in which the people around me did not have such a strong sense of individuality as North Americans do. She explained that the other drivers would think that the other bike or car is actually part of themselves, therefore drivers seem more responsible and aware of distances between things. It also makes no sense to get angry with you, because if you are part of me, then I am only getting angry and being disrespectful with myself! This amazing lesson taught me to become more aware and be more responsible. I learned to navigate through the chaos of traffic on my bike, and actually enjoyed it once I discovered that the chaos had its own special rhythm to it. It was quite a shock coming back to North America, and the driving standards we have here – drivers giving the finger and getting upset at how everyone else is a bad driver!

Now that I've given you a cultural lesson, you can move into a frame of reference that will help you become less angry and be more compassionate with people. As I learned how much of a resentful and angry person I had become, I made a conscious effort to improve my attitude. I was constantly noticing how I was responding to challenging technical situations at work or how I was contributing to complaining and negative behavior. As I became more aware, I consciously tried to censure myself and have more control over my reactions. I learned that there are four pillars to the development of non-angry behavior and put them into practice. The four pillars are compassion, control, wisdom and cheerfulness, forming the "CCWC" of this chapter heading. I know now that all four must be present —the first three begin with me and are more internal, however the fourth pillar - cheerfulness, is an external expression to others, so that my kind, compassionate attitude can be shared.

In order to deepen my practice of this concept, I have practiced the auto-response training that was popular in the sixties and seventies. The auto-response training technique involves placing yourself in a desired state of mind and then associating a word or phrase with that state. When feeling challenged, impatient or sensing a loss of kindness, I simply repeat the phrase "CCWC" in my mind to remind myself of my practice of compassion, control, wisdom and cheerfulness. The sense of calm, focus and purpose returns instantly! This practice helps me in my efforts as a Buddhist and Christian to see a Buddha, or Christ child in the eyes of other people, even if they have harmed us, for in the harm there is some lesson to be learned. With this attitude, you find that if you are angry with someone else, then you are being angry with Buddha, God, or Christ, and doing harm to another sentient being created by a power greater than yourself. See that everyone else is a Buddha or Christ child even if they hurt you. Buddha does this to teach you a valuable lesson.

Wisdom – The Cure for Anger

In "Anger – Wisdom for Cooling the Flames" Thich Nat Hahn says that anger is like a fan that has just been shut off in that even though the power may have been turned off, the fan keeps spinning. Eventually though, it loses momentum and slows down. Our anger can be very similar to the energy of the fan blade. It may take some time for your body to recognize that you are no longer angry and to cleanse itself.

Again, practicing firmness with compassion will prevent the development of an anger condition. However like myself, many have already developed an anger habit and need to resolve the fact that we are already angry and our body has responded with muscle tension and chemical changes. This anger I found more difficult to deal with, but learned that forgiveness and compassion were the tools that helped me. In understanding that, by being betrayed and becoming angry about it, I had become a betrayer as well. My anger at people in my life was the result of an underlying judgment of these people. By realizing that I was betraying their goodness as well, and working to see the good in them, and forgiving myself for betraying them, I was able to heal a great number of relationships.

I have learned that to heal anger, I must sever the injury from any contempt, recognizing the hurtful incident as ignorance, misunderstanding, fear, or passion. The way to end anger is to become wiser, to plan your thoughts and reactions, not expecting the other to change, to give love, to be kind and develop compassion, see that in everyone else there is some good.

Changing Your Expectations

It is a fact of life that people often let us down. When this occurs the untrained mind may feel disappointment, resentment, anger, or a range of other emotions. Although it is reasonable to expect people to keep appointments and promises, you must remember that others, being human, are subject to their own strengths and weaknesses. By continually placing expectations on others, you are likely to be more often disappointed and angry. This is especially true if our belief system and expectations do not allow for the occasional failure. To expect means to also accept disappointment in your life. You cannot change others, but you can change yourself. You want to maintain standards in your friendships and relationships, but if your expectations are unreasonable, you are bound to end up disappointed at times unless you become more tolerant.

An example that comes to mind is the fact that I used to have an unreasonable expectation that friends would be around forever. It is a fact that people grow, and as a result, sometimes you outgrow your friends or your friends outgrow you. Because of my unreasonable expectation and my inability to let go, I found myself constantly fretting and getting angry over the friendships that had faded away. By recognizing the nature of these friendships, and acknowledging that one or both of us had moved on, I was able to change my expectations and therefore reduce and eliminate my anger. The way to end anger is to become wiser, to plan your thoughts and reactions.

Anger Resolution Exercises

Jump Forward In Time

This exercise comes from Rebbe Nachmann, an eighteenth century teacher of Kabbalah mysticism and founder of the Hasidic movement. He suggests "when you feel yourself getting angry, stop! Imagine yourself as having already exploded and you now feel wasted. For that's what happens when you are angry. Your soul leaves you. Do this, and your anger is sure to dissolve."

191

Mark Linden O'Meara

Breathing Purification Exercise

At times when I am angry, I have found that meditation has helped reduce my anger. I imagine breathing the anger out of my body, and as I do so it passes through a filter. Out of the filter comes love. This exercise helps transform our anger into a more positive energy. In many cases, the root of anger comes from your frustration in your desire to love and be loved. Through this purification you can connect with your deeper desires. Remember, anger is usually a secondary emotion resulting from unmet needs!

Give Your Anger to Nature

A Native American exercise to dispel anger energy is to go to a riverbank and pick up six small rocks. In quick succession, throw the rocks out into the water as hard as you can, imagining the anger energy leaving your body with each rock. Watch the river cleanse and take away your anger in the ripples that the splash of the rocks creates. It is a Native American Indian tradition to speak to the earth to heal yourself. This is also reflected in the bible - "speak to the earth and it will teach you."

Meditation

Meditation calms your blood pressure, helps you focus your breathing, and improves your sleep. Meditation teaches you to sit quietly and understand yourself better. Learning to tame and calm your mind is a prerequisite to developing the skill of practicing forgiveness and compassion. Instead of trying to change the world, you change yourself. It's actually the easier way! According to a study by Daniel Kenneth Oxman, mediation can help reduce anxiety, fearfulness, and nervousness. Meditation also seems to raise the body's energy level, as well as increase your sense of peacefulness both at work and at home. Best of all, it's free!

Practice Random Acts of Kindness

If you learn to take the emphasis off yourself, and have compassion for others you can reduce your anger. I remember a friend telling me how a person she was driving with was in a very angry mood. As he pulled up to an intersection, a squeegee kid ran up to the car. He rolled down his window and instead of yelling at the kid as my friend thought he would, he instead gave the kid a couple of bucks. Turning to my friend, he said "It's amazing what a charitable deed can do for your spirit!" My friend said that he was calm and relaxed for the rest of the trip home.

Regain Control

Should you be in a situation where you find yourself very angry, it is important to tame the anger and to lower the energy level of the anger. There are two techniques I can recommend. The first is to breathe deeply. When filled with anger your breathing is usually quickened, short and in the upper chest or in some cases you may completely restrict your breathing. Breathing is one of the easiest things to control. By slowing your breathing and breathing deeply into your belly while telling yourself to relax, you can give yourself a few moments to regain control and to process the anger and think about a calm response.

Running Man Exercise

Another method is to imagine your anger as a man running. You can imagine the man gradually slowing his pace down, to the point where he is walking, and then eventually have him sit down and meditate. This mental exercise has been very helpful in calming both my thoughts and emotions.

Express Your Energy through Creativity

On a day that I felt particularly frustrated and anger, I sat down at my electronic piano, put the headphones on and called up all the percussion sounds I could find. My keyboard became a complete drum set through which I could make lots of sound and noise, and express my anger and frustration. It is now rather humorous, but I remember as a teenager being asked by a counselor how I let out my frustrations. I replied, "I use my drum set." All of a sudden he became very quiet and serious and said "Are you planning to use it on anyone?" I looked at him rather quizzically and said, "Well, I plan to make some noise, you know, like bang, bang!" He seemed to become even more perturbed and said "Are you thinking of using them on yourself?" By now I thought he was really weird and I replied "What? Hit myself over the head with a drum?" Immediately he slumped in his chair with a look of total relief as he exclaimed, "Drum set!!! I thought you said gun set!" He took about half an hour to recompose himself! He stopped looking at the phone as if he was going to call the police!

Obviously there is humor in the above story, but sadly, some people do resort to violence thinking it will resolve their anger. In their clouded state of mind, they have rationalized that their actions will bring about change. It never works that way. They end up leaving a trail of people victimized and traumatized with their actions and no healing occurs. Find a safe way to deal with your emotions. Never harm anyone or any animal or thing through your expression of anger.

Mark Linden O'Meara

Reclaim your Soul

A helpful exercise to regain a sense of control and reduce victimization, and to strengthen your sense of self is to perform a ritual or a visualization in which you recover the parts of your soul you feel you have lost from those who have harmed you. It is not necessarily a physically exercise, but is spiritual in nature. Simply close your eyes and imagine yourself feeling grounded in your body. Imagine traveling to the place where one of these people are and imagine yourself spiritually recovering what you lost. Wish them well, and then return to your present moment and place. Sense the renewal in your body!

Change your Reaction and Behavior

In many cases, anger arises from not accepting "what is." When our needs are not met, the combined frustration leads to resentment and more frustration. At a talk by vegetarian author John Robbins, I was deeply moved by the words of a man in the audience who spoke about how his anger as "love with no place to go." His wife had divorced him and had started a relationship with a new man in her life. She had custody of the children. He described how he admitted to himself that he was angry because he missed his sense of family. He decided to let go of the relationship, and communicated to his ex-wife that he accepted the divorce and that she was now with a new partner. He forgave her, expressed his wish for her to be happy. In the end he became friends with all of them, restoring his sense of love in his life for their kids, his ex-wife and her new partner!

Separate the Person from the Event

One of the most difficult things for me to forgive resulted from an injury that caused a great deal of physical pain. A friend jokingly stomped on my foot, causing painful arthritis in the joint that lasted for over a year. Every day I was reminded of the pain, yet had to learn to forgive in someway. It was easy to forgive on one level, but on a deeper level, it required a constant effort, even though she had apologized. The difficulty came from the fact that although she had apologized, I was still suffering. I realized that when my foot hurt, a picture of her would pop into my head and I would feel angry towards her. It became much easier to deal with my anger as I learned to visualize the event as being separate from her. I imagined a cloud forming over her that represented the event. The cloud then moved away from her, allowing rays of sunshine to illuminate her in love. I would then visualize the cloud moving away, and then turning into a rainstorm that dissolved away, nurturing the plants and animals. This meditation has helped me to understand that anger results from the event, but it turns to resentment when it is directed at a person. I now believe that there are no justifiable resentments. Love the person, but challenge the behavior!

Learn to Listen Deeply

My healing process has helped me to increase my ability to love unconditionally the people who trigger me the most, and to understand that I may have incorrectly assumed that others are conscious of what they are doing. I often would quote the words attributed to Jesus "Forgive them father, for they know not what they do" yet have now learned that these words must be said without a tone of judgment. I've learned to be more compassionate and understanding of other people's points of view and to listen instead of arguing my point. My friend Phil wisely says "Being right and proving your point prevents real listening and understanding. When trying to prove our point, we are always thinking of what to say next rather than listening fully." Many of us have heard Thich Nat Hahn's response after Sept 11, 2001 that if he met Osama Bin Laden "the first thing I would do is listen, and would try to understand why he acted in that cruel way." By understanding how someone would come to such a horribly painful action, one would be able to respond firmly and challenge inappropriate behavior. These are wise words that hopefully you can apply in your own family situations, to listen without judging. It should be easier to listen to family, but most of us find this to be the most challenging!

Physical Exercise

Becoming involved in sports can greatly reduce tension. Even a walk or stretching exercises can help in improving our health. In addition to numerous benefits, exercise has been shown to increase levels of serotonin.

Sports, such as racquetball, that provide indirect competition with another player by bouncing a ball off a wall can be an excellent means of clearing your tension and anger. It is important to ensure that the anger does not turn into inappropriate aggression, otherwise the sport will not be as enjoyable for you or other team members. If it is not possible to make it to the gym, you can go for a brisk walk or bike ride. One of my friends has a trampoline set up. She says it's a great way to release energy!

> People will forget what you said.
> People will forget what you did.
> But people will never forget how you made them feel.
> - Author unknown

19. Remember and Forgive

> Growth in wisdom may be exactly measured by decrease in bitterness. - Friedrich Nietzsche

In your healing process you may ask yourself whether it is necessary to forgive those who have harmed you. But first it is important to also ask whether the person needs forgiveness at all. Suggesting that you need to forgive someone implies that they have done something wrong. First you must evaluate whether the issue is a serious one that requires forgiveness or whether it is just a misunderstanding or difference in viewpoint that caused the disruption in the relationship.

Once you decide that forgiveness is a desired goal, you need to evaluate and clarify your understanding and definition of forgiveness. First and foremost, forgiveness is something you do for yourself and the good of all people. It is an act of restoring sanity to yourself by changing your own attitudes and feelings. In forgiveness, you do not condone the actions of others, nor do you minimize the impact that those actions had on you. It is not a process of wiping the slate clean. It is a process of acknowledging what occurred, the impact of those actions or events, and the work you have done to cope and resolve the problems. It is not a method of minimizing or denying your pain.

Secondly, forgiveness does not always mean reconciliation. Forgiveness can occur without reconciliation or an apology from the offender. It is also important to note that forgiveness is not something you do only once. It is an ongoing process.

If you do not forgive, then you end up living with resentment and bitterness. By not forgiving, you end up harming yourself. Most definitions of serenity include not only acceptance and empathy, but include forgiveness as being fundamental to attaining it. Others have stated that a lack of forgiving imprisons your soul. Terry Waites, upon his release from his hostage ordeal, stated that he had to forgive his captors; otherwise he would remain captive forever.

In my own path of forgiveness, I found that there was a very spiritual dimension to the process. In doing forgiveness work, I found that I discovered a greater sense of being human, and discovered more about others. I learned about the frailty of the human condition, and the difficulties people had faced.

I also learned not to judge, to be mindful of my own limitations and to maintain a spiritual practice of love for myself, and others.

Still, it was a difficult process, as I needed to examine the nature of my anger and attributions and self-doubt. With situations of abuse, it became necessary to move towards seeing the abuser as a human with weaknesses and someone who was not totally evil or bad. It is often easier to hate than to forgive. Naturally I was very angry with a number of people who had treated me poorly and verbally, emotionally or physically abused me. At times I felt like I would like to confront them and hold them accountable for their actions. To heal it is necessary to gain understanding beyond these feelings and healing yourself.

While moving forward in your healing process you may consider confronting the offender. In such cases it is extremely important that you understand your expectations regarding the confrontation. It is important to stop further incidents, however additional pain can occur due to your expectations of the offender. You may expect them to apologize and dramatically change their behavior. Some people will deny the offence. Others may admit to it and apologize, yet continue with offensive or abusive behavior due to their own difficulties and problems. Others may begin their own process of healing, while others may be resentful.

In your quest to forgive you need to give up the notion that the offender owes you something or needs to make up for what they did or did not do. Only when you give up this notion can you have truly forgiven them.

While you may feel that confrontation is necessary, so is forgiveness. Healing involves forgiving yourself as well as others. It is a step that you take to rid yourself of resentment and bitterness. It can be a difficult and challenging, yet rewarding, process in which you free yourself of a burden and release others from your expectations.

Forgiving involves a lack of a need to retaliate. It also involves accepting an apology if one is given. One of the most difficult things to do is to accept an apology when you are still very angry. You may not be at the same healing place as the other person is and as a result of the timing, healing may not occur if you do not acknowledge the apology and modify your thoughts accordingly. You may be still investing in being angry and judging the other person. To heal and forgive you must begin to see the good in others. Remember that apologies come in many forms. Sometimes a gesture of goodwill, special eye contact, a hug or other body language, will suffice when words are hard to speak.

One of the most difficult types of forgiveness to achieve occurs when there is no acknowledgement of the incident or hurt. In this situation, you need to discover for yourself what you need to forgive. Essentially, you need to master your own healing process.

Another challenge for many is what is called pseudo forgiveness. You may go around saying "I've forgiven" but it is really only a state of denial. You haven't really done the work, only blocked out the feelings and are avoiding the necessary healing work. Forgiveness involves giving up your sense of hostility and need for amends from another person or organization. To do so allows you to move on to greater things in your life. Studies of forgiveness have noted substantial improvements in peoples lives in the area of mental health when they forgive. These improvements include relationships, physical health, hostility, anxiety, self-esteem, depression and social activity!

The Skill of Forgiveness

According to the latest research, forgiveness actually seems to be a learned skill that comes with age and is learned over a total life span. According to a French study, adults are more likely to forgive than adolescents, and seniors are more likely to forgive than younger adults. There are also a number of factors that facilitate or make forgiveness more difficult. The first aspect is the degree of harm that was experienced. Obviously, a simple mistake by another person that has little impact on our lives is much easier to forgive. Secondly, if you have been adequately compensated in some way such as through an apology or kind deed, then you will be more likely to forgive. Furthermore, strong emotions regarding an incident tend to make it more difficult to forgive. It is necessary to work through the emotions in order to bring the incident into a process of forgiveness. Finally, if you have a reason for why someone did something then it is much easier to forgive.

In a forgiveness study, college students were told that a dog had bit another person. One group was told the dog had been abused, while the other group was not given any reason. The first group exhibited far more compassion for the dog than the second group! If you can gain some insight as to why the incident occurred then it is much easier to forgive. By gaining a view of the other person as being human with flaws just like yourself, it becomes easier to forgive. One thing that seems to help forgive is to tell your story. Journaling can be very helpful. I remember an incident that happened years ago that I was angry about. I took some time and wrote out what happened as I remembered it. As the details flowed out, my ability to see other aspects of the incident increased. I ended up with a much greater understanding of the dynamics in the situation. Forgiveness became easier!

Blocks and Catalysts to Forgiving

Of all the factors that stop us from forgiving, age is not one of them. Study after study has shown that forgiveness is a learned skill and habit that seems to increase with age, not decrease like so many other aspects of living. It seems that as you get wiser in your older years, you learn to forgive and increase your sense of well being. Another factor that helps you forgive is the closeness of the person you wish to forgive. You might find it more difficult to forgive a colleague than a close family member. What helps you forgive is a desire to restore the relationship especially when the other person is a member of your close community.

From the studies I have read, there is very little difference in willingness to forgive and your gender. Mood is also a factor in willingness to forgive. It is easier to forgive when you are in a good mood. Generally speaking, people find it easier to forgive if there was no intent to harm, or if there was no negligence. The more severe the consequences, the harder most people find it to forgive.

There are other blocks to forgiveness that we can examine. First of all, some people want revenge or punishment. This is clearly a block to forgiveness. Others want to somehow cancel the consequences and return to the state that they had before the incident. Often this is not possible and therefore blocks people from forgiving. Many people believe they cannot forgive if they have not received an apology. On the other side of the coin, many people find it easier to forgive if there is repentance and remorse on the part of the offender.

In some situations, people will forgive only because of social, peer or authority pressure to forgive. This type of forgiveness is not as effective in reducing anger and generating healing between the offender and the injured person. Forgiveness out of obligation is less effective than forgiveness derived from a sense of love and compassion for yourself and others.

Finally some people find it easier to forgive after a period of time has elapsed since the event. Perhaps as you acknowledge and healthily express emotions and the event fades into the background, friends, family, and colleagues realize the value of the relationship and are willing to make amends or let go.

Seven Steps to Forgiveness

Much has been written about forgiveness. Everywhere you turn people are saying you have to forgive, yet few people likely understand the process of true forgiving. For true healing, forgiveness is essential. The same holds true for the idea of compassion. Yet I have learned that going from anger straight to compassion does not bring about true forgiveness. It only creates a sense of pseudo forgiveness. Many people try to go from hurt or anger straight to compassion.

It most often fails unless they fully understand the deeper process. In most cases the shortcut backfires or they have only repressed their anger. While you maintain an air of forgiveness, you may find yourself easily triggered when speaking of the original event, or you find yourself reacting emotionally when the issue is raised.

I have found that the following steps bring about lasting forgiveness when implemented and practiced on a daily basis. I've had many things to forgive, so I've had practice. I've noticed that it is easy to fall back into a trap of non-forgiveness and resentment unless you make it a daily habit to forgive. Why forgive? You forgive so that you can stop harming yourself through resentment and begin to move into a state of happiness and gratitude.

Stage 1- Admit You Are Angry!

Many of us will echo the thoughts "What? I'm not supposed to get angry! I've done all this healing work!" I've learned that it is harmful to get angry but it is more harmful to be angry and not admit it! The way to check if you are angry is to observe your inner dialogue about how you are relating to yourself and others. Are you finding yourself being negative, critical or frustrated? Do you find yourself being impatient with people and critical of how things are done? Are you constantly blaming others for your troubles, wishing that others would change? If so, then it is likely you are angry. Try to recognize what you are angry about. It may not be the little things, but something that happened months ago. Look back in time to what might have triggered your anger and where your expression has been blocked. Bitterness is anger with no outlet to be heard or feeling that you can not change anything. It is a form of helplessness. Try to discover what you are bitter about. Make a list of resentments. Don't hold back or edit your thoughts. Being honest with yourself is the first step in healing anger.

Stage 2- Acknowledge the Loss and Consequences

In order to fully forgive, you need to look at the consequences of the event. By consequences, I do not mean just emotional pain. Look at the past and the present, and honestly note any changes. Were you physically injured? Were you emotionally hurt? Did you suffer financial loss? What other types of losses occurred? Was there harm to other relationships? To achieve lasting forgiveness it is important to acknowledge all the losses, otherwise forgiveness will have to be revisited. When listing the losses and consequences, try to look objectively at the incident without investing in the emotions around the losses at this time.

Stage 3 - Submit to a Feeling of Vulnerability

The next stage in forgiveness is to open your self up to change and dissonance. You can not spread butter when it is hard and cold. Forgiveness does not come easily when your ideas, thoughts of revenge or justice are hardened. You must retreat and re-examine your approach. Just like a pound of butter, if you want to forgive and heal, you need to let your ideas thaw and be molded into a new perspective, combined with other ideas and views. You need to admit that to harbor anger and resentments violates the laws of kindness and compassion both for yourself and other people. You must realize that in not forgiving, you are now betraying the person at whom you are angry. This is not an easy step. It can be painful to realize that it is you who needs to change, and that it is you who has the poison of anger and resentment. It is easy to build up a wall of justification around your thoughts, actions and feelings regarding the harm done to you. In order to heal and forgive, you need to break through the wall and tear it down completely!

This stage of forgiveness also requires you look at whether there was any responsibility on your part. In some cases there was none, in some cases, you may have taken action which contributed to the decision. In this case, it may be hard for you to admit that you caused part of your own suffering as it is easier to blame others than to take any responsibility. This stage requires an honest, fearless, kind and moral inventory of your own actions and behavior. Sometimes you may not like what you find, but facing your shadow can be one of the most powerful healing experiences. See if you can find some common ground.

Stage 4 – Stop Punishing

One of the common behaviors of people is to try to punish those who have harmed us. Most studies have shown that punishment rarely teaches anything other than to resent the person doing the punishing! Some of the ways you may punish are by withholding companionship, giving someone the silent treatment, or even giving compliments but then taking it back with an insult. You may try to go further with legal action, or you may try to damage things that the other person prizes. Another method of punishment is gossiping about the other person. In order to truly forgive, you need to give up the expectation that the other person will be punished. You can ask that the other person make amends for their harm, but if they refuse or are unable to make amends, then releasing them from the idea of punishment frees you from lingering resentment.

There is great wisdom in the following Buddhist teaching – "Should one person ignorantly do wrong, and another ignorantly becomes angry with him, who would be at fault? And who would be without fault?" It is far better to try to forgive, and reintegrate your friends back into community than to ostracize and alienate them through punishment. Try to practice compassion, work at developing a deeper understanding of how and why people behave. It seems that we prefer a simple explanation of things, yet you need to understand that human beings and the relationships between each other are complex. Understanding the ways of the world and the people in the world requires wisdom and self control. Use the opportunity to forgive as a means of growth!

Stage 5 – Identify Some Good in the Other Person

This step, finding some good in the other person is probably the most crucial step in bringing about lasting forgiveness. It can also be the hardest depending on the severity of the event you are trying to forgive.

According to Francis Bacon, the key to forgiveness is in "not expecting the other to change, to give love, to be kind and develop the ability to see that in everyone else's eyes and heart there is some good." In forgiving, you try not to think of yourself as being good and the other person bad. You can find it easier to forgive if you can understand that the other person has difficulties too, or was harmed in the past.

If you do not practice this step, then forgiveness will be futile because it will be done with a sense of contempt for the other person. If you can not find good in the other person, then at least pray for them. A wonderful technique for developing your vision of good in another is to imagine a seed of goodness in their heart, and in prayer imagine that both you and God are watering it to make it grow stronger. Better yet is to image that each person already has this great flower of goodness in them already. Admit that it has been obscured from your view because of your anger, resentment and justifications. Learn to look for the good. At first, like developing any skill, it is challenging. You will become better at it with practice!

Stage 6 – Develop Genuine Neutrality

Hopefully in the process of forgiveness you will come to resolve any negative emotions and thoughts about yourself and the other person or organization. To do so requires that you do not expect or demand any payment or restitution after forgiveness. You must assume that there is no debt owed to you. Mother Theresa once said "it is between God and myself, it was never between me and them anyway." This must be practiced daily. It is easy to slip into anger and resentment if you do not cultivate a practice of neutrality. Depending on the severity of the event, you may choose to not have any further contact with the person, but if you meet them by chance, you want to have a sense of neutrality and a sense of calmness instead of avoidance.

Stage 7 – Stay in the Present

"Bury the hatchet" is a phrase you may have heard many times. There is wisdom to this phrase if you understand its original meaning. The phrase comes from spiritual traditions of North American Indians who would put all weapons out of site while smoking a peace pipe. For your own forgiveness work, you must keep the original wound out of sight, or out of present mind. It is necessary to acknowledge what happened, to not forget it, but also not drag it up again as a fresh wound. Resurrecting the event and bringing it up again with the person who harmed you will cause you to feel the associated feelings again. Balance your memory of the event with your memory of the forgiveness work you have done. Practice loving those you dont feel warmth towards.

All of your forgiveness work can be undone, and the resentment rekindled if you begin to dwell on the event again. If you begin to rerun your mind's movie of the harm, then you may find yourself in an angry and hurt state again. It is the nature of your mind to ruminate, and therefore you must develop self-discipline and remind yourself that you have completed forgiveness work around this issue. Thank your mind for the intrusive thought, and send it off into the far reaches of the universe! Refuse to bring the past into the present again, as it will re-trigger you back into hurt and anger. Continually rise above the injury! Practice compassion and unconditional love towards all people!

Making Amends

There is great wisdom in one of the most critical steps in twelve step programs which occurs when you make a list of all persons you have harmed and make amends as long as doing so will do no harm to others. I believe this step is a very powerful example of doing onto others what you would have others do unto you. It is also a powerful step in self healing, respecting others boundaries and taking ownership of your own behavior and issues. We have all hurt someone at sometime in our life. Examining the impact that it had on yourself and others and looking at how your own character may have negatively affected someone else requires self love and a degree of caring for other people.

While attending a dinner I bumped into a woman that I dated briefly after completing my master's degree. At the time I dated her, I was physically and emotionally burnt out and wasn't warm and accepting of her kindness. I told her how I felt badly about how I treated her. Although I conveyed that I was not in good shape, and that I wasn't really capable of giving at that time, it wasn't she who had a problem. I said I was sorry for not recognizing the gifts she had to offer. I could tell from the sense of relaxation that came over her and the unspoken reduction in tension between the two of us, that my words meant a lot to her.

Clearly this was a case in which contact between the two of us would not harm her, however in some situations an apology will bring about more harm than good. When a secret has been kept from someone and then you tell him or her and also apologize, you have to wonder if the apology is meant to help him or her or yourself because of guilt. For this process to work, I would suggest that the apology must occur for some event that both people are already aware of as having happened. In apologizing, you may be bringing up old wounds in the other person that they are not ready to deal with. It is best to ask whether it is okay to talk to them about it. If they say no, then their wishes should be respected. If you apologize for something you did that the other person was never aware of, you may end up hurting someone with new information and end up dumping your problems onto them and causing pain about a closed chapter of their life.

Making amends can mean a number of things too. If there is someone you cannot contact and you wish to be forgiven for some deed, create a simple ceremony in which you do something for a stranger and in silence, release yourself from owing the apology. You are still accountable for your actions, but in some way, you are giving out the energy of health by completing the issue for yourself. If you are fortunate to have that person come into your life at sometime, you can tell them of the ceremony you did for them.

Self-Forgiveness

In my healing, it was very important to forgive myself as well. There have been times when I have let myself down, regretting the things I had not done or wish that I had done things differently. Self-forgiveness is needed just as much as forgiving others, yet it is just as difficult. Self-forgiveness is accepting yourself for the things you have done with the knowledge you had at the time. It is accepting your limitations, yet not limiting your capacity for change. Self-forgiveness requires that you look at your shadow, or the secrets you hold that you hope no one will ever find out. It is about acknowledging your deepest fears.

I was twenty-three when I was told that my mother was terminally ill. I simply could not accept that she was going to die. I was also quite busy with starting my undergraduate degree, and was playing in a rock band. I postponed going to visit her at the hospital. When I finally did, she was unconscious. I never got to say goodbye to her. It was always difficult to forgive myself for this, then I realized that there was no way I could have held my life together other than to deny my fears and to rationalize that she had bounced back at other times and this would be one of them. Being gentle with myself, accepting the place I was at during those weeks, as well as sharing these feelings with a counselor has helped heal this shadow. I have come to accept that my mother knew far more about me than I realize. At the moment she passed away, I was setting up my drums for a high school dance. As she departed this level of existence, I felt her presence sweep down on me, hug me, and then move off towards a great expanse of freedom. I knew that she was gone, and that she loved me deeply enough to say goodbye. Her final words to all of us, dictated to my father were "be good and be happy!" She wouldn't want me to feel remorse, and she certainly wouldn't want me to punish myself.

Try to discover which events in your life you have regrets about. Find practical ways of self acceptance and forgiveness.

Compassion....
Does a true hero have to be heartless?
Surely a real man may love his young son.
Even the roaring, wind-raising tiger
Turns back to look at his own tiny cubs.
- Lu Xun

20. Soul Medicine

"I've hundreds of things to say but my tongue just can't manage them, so I'll dance them for you"
- Nikos Kazantzakis, Zorba the Greek

As a counselor, I have often wondered about the limitations of talk therapy, given the wonderful ability to heal through the expressive arts. My own healing journey would not have been possible without the writing, singing, dancing, drawing, and drumming that I did to express my feelings. Of course, speaking with a counselor was also integral to my growth, as it provided an opportunity to reflect and examine my worldview. The process of therapy also gives you a chance to conduct a moral inventory and express it to another human being, as described in twelve step groups. In counseling, your therapist becomes a witness to your process and facilitates your growth. Both counseling and expressiveness are valuable and one should not be discouraged over another.

In my own counseling training, we were encouraged to use tools that helped the client. In some cases, a block of clay was provided for the client to mold. I was amazed how some clients would create beautiful images while talking - seemingly unaware of how their hands were creating metaphors for their inner world. I distinctly remember a client shaping the clay into a vulnerable newborn while talking about herself, yet changing the clay into a round metallic like cylinder when talking about her mother. Examining the view of her mother also being a vulnerable child at one time opened new pathways to healing for this individual.

In using the expressive arts, you can come to realize that you do not have to be a professional artist or musician to show your gifts for being creative, although you may be surprised to find a hidden talent. Though many have been discouraged, many have also persevered in recovering their artistic abilities. Gradually as you create, you learn to become vulnerable and to share your thoughts, works, poems and voice. The process of writing and sharing this book began with baby steps of writing a few words, taking singing lessons, then eventually sharing my creativity.

For many, the artistic world is what keeps people connected and sane. Musician Bill Henderson writes:

206

"When I was young I was very shy and had a rough time talking to people... there can be heavy duty pressure in school when you are growing up. Music was the only way that I could communicate with the world that actually worked. Music saved my life. When you create music, you are finding something that makes you feel better and when you give that to someone it's a wonderful thing. It helps our culture become saner. The artists view point is one our society needs more of."

For those who have been discouraged from singing and have based their own evaluation of their artistic ability on others' opinions, the following words from Ron Dante, the voice behind The Archies, The Cuff Links and numerous other bands may provide some encouragement:

"At my first recording session when I was about 14 years old the owner of a well-known recording studio in NYC told me after listening to me sing in front of a microphone that I had no sound to my voice - that it did not record very well. Even then I knew that he was dead wrong. My sound became one of the most famous vocal sounds on records and commercials. A few years later my recording of "Sugar, Sugar" sold more than 6 million records."

Ron provides further inspiration to keep going and never give up!

"I started to sing at about 7 or 8 years old and knew I could do it by the age of 14 when I recorded my first record. I was encouraged to sing by my parents. They loved to hear me sing. Being encouraged when very young helped me be successful. I got discouraged many times when starting out but always believed I could achieve big things in the music business. When something bad would happen I would just reaffirm my conviction that I would do better next time and upgrade my game so to speak. I love to sing because it puts me in the zone that sports players like Michael Jordan speak of. It's that place where you were born to be. Anyone can sing but most do not have the ear to know when they are in tune or out. People who can keep rhythm can be taught to sing. It takes practice and learning how to count bars and things but they can learn. Pat Boone was one singer who learned to sing by counting bars."

While not everyone feels a calling to become a singer, it is important to discover your own medium for expressing your soul's nature. This can be done through your hobbies, through your career or even through your family life. We long to enrich people's lives. In reading the next few pages, try to think of what you would like to do to express yourself. Try a few new things. Sing in your car! Buy a sketch pad and some crayons. Learn to play again!

Artistic Expression

Pablo Picasso was quoted as saying that "art washes away the dust of daily living from the soul." Art of any form has been known for ages to have tremendous healing powers when some medium is used to express the feelings and creative center of the artist. In referring to artists, we wish to include all forms of art — dancing, music, painting, sculpting, or any other form of expression. Art therapy has been a very successful treatment for those who are recovering from the trauma of being sexually abused.

In using art as a healing medium, it is important to create art that is expressive. If you place an object on a table and paint it, then the exercise of painting will be relaxing but not as healing as using a canvas or other medium to express your feelings and emotions.

One of the greatest healing tools is a sketchpad and a package of crayons. Planning ahead, I would always make sure I have paper and the drawing tools available. I often draw the emotions I am feeling by picking colors that I felt would represent the emotions I am experiencing. Using reds and dark blue for anger, I would simply shade in areas of the paper to express my emotions. I might add in lighter colors such as yellow and sky blue to express more joyous states. I would often create two or three drawings, resulting in a progression of expression that would lead to healing the emotions. I have always found this technique to be stress reducing and a method of externalizing the emotions I was feeling. While I do not consider myself an artist, I have learned the art of emotional expression!

In times of healing, many people re-discover a talent they had abandoned. Others may discover a talent that they never knew they had. In many high schools we see a great deal of artistic talent that falls by the wayside upon graduation. Perhaps it may be time to try things you always wanted to or were afraid to do.

You may wish to start your own "School of Self Expression," where you are both the teacher and the student! In reading *The Importance of Living* by Lin Yutan I learned that in the 1600's, three Chinese brothers started such a school, called the "School of Hsing Ling".

Lin writes "Hsing Ling translates to self expression, but in the true sense it means Hsing - personal nature and Ling - soul or vital spirit… The School of

Self Expression demands that we express … only our own thoughts and feelings, our genuine loves, genuine hatred, genuine fears and genuine hobbies. These will be expressed without any attempt to hide the bad from the good, without fear of being ridiculed by the world and without fear of contradicting the ancient sages or contemporary authorities." The key to immersing yourself in the creative arts is to accept whatever you create and avoid judging it as good or bad.

In the following pages you will find a number of techniques that I have come across that can be used to facilitate emotional expression. One aspect to be stressed at this point is that each person's emotional healing process is personal and unique. In reviewing the techniques below, you may find that some of these will suit you while others may not. Just as the interests of people vary, so do the ways that people express themselves and heal. Keep in mind that there is no right way or wrong way to express yourself as long as your method does not harm others.

Pablo Picasso was quoted as saying "There are painters who transform the sun into a yellow spot, but there are others who, thanks to their art and intelligence, transform a yellow spot into the sun."

Dance and Drama

Healing through expression is not limited to art alone. Meditation, visualization, singing (a form of meditation in some cultures), chanting, role-playing, and dance can all play an important role in the healing process.

In *Creative Therapies in the Treatment of Addictions*, author Lynn Johnston states in her abstract that "the core issue in addiction is shame, and creativity can serve as the antidote to this shame. Creativity may take the form of poetry therapy, art therapy, dance therapy, or musical/dramatic performance."

In another study entitled *Dance Movement: A therapeutic program for psychiatric clients*, author Lou Heber reports that when using dance therapy, patients reported an increase in self-esteem. Fern Leventhal, in *Dance/Movement Therapy with Battered Women*, reports that "by motivating female victims of domestic violence to act, dance/movement therapy addresses patterns of helplessness, ambivalence, and inactivity. Dance/movement interventions help women (and men) internalize a positive self-concept as well as gain physical and emotional control."

Musical Expression

Musical expression can also be very helpful in the release of emotional energy. In *Care of the Soul*, Thomas Moore writes "one of my own forms of expression is to play the piano in times of strong emotion. I remember well the day Martin Luther King Jr. was killed. I was so overwhelmed that I went to the piano and played Bach for three hours. The music gave form and voice to my scrambled emotions, without explanations and rational interpretations."

As reported by Judith Ginzberg in "*In Search of a Voice: Working with Homeless Men,*" music, ritual and dance can help the men to enhance self-esteem, establish trust, reduce tension, and promote group interaction.

As a singer myself, I have often noticed how singing lifts my spirits. I also noticed that as I released and resolved anger, I discovered that I had a clearer, more resonant voice with greater range. My singing instructor claimed that a number of her students often experienced singer's "buzz" -a sense of joy and elation from singing.

Keep in mind that you do not have to be a professional musician or singer to enjoy these benefits. The key is to accept whatever sounds you make without judgment. I have often found that I could relax a great deal simply by playing whatever came to mind on my guitar. As the famous Beatles' song goes - ."as my guitar gently weeps."

Expressing Yourself Verbally

To avoid resentment it is necessary for us to speak up about incidents as and when they occur. For some of us this may take some effort and practice. Not only must you speak up about irritants, you must also express your love and concern for others. When you let things slip by, you end up internalizing them. They then become harbored resentments that you will have to deal with at a later time.

To improve your emotional health, practice being less timid and set boundaries for yourself and with others. You have a right to stand up for yourself and to speak up when anyone does something against you. It is usually easier to deal with an issue at the moment it happens, rather than later on, after you have stewed over it!

Writing and Journaling

Keep a Diary or Journal

Writing can be a great way to release emotional tension and promote healing. Journaling can even improve your health and psychological well-being according to the Journal of Experimental Psychology! Putting thoughts down on paper can help clear the mind of its cobwebs. It is a great technique for getting your thoughts out of your head and onto paper where you can look at them more objectively. If you are afraid of someone reading it, then find a safe place for it or keep it under lock and key if that helps. Writing out your thoughts may seem strange to you at first, but with practice it will become easier and easier. Most of you wish you could faithfully keep a journal but realistically, few of you do. Simply be content to write in your journal whenever you feel like. It is unwise to create an expectation of writing faithfully. Be content with whatever and whenever you write.

Writing also has a second payoff as it allows you to look back over time and measure progress over weeks, months or years, noting the issues you have resolved. If an issue is still in your mind you can continue to work on it. Problems are often resolved and forgotten. The absence of a problem needs to be acknowledged as a success. Journaling helps you to look back and see from where you have come. Go out and purchase a journal. Pick one that has a cover that you like. Many stationery stores carry books with empty pages. Even if you do not plan to write today, purchase a journal so that it will be ready for you when you are ready. In journaling, try to describe what happened, how you feel about what happened, what you would have like to occur differently, and what you need.

Write or Tell Your Story

A larger writing project may involve writing a two or three page summary of your life story. This exercise can help in noticing the important events that have occurred in your life. In writing your story it is important to use "I" statements and to describe the feelings you had at each event. While therapeutic, this exercise has been known to be somewhat exhausting. Tackling it in portions can make the task a little easier. Many therapists ask their clients to write their story in order to get to know their client better.

In my own inner work I have found that sometimes I needed to tell a particular story more than once. I would suggest that there are different stages of telling a story, and therefore going through it a few times may be helpful, especially for more traumatic events. The first time you tell your story, simply acknowledge the event. The second time, you may be more ready to acknowledge the feelings and emotions. As you become more aware of the emotions and can express them, you may want to begin to talk about the impact and consequences of the event. From this point you can move into an evaluation phase where you look at all perspectives. Finally you can develop a new paradigm and integrate the story into your personal history.

Write Letters of Letting Go

There are times when you would like to express yourself to someone yet conversations don't always go the way you want them to. You may also find that the other person will not listen or perhaps they are no longer around you to hear the communication. The person you wish to communicate with may be miles away, you may not even know their address, or they may have passed away.

Too often you have unfinished business with someone and need closure. What you want to communicate may vary from relationship to relationship. You may be angry and hurt, or you may wish to tell someone that you love him or her and have never told him or her. Writing a letter to that person can help you express your feelings and give closure, even if you don't send it.

More often than not you never end up sending the letter, but like keeping a diary or writing your story, writing a letter is an excellent way to get your thoughts and feelings out of your head. It helps greatly if you write the letter using the words "I feel..." in the letter rather than the finger pointing "You...."

Whether or not you ever send the letter is not important. What is important is the expression and release of your feelings. You can write the letter and then, with a clearer head, decide whether to send it or not. Keep in mind that the purpose of writing a letter is to provide release for your thoughts and emotions, not to try to change someone else's thinking or behavior. What seems to be unfinished emotional business with someone is often an indication that you need to face something in yourself.

Create Poetry

While I am more inclined myself to write in my journal, I have met many people who can communicate far better through poetry. Like a painting or piece of music, poetry can express deep feelings, wishes and desires, or anger. Yet poetry can present your thoughts in images with rhythm, metaphors and in some cases a wry wit. Try it! You never know what you will come up with!

Write the Letter You Would Like to Receive

Along with writing letters that you may never send you may wish to write the letter that you would like to receive from people we are no longer in contact with. The letter you write could be the words of an apology you wish for or the words that you need to hear to obtain closure and to let go. After writing the letter you can read it back to yourself and have a ceremony of completion.

Create a Collage

Gathering magazines, pictures, pens and paper to create a collage of what you desire and hope for, can be a great exercise in visualizing your goals. Cut out pictures and words that remind you of a healthy life and arrange them on a piece of poster board. This is a great exercise in creativity that brings out an image of hope and direction.

Ceremonies of Completion and Letting Go

In some cases it may not be possible to send the letter you have written and often you may not want to. Keeping the letter in a drawer can often result in a lack of closure or a sense of holding on. To complete the unfinished business you can have your own ceremony of completion. By ripping the letter, shredding it or burning the letter safely in a fireplace, and saying a phrase to yourself such as "I let go" you can create completion for yourself.

The Empty Chair

It is often very healing to place an empty chair in front of you and imagine that the person you wish to communicate with is sitting in the chair. Proceeding to tell them exactly what you would like to say to them and how you are feeling is a technique often used in therapy. Your mind will become clearer through this opportunity to express yourself. The next step is to imagine hearing them say what you would like to hear from them to help you heal.

Graveyard Visits - When Someone is no Longer With You

Many of us have lost family members or friends. Again, you may have unfinished business. In some cases you may want to express your love, in other cases you may want to express your anger over their leaving. Because someone has passed on does not mean that you should not be angry with him or her. Going to a graveyard and saying what you want to say can be a tremendously healing experience. Dr. Wayne Dyer described that going to his father's grave and expressing his anger, disappointment, and forgiveness was a catalyst in creating his highly successful book *Your Erroneous Zones*. Go to a graveyard and say the things you want to say. Remember to forgive!

Physical and Emotional Catharsis

Massage and Healing Professions

In your emotional healing it is important to nurture yourself and promote relaxation. Emotional expression involves the contraction and relaxation of muscle tissue and emotional blocking leads to an increased level of muscular tension. Releasing the muscular tension will often help you release some of the emotional energy. A well-trained massage therapist will be able to assist in your healing process. Massage can bring about a better state of relaxation, which in turn will bring about emotional release. Often you may find yourself moving through various emotions when receiving a massage. The latest research has indicated that touch and therefore massage, can result in changes in serotonin levels which are clearly linked to healing from depression.

Besides massage, there are a number of other healing professions such as acupuncture, Reiki and aromatherapy. What works for you may not be the choice of someone else. The key is to feel comfortable with what you are doing and to ensure that it promotes healing.

Crying and Crying Substitutes

Often tears well up but you do not give yourself permission to cry. You may experience tension in the chest and throat area, but you do not cry. Often it is very easy to stifle the tears and continue on with your tasks rather than express your feelings. If you pay attention to these signals and give yourself permission to cry and let go, then crying will usually follow. Noticing your breath at these times can also help you let the tears flow.

Often though, you may not be ready for tears and may develop your own crying substitutes. Often, adults will learn whole repertories to substitute for crying. The simple act of talking and sharing in a support group may be one of the first stages in allowing release to occur. If your tension level lowers, and you experience enough self-acceptance, then tears will likely follow.

Sobbing or Crying

The earliest tears will be usually experienced with tension in the upper chest and throat. However, a deeper type of release is possible. Crying can often lead to a deeper sobbing if you accept the pain you are feeling and allow the tears to fully flow. This type of release is centered more in the stomach area and will involve more of the body, particularly the abdomen and shoulders. A deep body sob promotes healing and is a deeper release of emotional tension. The sobbing with the whole body can be quite exhausting and a period of rest afterward is a good idea.

I clearly remember a time when some painful memories were triggered while watching a movie with a friend. I became aware of a deep-rooted sense of loneliness and pain that had long been forgotten. I asked my friend to stop the tape and she held me as I cried. As I took deep breaths, the crying came from deep within my chest. I could feel a knot of energy being released from deep inside of me. Although painful and exhausting, I had acknowledged a deep sense of pain which my friend reflected back to me when she said, "you've really been hurt." After resting, I felt a sense of calmness and serenity, and a stronger connection with my friend for supporting me through this.

Laughter

While tears are often credited with healing, so is laughter. Rent a funny movie, go to see a comedian, or call a friend with whom you share laughter. Finding humor in your own situation or mannerisms helps you to accept yourself. Laughter can restore vitality and produce chemical changes in your body. Laughter reduces your susceptibility to disease and enhances your coping abilities.

Make Use of Emotional Movies etc.

Often you can bring about healing tears by making use of emotional movies or music. If you find that some sentimental movie, a piece of music, or a poem helps you to cry then, by all means, use it. Sometimes all you need is a little extra to help get the release started. Sometimes a movie or song will trigger a memory or release for reasons that may be unknown to you. Seize the moment as an opportunity to let go and be free of whatever has been bottled up. Keep a box of tissue handy and let go! On the other hand, remember that you can also use various forms of entertainment to help you laugh.

Research Your Family Tree

Researching my family tree has provided me with a greater understanding of my roots, and what my parents and grandparents experienced. It can also be a safe way to discover other relatives, or even to get a sense of a larger family that you belong to rather than just your own immediate family. The Internet has made searching easier and the resources of the Church of Latter Day Saints provides valuable information. In researching my family tree I discovered that my father had lost both his parents by age twenty-five, his father dying when he was twenty-one after only a brief two week illness. I learned that his parents lost their parents early as well, and one of my great-grandmothers lost her husband when her children were only four and seven. On this side of the family, a number of children died young. All of this gave me a greater sense of compassion for these people who had endured a great deal of suffering, and helped me to understand some of the key events that shaped their lives. This type of research can also help you to forgive your parents if you understand their circumstances better.

Creative Visualization

Visualizing a Different Outcome

Creative visualization is a powerful technique that can help you move into the type of lifestyle you wish to have. It can also help you develop a more positive attitude or assist you in the development of a sense of competence and serenity in dealing with others. There is some sound wisdom in the words "whatever you tell yourself and believe is then true for you." Using techniques of visualization, you can work on your beliefs and begin to train your mind to operate with new beliefs about yourself. By visualizing yourself being success-

215

ful, so you become. If you imagine yourself being relaxed around others, it is likely that you will become that way. There are numerous books on creative visualization, meditation, and affirmations. You may even want to create your own affirmations!

The Birth Order Exercise

A wonderful technique for promoting understanding of family issues and discovering the humanness of your parents and family members is to guide yourself through the following exercise.

Imagine your parents, as they were when they met. Imagine the conditions they were living under when they married. Go on and imagine what it would have been like if you had been born in the order you wish you had been born in. With each birth, imagine the circumstances and stresses on the family. Then imagine the way it actually happened. What were your parent's emotional states? What would the state of each of the other family members be? The purpose of the exercise is not to release others from responsibility for their actions but to gain a better understanding of where you came and the environment in which you were raised.

Cultural and Religious Healing Practices

With the exception of the Native Indians, North Americans are one of the few cultures who lack healing ceremonies. Native Indians practice and partici-pate in various healing rituals such as sweat lodges, and talking circles. As a participant of a healing circle, I was invited to partake in a sweat lodge, which is a very spiritual and sacred ritual, led by an elder. While I remained skeptical about the possibility of experiencing a vision as others had described, I was open to receiving guidance in this sacred ceremony. Participating in a sweating ceremony involves going into a covered dome that represents the mother's womb. In the ceremony, rocks heated in a ritual by itself, by a fire maintained by a designated fire keeper, are brought into the sacred space. Fully describing the depth and sacredness of this ceremony is beyond my ability, yet I can describe the beautiful message I received from images that appeared to me during this ceremony! At one point, the image of a wolf placing its head in the palm of my hand and looking up to me vividly entered my mind. What struck me was the look of the wolf's submissive eyes. A moment later, the same wolf appeared, staring deeply and lovingly at me at eye level, conveying a sense of equality between myself and others. Improving my self-esteem by beginning to live among others as an equal was a key lesson I needed to learn and begin practicing! I was very thankful, grateful and humbled by this experience!

Other cultures have various beliefs and practices that promote healing. Various religions have services that are related to healing. Learn more about what your culture or religion may have to offer you. Again, your healing is a personal adventure therefore what you choose may be different from another. Discover what works for you, while respecting the traditions of others.

21. Finding Your Community

The Roots of Loneliness

It has been said time and time again that you are born alone and you die alone. Although at times you may feel alone, there is a difference between being alone and being lonely. Although you may live in a city with thousands of people, loneliness is a very common problem. I once spoke with the director of a crisis line who advised me that over 60 percent of calls to their lines were due to social isolation and loneliness.

It is clear that periods of loneliness can be painful. Yet solitude can be a valuable time to reflect, examine our needs and goals, or simply to re-connect with your self on a deeper level. Like most things in life, too much of something is not good for your spirit. The same holds true for loneliness.

My dear friend Estelle wrote the following in a poem about traveling "You will find the feeling of being along is quite beautiful, but at first you must feel the sadness of loneliness. Nobody wants to feel this sadness, so they never know how beautiful feeling alone can be. Just like the taste of coffee, aloneness tastes bitter at first but as you get used to it, it becomes less and less bitter. Eventually you grow to like it."

While traveling in Ireland to research my family tree, I came across an interesting story of a pilgrim who, hundreds of years ago, placed himself voluntarily in a position of wandering the countryside. The early Irish legal and social system was based on ties between families, their chiefs and their lands. The worst crimes were punishable by exile. A landless person without kin was regarded as an outcast. Perhaps the people of the time, and the pilgrim, were keenly aware of how deeply isolation and loneliness could trouble one's spirit, thus the punishment was deemed a fitting one for serious crimes.

The issue of loneliness is rampant throughout our society. Loneliness can be the root of many personal problems. I think there is also a fundamental difference between choosing to be alone to recharge yourself and forced aloneness due to life circumstances. When choosing to be alone, you are exercising free will. When circumstances in life bring about loneliness even though you try to connect with others, you may end up feeling helpless and unable to control this aspect of your life, leading to a sense of alienation and pain.

Retired psychologist Boris Blai Jr. states, "investigations... show a connection between loneliness and depression, substance abuse, suicide and other forms of psychopathology." Blai also describes two types of loneliness: a feeling of aching due to the absence of an attachment figure; the other a sense of being excluded or not being accepted in some form of community. Blai states, "There is also some evidence that either form of loneliness is more apt to be present when the lonely individual suffers from feelings of low self-assurance." Research has indicated that it is your attitudes and sense of self-esteem that have a greater impact on your sense of belonging rather than the number of clubs you join. Often it is not the state of loneliness that is painful, but the old and new feelings that arise and the thoughts you have about yourself and your experience of loneliness.

While loneliness can seem difficult it is also a time to reflect and renew. In his book on loneliness, Clark E. Moustakas writes "man's inevitable and infinite loneliness is not solely an awful condition of human existence but that it is also the instrument through which man experiences new compassion and new beauty." In the realms of creativity, there is almost a necessity of loneliness and reawakening of the self in loneliness, as described by Christy Brown. Christy was born with cerebral palsy and learned to paint and write with his left foot. In spite of having a successful career as an artist and author, he wrote:

> "It would not be true to say that I am no longer lonely. I have made myself articulate and understood to people in many parts of the world and this is something we all wish to do, whether we are crippled or not. Yet like everyone else I am conscious sometimes of my own isolation even in the midst of people and I often give up of ever being able to really communicate with them. It is not only the sort of isolation that every writer or artist must experience in the creative mood if he is to create anything at all. It is like a black cloud sweeping down on me unexpectedly, cutting me off from others... a sort of death. I lay back in my chair while my own left foot beats time to a new rhythm. I could enjoy myself completely. I was at peace, happy!"

Brown's words reflect what Moustakas also eloquently writes:
> "Loneliness involves a unique substance of self, a dimension of human life which taps the full resources of the individual. It calls for strength, endurance, and sustenance, enabling a person to reach previously unknown depths and to realize a certain nakedness of inner life. Being lonely is a reality of far-reaching social consequence, yet it is distinctly a private matter."

219

For myself, loneliness has been a major issue for me to deal with. At times I was so busy and numb that I was unaware of my loneliness. Due to my upbringing, social conditioning and unresolved grief I was always feeling a sense of emptiness and disconnection. Although I had become involved in a number of volunteer organizations and made a number of friends, I was still experiencing a strong sense of loneliness and aching regarding the loss of a parental figure, as Blai described. I have since learned that my attitudes and beliefs play a greater role in dealing with loneliness than I had previously thought possible. I have discovered that a strong and healthy relationship with myself is critical. I had to examine whether I could be comfortable with myself when alone, and whether I could become my own parent. I also had to review the nature of people and learn to accept the nature of society and then adjust my attitudes appropriately.

Whether you have living parents or not you may have experienced a separation from your family of origin. In the case of abusive parents, part of the solution to your problems has been to strike out on your own and to forge healthier relationships. In some cases, it is healthier to be away from your family of origin than to participate in the dysfunction and denial of issues. Perhaps at times your need to remove yourself from the family situation will only be temporary. In either case, a question remains regarding how you can obtain support and friendship and find a community in which you can also give.

Although some of us have been able to find a sense of familiarity with friends or perhaps a mentor, it can be difficult to maintain long-term support. Friendships can be very fluid. Just as I change and grow, so do friends. I have learned to recognize that friends may move, change interests, pursue other friendships, or may be unavailable perhaps due to the demands of their work or study.

There is also the need to recognize that any one friend cannot meet all of my needs and that at any one time I may need a number of different friendships. In addition, some friends may be an acquaintance; others may be closer, while others may be friends that I can share my deepest thoughts and feelings with. One may be a partner or lover. I have often heard that most people have only two or three close friends and that these friendships take time to develop. This may prove advantageous, since a smaller number of close friends are more likely to provide a greater sense of belonging than a larger number of acquaintances.

Developing friendships also involves developing the ability to choose your friends appropriately. Not being selective in your choice of friends can often result in disappointment. Too often, perhaps due to previous patterns of loneliness, you end up being friends with whoever will reciprocate friendliness. Once you realize that there really are an abundant number of possible friendships out there for us, you can learn to be choosier. I have also learned that diversification in friends can be beneficial, where previously I may have put all my eggs in one basket. The same holds true for the places that you meet your friends. It can be helpful to develop a number of interests and goals that bring you into contact with a variety of people. If you choose to give up a particular activity, you do not end up losing your base of friendships.

With regard to creating friendships, I have learned that being open is a first step. I've also learned that it takes time to develop a sense of trust and openness. At one time I was like a closed book with very little self-disclosure. Then came a period when I was open with whoever would listen. I have since learned that sharing intense feelings can scare some people away. I then began to develop the skill of testing the waters with friendships. I have learned that there is a difference between being open and seeking help for my problems. When starting friendships, a certain amount of openness will draw others to me. However, seizing new friendships as an opportunity for unloading problems can scare people away. At some times, it is necessary to put on a mask with others.

While you need support, it is important to look in the appropriate places. Although you are often asked how you are doing, answering honestly can frighten others away. The outpouring of your problems can result in receiving less support than if you had been able to simply spend time with someone without actually discussing your problems. During my second year of my masters program, I experienced a number of financial setbacks and the loss of a wonderful pet. During this time a fellow student and I would go for coffee. The sense of encouragement and support I felt from this person occurred without directly bringing up the losses. I believe this situation is an example of a popular 12-step group saying. Alcoholics Anonymous members and Al-anon members often hear the phrase "fake it till you make it." Striving to be healthy and happy will attract people to you. I now believe that sometimes it is appropriate to withhold issues from others, or to simply disclose the issue as working through a transition, health or family issue. Just as if you are over-watering a plant, a substantial outpouring can drown the seed of friendship. How then, can you be truthful to others and yourself when you are asked how you are doing? Perhaps another 12-step saying is appropriate. If someone asks you how you are doing, you can answer "fine", while remembering that "fine" stands for "Freaked out, Insecure, Neurotic and Emotional!" Another good reply is "As well as can be expected." This leaves an open door. If the enquirer is actually interested they may ask further upon which you can go deeper. A sense of humor can help as well. When asked how things were going, I sometimes replied "I've had better past lives!" This gave the message that I was dealing with challenges, but also open to humor and inquiry.

It is important to remember that, as a human being, you often have limits as to the degree of support you can give. If you are constantly in need of support and constantly focusing on your problems, then others may shy away from you since their own limits are being reached. You may also be triggering their issues. Friendships are complex. Rarely do two people say "I have a problem, can we be friends?" but over the sharing of interests and values, you come to know and trust one another. You learn to give and receive from your friends in a manner that is appropriate for the level of friendship. It is important to have clarity in your goal of seeking friendship. We've all heard the saying that misery loves company, but this will not help you in your goal to heal. Finding people who validate your feeling miserable will likely slow your growth. You need to find positive, healing people who will teach you and learn from you as well. Part of attracting people involves marketing yourself and putting your best foot forward, and recognizing your gifts. You can be in pain, but still be positive about outcomes. Sometimes just having a goal of being happy will bring positive results, again if you have reasonable or perhaps no expectations of others. You do need friends, but no friend can ever meet all of your needs. It is important to recognize the limitations of others without being judgmental. Friends usually will try to support you in the best way they are capable.

In my counseling courses I was taught the value of a support network. A counselor I was seeing aptly pointed out that having a support network does not mean being propped up. A support network should involve mutual encouragement of each other. To do this you need to be able to stand on your own. In the transition from teenager to adult you need to learn the concept of self-reliance, of being able to take care of yourself. When you have a sense of this you can truly give unselfishly and can be your own best friend. Granted, at times you experience life events or lonely times that leave you vulnerable. At these times you need to choose your friends and support with care. Some people will run from you, more because of their own fears and issues, but you will also find those who will have a healthy sense of boundaries and distance and will be able to encourage you without becoming enmeshed in your difficulties. Ultimately you must pull yourself out of a social, emotional or mental rut.

Whenever I have traveled I have easily made friends, yet in my own city I have found some lonely times. It is clear to me now that the reason for this simply is that while traveling, I was mixing with others who shared my love of traveling. Back at home, once I stopped "searching for friends" and concentrated on developing my interests, friendships flow freely! There are millions of people on the planet to meet, the challenge you face is to discover what talents and interests you have that will bring you in contact with them. Yet at times in your life you will again be lonely. It takes courage to accept this, to learn to move through these times of loneliness, realizing that in life there is ebb and flow. The flow will come again!

Unconscious Bargains

The creation of this topic came about after a challenging time when a number of friendships ended in disintegration. It was a very painful time, as I learned how I had essentially built some of these friendships out of neediness rather than on the basis of whom these people were and why I had chosen them as friends. I have learned that neediness can cause the loss of our discriminating guide in who we choose as friends.

Neediness involves trying to get others to tell you that you are good and valuable, rather than telling yourself and believing in your goodness. Neediness involves trying to get others to fill your cup and trying to get energy from others rather than understanding that you have an unlimited capacity of love for yourself that you can tap into. All it takes is thought! When you are needy, however, you end up taking your friends as hostages to combat your feelings of inadequacy, loneliness or need for validation.

Because of my need for someone to tell me that I was OK, essentially I was making an unconscious bargain with these people that I would do something for him or her, and in return, they would be my friends. It is no wonder then, with the lesson I needed to learn, that these friendships vanished. In examining my remaining friendships, I realized that these were based on an equality of needs as well as a greater willingness to support each other. This process of discovery led me to face a problem that had been following me around for a number of years. As my friend Bruce put it, "this is your beast or shadow that you need to tame or learn to live with."

As a result, I was trying to find a sense of family in friendships, acquaintances and people I met. It was the searching in others for this sense of belonging and love that reflected an un-resolvable neediness. This was my beast or shadow. I also learned that I was ashamed of my current loneliness as well as being ashamed of the loneliness I experienced as a child and teenager. These dynamics created a heavy burden and an ongoing sense of sadness, loss and depression.

After the loss of three friendships, and recognizing that it was necessary to resolve this problem, I sought to identify ways of nurturing myself and to become my own best friend. I realized that I needed to develop my own self-parenting and nurturing skills and to accept that I was in fact alone and at times, always will be. Ironically, doing so has created the sense of wholeness that had eluded me for so long!

While I do not expect to always be alone, I am learning that I can be comfortable with myself and self-loving. I am learning to lean on myself more, rather than to seek my sense of worth and validation from others. In doing so, I feel more complete and stronger, and better equipped to enter a relationship or friendship. Instead of developing friendships in the hope of cementing over or filling in the emptiness, I am recognizing the needs I have and the things I have to offer and how I may be able to contribute equally in a friendship. Sometimes the best way to develop a friendship is to be a friend to someone rather than looking for a friend. Another predictor of successfully combating loneliness is to be hopeful and optimistic about your life and chances of developing new friendships.

The difficulty though, is that as humans we have a basic need for companionship and involvement. We need to be plugged in to some form of community or association. When I have been lacking this, I have found that by summoning up the energy to give, rather than trying to receive, reduces these feelings of neediness.

Life is full of ebb and flow. There are times when you will have fewer friends than you would like, and times when you will have too many social responsibilities. It is also important to note the role that synchronicity and timing play in meeting new friends. Sometimes you are just at the right time and in the right frame of mind. Having learned a number of valuable lessons, I took some time off to relax and integrate the things I had been learning. I went to a small island for a retreat. While there I happened to meet a friend I hadn't seen in a while and also met up with another traveler. Many people have echoed the thought that you often meet special people at the time you are ready. After this challenging time, my Graduate Advisor jokingly said, "finally, fate is working for you." Looking back, I believe it always was.

Healing Neediness

I have often found that it is most easy to attract friends into my life when I am in a positive frame of mind. With the exception of people I have met in support groups, this support is hardest to find when I am down and in need of nurturing. It has been interesting to note the habits of other people in times of trouble. I have observed that quite often people will withdraw and retreat rather than lean on others for support. This is an important concept to keep in mind when looking for support from others who are going through difficult times. Although the support of others can be beneficial, there are times when you need to retreat for a period of self-discovery. This self-discovery period may be a time of re-discovering your goals, reconnecting or examining your purpose. Having experienced this period of loneliness, you often emerge stronger and more aware of your desires and capabilities. You often develop a stronger sense of self and personal strength. Often the reality of loneliness is less painful than the fear of being alone.

The paradox of loneliness lies in the notion that the more accepting you are of your aloneness, the more likely you will be able to attract people into your life. It seems that neediness is not a valued commodity in relationships. People have an uncanny ability to sense neediness in others. While it is important to be able to express your needs to others, this should not be confused with neediness. Neediness is an inability to nurture yourself, to be incomplete on your own, a strong requirement to have someone else fill emptiness inside yourself or an attempt at avoiding responsibility for parenting yourself. As my friend Daniel told me, "There is a subtle difference between wanting to be helped and wanting to help yourself." People tend to want to help those who are in the process of working on solutions to their problems. In developmental terms, you may not have matured to the point where you have developed our own autonomy and self-direction. Like the child who says, "Hey, look at what I did", you may lack the ability to give yourself the acknowledgment you need.

I have found that when I am feeling needy, I can now heal this feeling quickly by first of all acknowledging that my desire to connect with people is a healthy one, and then practicing some self-talk that helps to build my character and self-esteem. By reading my "rainy day list" of things that I like about myself, telling myself that I am capable of looking after myself, journaling and by giving myself some empathy I can build on my sense of self fulfillment. Think of my accomplishments and times when I did well looking after myself, I can build a feeling of self love that comes from being an observer of my own accomplishments, realizing that I can give myself, what I have been desiring from others!

Even if you did not receive much love and nurturing as a child, you can learn to "re-parent" yourself as an adult. Part of growing up involves separation from your parents. You can learn to nurture yourself and give yourself what you need. You can even visualize times when you did not receive the encouragement you needed and imagine a part of yourself giving yourself the encouragement you needed.

"It takes creative courage to accept the inevitable, existential loneliness of life, to face one's essential loneliness openly and honestly. It requires inner fortitude not to be afraid or overwhelmed with the fear of being and the fear of being alone." - Clark E. Moustakas

The Developed Self

I think we have all heard some variation of the phrase "you have to solve your own problems before you get into a relationship." Although it is impossible to solve all of your problems before getting into a relationship, it is important to have a healthy sense of your values and the gifts you have to offer others. This is the essence of self-esteem. I believe it is also healthy to have developed a sense of one's interests and talents, which will then assist in the creation of suitable friendships outside of the relationship. I have often heard from people that when a relationship ends, they find themselves very alone, having given up many of their friends and interests. In love, sometime people devote themselves entirely to the other person and abandon their friendships.

Perhaps the following can illustrate a healthier attitude towards the maintenance of the individuals in relationships. At some weddings a ritual is followed involving the lighting of a larger candle from two candles, and the extinguishing of both of the smaller candles. The romantic thought is that the two people are now joined as one and that the individual lights are merged. There are still two people who have different interests, needs, goals, and communication skills. I have recently witnessed ceremonies in which the new couple leaves the two individual candles burning with the larger candle representing the light of the relationship between them. Whether married or simply dating, the lesson that often needs to be learned is that it is unhealthy to totally lose your sense of self in a relationship. Too often, one of the partners begins to grow, touching off a reaction of issues and changes.

With regard to having to solve your problems before getting into a relationship, I believe a more appropriate statement is that your chance of a successful relationship will increase if you recognize that you have emptiness and can learn to fill that hole before getting into the relationship. Human beings are social. We need community, connectedness and support. These three aspects of your social life are experienced differently when you seek them to fill emptiness rather than to love and give to others. Resolving past issues and losses also helps. When you walk into a relationship or friendship with a cleaner slate built upon a more solid foundation of self, relationships work out better and are healthier.

In examining my own situation, I made an important discovery regarding my expression of emotion that has impacted the nuance of my friendships and relationships. It is important to recognize that you may be doing your own healing work while you are meeting new friends and becoming involved in organizations. I came to realize that much of my emotional energy was being directed at these people with the expectation that they would help me deal with it, resolve it or simply acknowledge it. In this essence I needed to have my emotions validated by others and was therefore once again needy. Since a substantial part of communication is non-verbal, I have learned that it is important to learn to own the emotional energy and be able to appropriately direct it through other forms of release. This is a subtle concept. When we are aware of our own emotional energy we can learn how to direct it and release it appropriately. This can allow others to feel less burdened in their endeavor to support your healing work.

Replacing Lost Family

Since family is considered to be an important aspect of being human, how do you replace the nurturing and comfort that you can give and receive in families? In the following paragraphs I discuss a number of concepts regarding this issue. Although these suggestions have helped me, I believe there is no single or perfect answer to the problem. Take what you feel will help from this section!

Although loneliness can often bring about a sense of failure, it is important to recognize the nature of society. First of all, it can be difficult to find support, particularly when you are needy. People often don't know how to respond empathetically when you express your feelings. Quite often I've been told by well meaning people that I shouldn't feel so bad because others don't have family, or that others don't see their family. Although these people's intentions are good, I have learned to recognize that these statements, as true as they are, do nothing to recognize my own sense of loss. On the other hand, the message that "without family, life is empty" reverberates in church halls, on TV shows and is communicated to us time and time again during holiday seasons. How then does one cope with not having a real sense of family?

To obtain answers to this question, I asked those who had lost the connection with their families in some way or another. In particular, I sought answers from those who had successfully managed to deal with their situation. A posting to the support groups on the Internet brought numerous responses and suggestions that I will share with you.

First, the consistent suggestion in a number of messages I received was to learn to be your own best friend. This means learning to nurture and accept yourself and to develop your ability to be alone as well as to be able to reach out to others. It is easier to attract new friends when you have a sense of competence and confidence. Secondly, friends and support groups were considered to be the next source of support and a place to give. You also need connection among your friends. Having friends that know each other exponentially increases your sense of connectivity and allows you to experience a sense of community with your friends.

With regard to friendships, there were some special ideas that facilitated a sense of support. Some suggested that developing two or three close friendships was much better than having a number of acquaintances. Secondly, doing volunteer work that focused on relationships was very rewarding. Some suggested becoming a school volunteer, a scout leader or a big brother or sister as ways of developing meaningful relationships in which you are giving support to others. Church was also suggested as a means of becoming involved in a community. The key to volunteer success is to join an organization that focuses on relationships or teamwork to accomplish the organizational goals.

One technique to combat loneliness and lack of family can be the development of friendship rituals. Much of what families do together consists of rituals such as sharing a meal or watching a movie. Even family day trips involve a series of rituals of preparation. One of the comforts I had in the previous city I lived in involved going out for springs rolls and hot and sour soup with my friend Cathy. We would do this on a fairly regular basis and talk about the things that were going on in our lives. Since moving, I have developed other rituals such as going for a coffee and chat with my friend Ross, or when in Beijing, going for ice-cream with my friend Phil. I have had to recognize the loss of my ritual with Cathy, but found new rituals to replace the old ones. Rituals seem to provide a structure for the sharing of personal stories, laughter and companionship.

As I found in posing my question, another form of ritual can involve regular reading and posting to the Internet support groups, giving a sense of being part of an on-line community. I made contact with numerous people scattered across North America in my endeavor to obtain a solution to the problem. One user even posted a message adopting me as a group member! I experienced a substantial amount of warmth and encouragement from these people. Similarly, attending a support group can bring relief to loneliness through the sharing of strengths, problems and experience. Groups are often accepting of newcomers. It is also possible to connect with similar groups when traveling or when moving to a new city. Involvement in a 12-step group can often mean that you never have to be alone with your problems, since groups exist in almost every town or city in the world.

It is important to recognize that pursuing a goal of bettering yourself can be more rewarding than solely pursuing a goal of finding a place in which you can belong. The search for belonging often leads you on a path of disappointment when you are let down by the human nature of people's shortcomings. Trying to find a place to belong can often heighten your sense of loneliness and isolation. Achieving a sense of self-worth and developing the ability to be happy and satisfied in meager times can be a powerful ally against loneliness and depression.

My friend Monika Hennecke shares these wise thoughts about family. Sometimes we need to reach for a more divine and soul level understanding.

"During the last years I have learned a lot about family-relations - and the most important thing I have learned is that there is, in the depths, always a very close link of love between all the family members. Often you would never think there is, but if you get a deeper insight, you happen to see that really strange behaviors can be motivated by love. Often, the love is buried under what happened in the past, but it always exists even if it has to be found beneath millions of layers of dust. I suggest that you just find your place in life where you are happy, knowing that your family indeed is close, even if it does not manifest in the physical world."

The Role of Grieving

As mentioned earlier, grief can be a very isolating emotion. During a period of grief, others may not know what to say to you. You may be lost in a spectrum of emotions. While others may mean well by telling you they know how you feel, you often feel isolated by such comments. Grief that goes unresolved can have a long-term impact on your ability to attract and build friendships. When I began my own grief work, I found that people became more open with me as I became more open with them. As I worked through the emotions I had long repressed, others began to feel more comfortable and relaxed around me. Some confided that I had been giving the impression that I wanted to be left alone - the exact opposite of what I really wanted. Unresolved grief can mask itself as depression, particularly if it has been carried for a long time. Obviously then, resolving grief can lead to greater openness and connectedness with others. It has often been said that time is a great healer, but it is not true if you avoid the grieving process.

In particular, the grieving process may also mean coming to terms with the abuse and harm you may have suffered from deceased family members. For the longest time I had the greatest contempt for the shortcomings of my father and the hurtful things that my mother had done. Although my parents had been dead for 10 years, I still carried them with me in my thoughts and these thoughts still impacted how I feel about myself. My unresolved grief towards my parents was still impacting my daily enjoyment of life and was contributing to my sense of loneliness.

It was while doing some work as a web page designer that I came across some research on child bereavement that was very helpful in dealing with my loneliness. A study had shown that children who had lost a parent fared better if they were able to maintain a positive emotional attachment to the deceased parent, while at the same time accepting the loss of the parent. Although this may seem contradictory that you need to hold on to a part of them yet still let go it has actually made a great deal of sense to me. Since coming across the research, I have learned to reconcile my own beliefs and ideas about my parents.

Previously, I had focused mostly on the negative characteristics of my parents. As I realized that my view was tainted by my anger, I came to see them as humans with shortcomings who did in fact love me, although they had great difficulty showing it. In a sense, I realized that I had to do some forgiving, and to realize that I was angry because they had, in a very real sense, left me. Instead of maintaining a negative internalized image of my parents, I have begun to focus on the ways that they did try to show they loved me. I remember being told by a friend of my father that he often told her how much he loved his five sons. My mother's last message to us before she died was to "tell the boys that I love them, and that God always comes through." There were times as well when my parents did show that they cared.

While attending a support meeting, I was deeply moved by the words of the son of a long time member who had recently passed away. The man's son believed that, although his father definitely had problems, in dying, his father experienced healing. I am now secure in knowing that my own parents are now free of their pain and issues. They are now free to love me in a manner that was difficult for them when they were alive. Due to my healing process, I am also freer to love them. My ideas, beliefs, and feelings about them have changed.

By recognizing the times that my parents did show love and were nurturing, I have been able to develop a more positive image of my parents. This new image of my parents seems to provide a greater sense of warmth thus lessening my sense of loneliness. As the research suggested, developing and maintaining a positive internal emotional attachment has helped. As in transactional analysis, perhaps those of you who do not have close contact with nurturing parents or siblings can develop your own internal images of nurturing parents.

The Art of Discernment

Almost everyone I know states that it is has been a struggle to choose friends wisely. I look around and notice the things we can build – computers, cell phones, the Internet, the space station. Yet can we build the most fundamental essence of being, a relationship with one another? Do we find it safer to provide unconditional love to those who do not trigger our own issues? Marianne Williamson says that "peace is not an absence of war, but a feeling of love between ourselves and others." Creating a sense of peace through love, personal warmth and connecting is a noble cause yet possibly the greatest challenge you face as an individual. So many times I've heard, "I've let go of those friends" or "I've moved on to healthier friends" yet I'm discovering that the greater challenge is to learn to accept others rather than simply moving on. I've also learned that friendship is not a singular idea or concept. Like dozens of eggs that will hatch into a flock, the practice of acceptance, compassion, self love and being able to listen are the skills that shape my behavior, thoughts and feelings. Boundaries, emotions, needs, self expression, forgiveness, beliefs, values, acceptance and prosperity are all eggs that need to be nurtured, hatched, and allowed to grow to form your way of being. I've learned to put these concepts into practice, but with some divine intervention. It all started when I was traveling in Australia. As I was surfing at an Internet café, a little boy appeared out of nowhere. He handed me a flyer and ran out the door, disappearing seemingly into thin air. It was a flyer for a psychic reader across the street. I finished my surfing and went for a reading. During which I was given some valuable advice. I was told that on my return I would have to look at my judgment of others and to entertain the possibility that in being betrayed, I had also become a betrayer. The words produced a deep resonance, having heard the same thing in a workshop a few months earlier.

My healing process has helped me to increase my ability to love unconditionally the people who trigger me the most, and to understand that I may have incorrectly assumed that others are conscious of what they are doing. I often would quote the words attributed to Jesus "Forgive them father, for they know not what they do" yet have now learned that these words must be said without a tone of judgment. I've learned to be more compassionate and understanding of other people's points of view and to listen instead of arguing my point. One of the greatest challenges to us all is to see the good in others and to truly connect with others without the expectation of changing the other person.

I have also learned to take it to a new level. While I see the good in people, it does not mean that I have to hang out with certain people. I have learned to be more communicative in my relationships, and with some people it comes back at me as criticism and denial, but with others it enriches the relationship. I used to think that if the other person responded harshly, then there was something wrong with me. I also lived in fear of alienating and angering others. I now know that if I have a set of expectations as to how I am to be treated, and

Mark Linden O'Meara

those expectations are consistently not met, I move on a lot more quickly than previously. I've also learned that it is much easier to set boundaries clearly earlier in the relationship than later! I don't have to make him or her out to be bad people or to be angry with them. I can forgive them and resolve any resentment so that when I come in contact with them, I do not feel emotionally triggered or charged! There are billions of people on this planet. You can't spend time with all of them. Whom will you choose to spend time with?

Pranic Healing

As you grow stronger in your ability to look after yourself, you may realize that although you are a social being, you can learn to nurture yourself and rely less and less on the strength of others and develop your own sense of stability and independence. A major revelation and change in my own energy came very late in my process of self discovery when reading a book on Yogi philosophies by. Yogi Ramacharaka. This self discovery helped me uncover my pattern and belief of expecting to be nourished by others. I learned from the readings in these texts that my energy should come from my food, air, and own personal nourishment and not be sourced from other people. This has always been a challenge for me to accept, but as I started to practice the exercise below, I found my own personal energy increasing and began feeling less of a reliance on others. When this realization came about, and as I began to practice this breath and energy work, I found others to be more relaxed around me and even received comments about the increase in my energy and how I seemed to have more to give, rather than my previous pattern of taking. The exercise is quite simple and you will get better at it with practice! Here is the exact text from this hundred year old book!

The Grand Yogi Energy Breath

The Yogis have a favourite form of psychic breathing which they practice to which has been given a Sanscrit term of which the above is a general equivalent. We have given it last, as it requires practice on the part of the student in the line of rhythmic breathing and mental imagery, which he has now acquired by means of the preceding exercises. [see page 172] The general principles of the Grand Breath may be summed up in the old Hindu saying "Blessed is the Yogi who can breathe through his bones."

This exercise will fill the entire system with prana, and the student will emerge from it with every bone, muscle, nerve, cell, tissue, organ and part energized and attuned by the prana and the rhythm of the breath. It is a general housecleaning of the system, and he who practices it carefully will feel as if he had

232

been given a new body, freshly created, from the crown of his head to the tips of his toes. We will let the exercise speak for itself.

1. Lie in a relaxed position, at perfect ease.

2. Breathe rhythmically until the rhythm is perfectly established.

3. Then, inhaling and exhaling, form the mental image of the breath being drawn up through the bones of the legs, and then forced out through them; then through the bones of the arms; then through the top of the skull; then through the stomach; then through the reproductive region; then as if it were travelling upward and downward along the spinal column; and then as if the breath were being inhaled and exhaled through every pore of the skin, the whole body being filled with prana and life.

4. Then (breathing rhythmically) send the current of prana to the Seven Vital Centres.

a. To the forehead.

b. To the back of the head.

c. To the base of the brain.

d. To the Solar Plexus.

e. To the Sacral Region (lower part of the spine).

f. To the region of the navel.

g. To the reproductive region.

Finish by sweeping the current of prana, to and fro from head to feet several times.

5. Finish with a complete breath, retain for a few seconds, then exhale vigorously, puckering the lips. This last stage is called a cleansing breath.

This breathing and relaxation exercise should help restore and revitalize your energy level. Practice it and see what happens! Remember that as you find your deeper source of energy and fulfillment you will attract greater abundance into your life. You will also be able to give more to others. By nurturing yourself you free yourself from the bonds of neediness and learn to be more self-supporting. You are a social being and you do have basic needs of companionship, interaction and friendship. This is not to be confused with neediness. Take care of yourself, allow others into your life, but accept that true self-acceptance and energy comes from within. With this foundation, your relationships become bonuses to your gift of living. You are more able to accept the impermanence of life and its constantly changing nature.

"Friendship is born at that moment when one person says to another. 'What, You too? I thought I was the only one!'" - C.S. Lewis

"Choose not your friends from outward show. Feathers float, pearls lie low" - Author unknown

Part Five - Teachings

22. Healthy Living

Healthy Things to Do for Yourself

The following are principles that will help greatly in your emotional and mental healing. Make a list of these ideas and place the list somewhere to remind you of them on a regular basis. These are principles and tools that have allowed me to progress through the process of emotional healing. During times of emotional pain and healing it is important to give yourself a break every now and then. Find something that soothes you, be it a favorite work of music, a warm bath, a massage, or reading a good book. Some people I know have even curled up in bed with a teddy bear! The point is that you need times to relax and bring down your stress level. These are important tips to follow even when you are emotionally healthy!

With the stress of a graduate program and the fact that I had moved to a new city, I found myself stressed and needing a recharge. My head was so full of the things that I had to do that I felt overwhelmed. A friend asked "what do you do to soothe yourself?" I could not come up with any answers. I have since learned that my stress level gets lowered when I set aside some time for relaxation - even if it is only a few minutes. During this time, I do one or two things that I have discovered to be soothing behaviors. I sing, play my guitar or spend time with my cat. Of course, the behaviors that you find soothing are personal. The things you find soothing may reflect your own interests and hobbies. Develop a sense of what works for you!

Learn to Put Your Problems Away

Often you need a break from your problems. You may also need to calm yourself and stop worrying. Worrying is a loop of asking a question that does not yet have an answer. The way out of worry is not necessarily to find the answer but to rest and accept that the answer will reveal itself or come to you at the appropriate moment. A wonderful technique to bring this about is to imagine putting each of your problems, one by one, into a strong wooden chest. You then imagine locking the chest with a strong padlock and dropping the chest off a ship into the deepest ocean.

This technique serves as a ceremony for putting your troubles away and helps to reduce your amount of worry. It is healthy because you are not denying that your problems exist, you are simply giving yourself a break from needless worry.

Eat Well, Rest Well, Exercise Well

At any time in your life, it is a good practice to eat well, get some exercise and rest appropriately. This is also very true during the healing process. Select your groceries well and prepare nutritious meals for yourself. Schedule some rest time during the day, and try to exercise even if it's only moderately. It will help you immensely to maintain better health during and after this process.

Create a Safe Place

Most of us do not feel comfortable expressing our emotions in public and society has not yet come to accept open expression of emotions. Perhaps this will come one day, however for the moment you may wish to follow the norms of society. You may not wish to force yourself to express emotions in front of others, but you will at least wish to be able to feel and express your emotions in the privacy of your home so that you may heal and move on.

Sometimes you may begin to experience an emotion that you want to release. How do you do so with people around? Once I was at a campground and another gentleman and I began discussing getting in touch with feelings. He expressed that he wished he had a place to go and cry. The solution was quite simple. He went for a walk along the road and found a quiet place for himself. In many cases you too can find a safe place when you need to. It could simply be in your parked car, an office washroom, or a room with a closed door where no one will bother you.

Let Your Healing be Personal

Your path is unique and belongs to only you. There are many things each of us share but your circumstances are unique in some way. Your healing process is the same. What works for someone else may not be what you would choose. Some of you are artists while some are writers. Some may use massage while some may use other alternative methods. Learn to share with others and to listen, but develop your own set of tools for healing. You are unique and you can develop a sense of what works for you.

Trust Your Intuition

Sometimes you may have a feeling that you should call someone, be at a certain place, or make a particular choice for no logical reason other than a gut feeling. Usually, these intuitive feelings turn out to be correct if you can measure the outcome. Sometimes you cannot measure the outcome so you may not know what the consequences of your actions were. In your journey it is important to follow your intuition.

One Saturday evening I was watching a movie with a friend and I had a very strong intuitive feeling to go to a dance that a friend of mine operated. I had been experiencing this feeling all day long. I explained to my friend that I had to go somewhere. I went to the dance and met someone who, a week later, gave me a book that was crucial to my healing. If I had not followed my intuition, my healing would have taken a lot longer and I probably would not have received what I needed at the time I needed it. Learn to trust gut feelings.

Develop a Relaxation Response.

Think of a word that you can repeat to yourself or an image that you can call to mind easily. Next, associate it with a feeling of being centered, relaxed, compassionate, rested, and forward moving. Meditate on these feelings while picturing the word in your mind. Use a positive word such as love, or an image of a peaceful place in nature. Imagine all of your muscles being relaxed and breathe deeply.

When feeling stressed, repeat the word or visualize the image and call to mind the body sensation you felt when meditating. This is a common technique for dealing with chronic physical pain. It can be also used to trigger an automatic relaxation response and help you create a sense of relaxation.

Take Your Time

Some things take longer than others to get over. It is important to give yourself as much time as you need to get over a loss or an event that triggers emotion. It is not how long you go out with someone that determines the amount of time it takes to get over a loss but how much that person affected you and how much you cared for him or her. Some people have a great impact on us in a short period. Healing will take as long as it takes. A study by psychiatrist Glen Davidson suggests that the length of time to grieve varies greatly, from 18 to 24 months. It can even be longer for some losses and some situations, without being considered abnormal. A shorter time is possible too!

Seeing the Positive in Losses

Although often difficult to imagine, positive things can come from losses. Often you learn a lesson or are assisted in releasing and resolving deeper issues. A few years ago I had a cat named Shadow. I got Shadow as a kitten in my second year of university. She had always seemed to sense when I was having a difficult time emotionally and would sort of whimper and curl up beside me. I remember when my father died. Shadow came into my room and placed her paws on my knees as I sat on the edge of the bed crying, she strained up with a sad but comforting tone in her meow. One morning I got up to go to work and Shadow did not answer my calls. I found her lying on the living room floor, her lifeless body missing the energy that had made her so special. It was a great loss.

I kept wondering why this had to happen. I had just started into working through my issues and this just didn't seem fair. I had a few good cries, got angry, even denied my loss in my dreams, but then finally I accepted my loss. I then realized that for the first time in my life, I had gone through a grieving process and had actually healed from the loss - an extremely important lesson to learn.

A few years later I volunteered with a senior's resource center. I was matched up with a kind gentleman named Victor who had recently lost his wife. We conversed many times and while he had opinions of his own, he was also respectful of other people's opinions, including mine. A few months later my friend Victor passed away. He had greatly missed his wife. His obituary contained this quote from Sir Henry Woolton: "she first deceased; he for a little tried, to live without her, liked it not, and died." The description of Victor's own loss moved me and I was also deeply affected by his death. The loss triggered my own unresolved grief. I was aware that in grieving my loss of his companionship, I was also grieving my own losses - that of a high school friend, and of the deaths of my parents. Denying my grief would have locked in my pain. Again, events happened for a reason.

Work on the Problem not on the Symptoms

For a long time I tried as hard as I could to feel happy. I tried positive thinking, seminars, etc. I also worked on communication, my loneliness and isolation, negative attitudes, as well as numerous other problems that arose from being emotionally numb. The resolution to most of these problems came from working on the main problem that I was experiencing, namely the suppression of all my emotions from a very early age. Keep your focus on the main problem at hand. As you make progress in your emotional healing you will likely find that the symptoms will become less and less noticeable!

Remember that You are a Thriver, Not Just a Survivor

Often you need to remind yourself that you have the strength and courage to face your problems and pain. You are much bigger and greater than your problems, although at times you may feel overwhelmed. The pain may be great and at times frightening, but you can overcome it. Remember that, as with all feelings that are allowed to follow their course, they shall pass. You can and will heal if you have courage and if you trust the healing process. During dark times remind yourself of your progress. Encourage yourself to continue your healing process!

Go at an Appropriate Pace

The purpose of therapy is to hold a mirror up to yourself. Often a therapist or a friend will try to guide you in opening up your blind spots. It is important that you set boundaries and agreements as to how far you can be pushed to discover things about yourself.

Identifying too many issues at once can cause an ignition of emotions that may be overwhelming and hard on your health. Your issues can be like a pack of matches - you take one match at a time and light it. If you were to light all the matches at once, the package will erupt in flames in an uncontrolled and dangerous flash of intensity. Your own issues can be similar. You need to look at a few issues at a time and deal with them without being overwhelmed and overloaded. Go at an appropriate pace. Your mind and your environment will help you bring issues to the forefront, as you are ready.

Accept that Emotions are Not Logical

If you were truly a logical being, then you would not be spending time to watch movies, listen to music, letting emotion play such a large part in your life. Yet there is also a part of you that navigates through life using logic and reasoning. Logic tends to demand symmetry and balance. However, the fact is that emotions are not logical. You can be angry with someone, and love him or her at the same time. Your emotions deny logic. Accepting this allows you to feel the emotions without judging yourself as being crazy.

In times of release you may be surprised by how much emotion is available to be released. You may find your patterns of behavior and consciousness shifting as you let go of what you have held onto for so long. Accept that the process will take place and that you can survive without control and logic.

Nurturing Yourself

Create a 'Bad Hair Day' List

Often we have difficult days. Unexpected things happen, you simply wake up on the wrong side of the bed, or as the popular phrase goes, you have a "bad hair day!" On these days it is helpful to resort to a list you have created on one of your better days. At a time when you are making progress in your healing, write down your accomplishments, the things that you enjoy, and the things that cheer you up. Perhaps you can make a list of your accomplishments or the things you like about yourself. Put the list in a place where you know you can find it. When you experience one of those "bad hair days" take out the list and do one or more of the things that cheer you up, notice the things that you have made progress in, and give yourself credit for the work you have done! Remember that just because things don't feel good, it doesn't mean they aren't getting better!

Visualization and Scaling

Visualization can be an effective method of reducing stress and anxiety, especially when combined with a technique called scaling. Imagine on a scale of one to 10 how stressed you are. Then imagine what it would be like to feel half a point lower. Again imagine what it would feel like to feel another half point less stressed. Repeat this process until you have lowered the scale. See if you feel more relaxed. Chances are you will. This is an effective technique that can work for a number of problems and issues. If you are feeling disconnected and ungrounded, the technique can be used in reverse to gain a sense of serenity. Simply reverse the process and imagine what it would feel like to be half a point higher on the scale. Again repeat the process, raising your level by half or full points.

Learn to Ask for What You Want

One of the most important life skills you can develop is the ability to ask for what you need or want. In our earlier years you may have been told that you were selfish, or your requests may have been ignored. As a result, you may have given up on asking. As a healthy adult you can rekindle your ability to ask and accept that others have the right to say no. I have learned that the best way to ask for something is to practice the art of ART. ART stands for Acknowledging, Requesting and Thanking. In a workshop I attended, we practiced the three-step process. We started by acknowledging and thanking the other person for what they had done in the past and how we appreciate them. Secondly, we made a request for something reasonable. We then thanked the other person for either granting or refusing our request, thus keeping healthy boundaries. At first it seemed awkward, as I was not used to acknowledging and requesting. Practice this three-step process and see what you receive and how others will value your acknowledgement and thanking.

Soothing Behaviors

Just as many of us have different interests, the things you do to relax vary as well. Since I did not want to list only my soothing behaviors, I posted a message on the Internet asking people what soothing things they did. Here are some of the suggestions:

- gardening: transplanting, feeding, watering and nurturing
- playing a musical instrument
- playing with a pet (pets are non-judgmental)
- singing
- listening to music
- talking to a (real) best friend
- drawing
- a warm bath, with the bathroom lit by candles
- watching a favorite TV show or movie with a friend or pet
- lie on a blanket in the backyard or park with a book
- go to the library, bookstore, arboretum, museum or art gallery
- cook or bake
- read a good book
- journaling
- drink a cup of tea, hot chocolate or steamed milk
- exercise (even just walking is fine)
- volunteer at a place that provides a sense of community
- make a list of things you like about yourself
- get away to nature
- cuddle up with a teddy bear
- have some chocolate (this was a common response!)
- take a yoga class
- laugh!

Often you need a break from your emotional work. You do not need to spend all of your time working out your pain or dealing with your issues. You need to find healthy distractions that will allow you to recharge. Meditation, theatre, a hobby, or socializing can be as much a part of your healing and renewal process. Read a book, rent a movie, talk to a friend, or listen to some music. You may need to learn to put aside your problems for a day or to have a vacation from them. It is OK to turn away from your pain until you are ready to deal with it. Most importantly, have a sense of humor!

Helpful Healthy Attitudes

Notice the Little Things

Very few of us frequently have events in our lives that rate extremely high on an emotional scale. A marriage, birth, winning a lottery, or a contest are wonderful events but they do not occur with great frequency (at least not for the author!). Troublesome events such as losses, illnesses, etc., are usually considered to be traumatic in nature. How do you achieve some balance? You can achieve balance by looking for and noticing the smaller nice things that happen to you. Sometimes this takes practice and you may need to get into the habit of doing this. At the end of each day, make a mental note of three nice things that happened to you during the day, however trivial they may seem. I guarantee this habit will start to lift you up!

Give up Control

You may erroneously believe that you are in control of your emotions. When you have stuffed or suppressed your emotions, it is really your emotions that are in control of you! You may be afraid however, that if you begin to let go, you may lose control. Since you have become so good at turning off your emotions you are usually able to do so again if the need arises. As you begin to experience your emotional self again, you still have the ability to numb out if feelings get too strong for you to deal with.

Let Go of the Fear

In the beginning of this process you may fear that if you begin to let go and release your emotions, you will not be able to stop. Remember that for a long time you have been able to hold your emotions at bay. You can still use that skill if need be. Try getting in touch with a small bit of sadness and see if you can immediately shut if off again. It is likely that you are able to do this. Most of us do have control of our emotions. You have the ability to turn them off at will. Turning them on has been your problem.

Do Things in Moderation

It is important to do things in moderation. If you have been keeping yourself extremely busy, then slow down gradually. If you are driving a car at sixty miles an hour and all of a sudden slam on the brakes, it creates havoc for the traffic behind us. The same is true if you need to slow yourself down. Coming to an abrupt halt may be overwhelming. Start limiting your activities or begin turning down new requests. Use the free time to try to relax. The paradox of the busy person is that he or she is hurting and needs to slow down but slowing down can result in beginning to hurt more. Moderation is the answer.

It may also be a time when you will want to put off major decisions until your emotional state has stabilized. You may have a great deal of energy available when releasing unresolved emotions. However, given that you are in a process of healing, major decisions may only add stress. A move or change of employment may create unnecessary upheaval when you need to find some anchors in your life at this time. A technique to improve your sense of grounding is to sit in a chair with your feet on the floor, breathe deeply, and focus on the sensation of your feet firmly planted on the ground below you.

Be Patient

Many small steps add up to full recovery and even going past your original state. Accept that full healing takes time. It may take months or even years. It is not something you can accomplish with a quick fix or a weekend seminar, although in one week you can make great progress. Be patient and give yourself time. Notice the little steps you have made and how they have added up!

Listen to Warning Signs

While completing my master's degree, there were times that I was exhausted from my studies. I remember how the director of the computer resource center spent a few moments with me and recommended that I take a few days off and go somewhere for the weekend as I was obviously exhausted. Being immersed in my work, I became insensitive to how exhausted I really was. When I got on a ferry to go to a small island near my school, I bumped into an acquaintance who upon seeing me said, "My God Mark, you look exhausted." It was at that moment that I realized how wiped out I looked and felt. She then gave me some valuable advice – the word HALT, which stands for the action that must be taken when any of the individual letters become true. Those letters stand for Hungry, Angry, Lonely, and Tired. If HALT applies to you, stop what you are doing and take restorative action.

Accept How Things Turn Out

Sometimes things turn out differently from what you had hoped for. Often you get what you need rather than what you ask for, yet you may lack the wisdom to see this at the time. Accepting what you get can be a very important healing tool, especially if you believe that there is a master plan for your healing that is being managed by a power that is greater than yourself.

Sometimes you do not get the job or relationship that you want. In the long run many people say that the pain they went through or the way things worked out was exactly what they needed in their lives at a certain time to overcome a hurdle or to learn something special about themselves.

Go Fly a Kite

For the Chinese, kite flying is therapy. They've been doing it for over 2000 years. There are a couple of things that kite flying does. First of all you are out in the open enjoying nature. Secondly you are looking up, and you are focusing on an object far away, relaxing your eyesight. Your mind is focused on the kite and is not easily distracted. You are less likely to think of your problems. You are also using many of your muscles to stabilize the kite. Your arms and shoulders will get a subtle and gentle workout as well as your mind. Flying a kite requires concentration. If you are concentrated on the kite, then your mind won't likely be given a chance to be distracted by the thoughts of the troubles of the day. With your mind focused on flying the kite, you will have time for restoration and healing. If you don't live in a windy area where you could fly a kite, find some other hobby that will distract you from thinking of your challenges and give your mind a period of restorative activity. If someone tells you "go fly a kite" perhaps you should consider it!

Choose What to Share

One of the most difficult things for me to learn in my healing journey was to remain positive in difficult times. I would want to share my troubles, thinking that would ease them. While opening up with a counselor can be helpful, greater discretion is required in social situations. I have learned to give hints to people, and test the waters. I can simply state, "I am going through some changes that are challenging, but I am confident that they will all work out." I then listen for clues. Do they ask me about what is going on, or just provide words of encouragement. The idea is to allow others to respond with the choice to inquire or not. My statement acknowledges the difficulties, doesn't trigger other peoples fear and previous losses, and lets them know that you are looking at the long-term outcome!

Set Goals

Both children and adults need to feel a sense of purpose in our day-to-day living. You need a sense of achievement or a sense that you are moving toward some ideal. Setting goals helps you to attain a sense of purpose. For many people in the healing process, their goal is to resolve some of their issues. This in itself can be a very noble goal and a source of inspiration. In setting goals, it is important to ensure that the goals are realistic, measurable and attainable. If you do not have any goals, try choosing a few small goals and identify the steps you can take to achieve them. Let go of any expectations or results and enjoy what comes your way!

Don't Give Up Too Easily!

As I mentioned in the first chapter, when I was in Beijing, I heard about a great massage hospital. Not speaking any Chinese, I knew it was going to be a challenge to find it. I eventually did, but with quite a story. The first time I tried to go I got totally lost. The second time it was pouring rain. One gentleman studied my map so thoroughly that he poked a hole in it with his finger! Now I had to replace the map! The third time I knew I was closer, but with no street signs and wrong directions, I ended up not finding it again. I asked for directions from a couple who spoke some English, but at the exact same moment they both pointed in opposite directions! The next time I tried, I walked for 2 hours and was tired so I stopped at a barber shop and tried to ask for directions. The woman of about twenty-five was helpful. I said "Beijing an-mo hospital' – an-mo means massage. "An-mo? Yes!" she replied and took the map from my hands and pointed to a chair to sit. She looked at the map briefly and the next thing I know she started touching me rather provocatively and where she put her hand next told me this wasn't really a barber shop. It seems she thought I was asking her for a massage and perhaps more! So I grabbed my map and knapsack and went for the door. My friends warned me about the girls in bars but not in barber shops!

I did eventually find the hospital! I began traction and massage treatments with a great doctor, who had just returned from vacation. My eventual timing was perfect. I made miraculous improvements in my health. Many people would think that after three times it wasn't meant to be. But my persistence in my efforts paid off with a life changing impact on my health. It is difficult to know when to persist and when to change directions. That is part of life. What you and I often need to do is look at the belief systems we have. Why is three the magic number? Why not four or five? Try to decipher the hidden rules you live by! The concept I now practice is to let go of outcome but always try my best.

Have Fun

A journey of healing can be a great time of learning. Many support groups are filled with the sound of joyous laughter, even with the serious nature of the issues that the participants are working on. Healing periods can be a time of learning and a time of joy and fun. Develop your sense of playfulness and allow yourself to be silly at times. When discussing his acting skills, Tom Hanks said that the best actors are those who allow the child in themselves to have a big role in their acting. Sometimes you have to remind yourself and allow yourself to feel more joy. Let your spirit soar!

If you love something,
Set it free.
If it comes back,
It's probably co-dependent!

23. Liberation - Creating Your Joyful Life!

Eggplant or Cucumber

Now that we have gone through our journey of The Feeling Soul together, there are some valuable concepts you can learn to continue to increase your level of happiness and to make sure you continue to benefit from your lessons learned. In doing your healing work, you can become a role model for others by choosing to be compassionate and above all, developing a positive attitude of gratitude and kindness. When having my picture taken in China, a friend yelled "Qiezi! bu shi huang gua!" which literally means "eggplant, not cucumber." In English this phrase has no meaning, but in Chinese, the pronunciation of "qie zi" forces your face muscles into a smiling position, while "huangua" shows the motion of crying or pouting. When you are faced with a challenging day, you can remind yourself to choose eggplant or a positive attitude over giving power to the negative, the cucumber!

As I began exploring the ideas for the contents of this chapter, I came across a tattered sheet of paper that my father had typed out years before. It was a summary of his notes on character formation and developing a happy disposition. My healing felt complete as I acknowledged the source of my notes for this section being guided by the help of my long deceased father. As I reviewed his notes, and also studied the works of Emmett Fox, I formed a picture of the concepts that I needed to learn myself as well as putting them into this chapter.

While I had shied away from positive thinking, I have learned that the power of a positive outlook has profound effects on health, both mental and physical. Part of this positive outlook is not only to be focused on yourself, but the good of others. While others may disappoint you, and while you may be discouraged at times by the things on the news, it is important to train your mind to be humble, kind, and diligent. It is easy when depressed and angry to resent others for their successes, or to envy others, to become discouraged from working harder, or to solely see the dollars in work rather than the joy in serving. By being humble, kind and diligent, you learn to stop finding fault in others and see their good qualities, praise others rather than criticize them, and to stop attributing their actions to negative reasons that conjure up in your mind. If events of the past are healed, but you still continue to think and act in negative ways, then you will not be modeling any kind of healing to others, nor will you be experiencing the benefits of healing work.

Finally, in developing a positive outlook, you need a sense of purpose. For this I turn to the words of Emmett Fox, founder of the Unity movement. Unity is a metaphysical approach to the bible, treating the bible stories as metaphors rather than taking a literal approach to the bible.

Emmett Fox writes:

"There are certain key tasks in which we must attain at least some degree of master in this life, if we are not to waste our time. These are:
1. Making personal contact with God.
2. Healing and regenerating our bodies and demonstrating health.
3. Getting control of ourselves and finding our true place.
4. Learning to handle other people both wisely and justly.
5. Perfecting a technique for getting direct personal inspiration for a general or a specific purpose.
6. Letting go of the past completely.
7. Planning the future definitely and intelligently.

To have made some real progress on each of these points, even though you may still be far short of mastery, is true success. Of course, you will advance farther in some of these directions than in others, but some progress must be made in each of them."

These words of Emmett Fox can provide you with a sense of purpose and what to do during your lifetime! Easier said than done, but a great journey of discovery!

What is Your Life Sentence?

The above section title has two possible meanings. The term "life sentence" normally refers to a lengthy punishment for a crime. "Life sentence" can also refer to a phrase, sentence or statement you continually say to yourself that reflects your life beliefs. A "life sentence" statement often becomes your "life sentence" or determinant of pain or happiness. How you talk to yourself imprints on your subconscious. What you tell yourself ends up being a "life sentence - a prison term" or an empowering statement that promotes happiness, wellness, personal responsibility, a positive outlook, and the freedom to be happy regardless of what is going on around you. Be careful choosing your phrase. With the power to choose new beliefs and a more positive outlook, you can change your destiny and ultimately your level of happiness. You can be released from the prison of your own mind's misgivings and faulty negative beliefs, leading to freedom to help yourself and to help others!

For some people, the time comes to break free from the narrow view of being an abused victimized person. You can expand to your true and full potential when you realize you still have the power of choice regarding how you react. No one can ever take the power of choice away from you!

It is your attitude and motives that seem to determine happiness, not the amount of money or the things that you have acquired. Workaholics who work excessively and do so because of social comparison, seeking power, or showing off, and overcoming self doubt are less happy than workaholics who work because they like the work they perform. The difference between the two groups is enthusiasm! Enthusiasm should be part of your life sentence as well. If it is lacking, try to nurture yourself and understand what can restore your enthusiasm. Perhaps rest is needed, but most often it is attitude and what you tell yourself about your work and playtime.

Try developing a personal vision statement for yourself. It should be a statement that you can live up to on good days and bad days, and one that will help correct your outlook. It can change and evolve as you go through life and expand your knowledge and views. It may even grow into a paragraph, or you many have many life sentences that will help you correct your behavior, thinking and emotions, deal with challenges. Ultimately it will help you build better relationships! My friend Stephanie tells me "Stay positive, it's your best defense and one of the things I've always admired you for." Practice the habit of using your imagination in a positive way. Take risks, hope for something better, and expect miracles!

Focus on Gratitude

Sometimes learning things the hard way teaches you very deep lessons. A lesson I needed to learn was that of gratitude and to not focus on what I lacked, but the blessings and opportunities that could be ahead of me. Deeply in debt for student loans and with significant medical expenses, I found that at the age of forty five I was single and had poor health yet almost all the people around me had recently bought or upgraded their houses, purchased new cars and were living a lifestyle that seemed beyond me at the time. I felt continually depressed seeing the financial and family achievements of those around me.

It was at this time that I learned that I needed to focus on the things I could rebuild. I began to counter each thought of what I was lacking with positive statements about a new friend I had made, my accomplishments, and sometimes simply telling myself that I was where I needed to be in my life. Slowly I started to pull out of my slump and began creating some fun in my life and recommitting to the things I enjoy. I recognized that I was in a period of re-building and to be patient. I also practiced "trusting the process of life itself." I started volunteering and finding places where I could contribute heart felt con-nection with others. Through focusing on gratefulness and adapting the strat-egy of searching out, noticing and feeling good about the positives I began to feel a greater sense of happiness with what I had in my life, while recognizing that this was the first step in moving towards improving things. I found that feeling sorry for myself or ruminating about the things I lacked did not help me gather them into my life. I also recognized that I could not immediately change some things but over time could develop a plan to improve the areas of life that I felt were lacking. Very quickly new opportunities began presenting them-selves as I worked on my attitude of gratitude!

There has been a great deal of research on gratitude that I can share with you. All of it is positive. Positive emotions and gratitude protect us in times of crisis. Those who practice gratitude tend to have lower incidences of depres-sion after a traumatic event or a crisis. People who are grateful tend to be hap-pier and have better health and relationships. Gratitude also seems to lower stress levels. It truly bestows happiness. Gratitude is not something that hap-pens to you, but is something that you create. Gratitude is a choice! It is there-fore possible to decide to be a grateful person, and become even more grateful. You can learn to be grateful. It is during the times that you are in a bad mood that you can use the corrective force of gratitude. Try to think of three things for which to be grateful. If that doesn't work, try doing something for another person. Giving always restores the soul and opens us up to gratitude. Give without expecting anything in return. If seeing the gratitude in others does not lift you up, at least be grateful for your positive qualities and your gift of life!

Learn Positive Words of Praise

If we gave to each other just one millionth of the amount of praise we give to God, this world would change overnight. Like many people you may not have fully developed your capacity for complimenting others. Here are some words you can choose from!

Amiable	Approachable	Articulate	Attentive
Big-hearted	Brave	Bright	Capable
Clever	Courageous	Dependable	Determined
Encouraging	Enthusiastic	Faithful	Friendly
Gentle	Genuine	Graceful	Harmonious

Honest	Humble	Inspiring	Keen
Kind	Learned	Lively	Loving
Loyal	Modest	Passionate	Patient
Polite	Radiant	Reliable	Respectful
Responsible	Selfless	Talented	Thoughtful
Tolerant	Understanding	Unselfish	Wise

By having these words in your vocabulary you can be ready to think positively about the people around you. What words from this list can you use to describe your friends, acquaintances, co-workers and family? Next, think of the people you dislike. Try to find positive words that describe them. I guarantee this exercise will challenge your beliefs and thoughts about others. So many people talk about unconditional love. Now is the time to put it into practice, for love truly does heal.

Looking Outward - With Empathy!

There comes a time as you move through your healing work that you begin to notice the things outside of yourself more than the things inside. This means that you no longer need to focus on yourself as much and you are ready to give more to others. As I healed some deep emotions and moved out of depression, I became more aware of the emotions my friends were having. I began to pick up emotional cues, and listen more empathically. I became a better listener by learning to ask questions.

Empathy, one of the most powerful counseling tools, is compassionate listening, acknowledging and reflecting the feelings of the other person. Empathy is the ability to understand and feel what other people are feeling as well as their perspective. When listening with empathy, you don't belittle, negate or minimize the other person's feelings. It is likely the best and most important skill that you can develop in your whole lifetime. If you have not worked through and experienced your own feelings, it is difficult to have empathy for others. Looking for emotional cues can develop empathy. The eyes reveal a great deal of emotion as people can only hide so much. Emotions are rarely put into words, but if you can sense what others are feeling, then your simple words of "I understand" go a long way. Empathy is a skill that can be developed. It has been shown to be present in young children. When you consciously commit to develop your empathy, you are committing to forming community and friendship. Empathy reduces everyone's sense of isolation, improves the self-image of the person you are listening to and improves their level of wellness.

It seems that the secret to successful relationships lies in self-knowledge, understanding the nature of difficulties and developing loving kindness. Buddhist teacher Lama Yeshi writes

"If you can understand the psychological aspects of human problems, you really generate true loving kindness towards others. Just talking about loving kindness doesn't help you develop it. Some people may have read about loving kindness hundreds of times but their minds are the very opposite. Its not just philosophy, not just words. It's knowing how the mind functions. Only then can you develop loving kindness; only then can you become a spiritual person. Be as wise with your mind as you possibly can. That's what really makes your life worthwhile."

Conclusion

In reading this book I hope that you have been able to develop some new attitudes and skills for dealing with and accepting emotions in others and yourself. Emotional work is a life-long commitment. It is something you do for yourself and for your relationship with others in the world. Many of us have had a difficult family upbringing or have experienced difficult times in our lives that, unless resolved, will continue to affect our behavior in subtle and sometimes not so subtle ways.

Through the healing and acceptance of your emotions you can break the cycle of how you respond to your emotions and thoughts. Fortunately, you now have the tools to gain greater understanding of yourself and of others. As an adult you can do a better job of ensuring that your unhealthy patterns of behavior and attitudes are not passed on to your children. You can become more loving and responsive to their needs and your own needs as well.

To work on your emotions and to resolve them brings you freedom - freedom to enjoy life more, to have closer and more trusting relationships and, most importantly, to have clarity of thinking when resolving problems and issues. All of these benefits will allow you to become better friends, teachers and parents. You are allowing greater opportunities for yourself and for others, lifting yourself above habitual patterns. You can bring about change, greater awareness, and can accept emotional expression in others. All of these benefits will allow you to foster creativity and more effectively nurture others.

Finally, to end our journey together, I wish to quote from Yogi Ramacharaka . I hope that you will be able to practice what he describes - a world of kindness:

"It follows that one who has grasped the fundamental ideas of this philosophy will begin to find fear dropping from him—for when he realizes just what he is, how can he fear? There being nothing that is able to really hurt him, why should he fear? Worry, of course, follows after fear, and when fear goes, many other minor mental faults follow after it. Envy, jealousy and hate—malice, uncharitableness and condemnation—cannot exist in the mind of one who "understands." Faith and Trust in the Spirit, and that from which the Spirit comes, must be manifest to the awakened soul. Such a one naturally recognizes the Spirit's guidance, and unhesitatingly follows it, without fear—without doubt. Such a one cannot help being kind—to him the outside world of people seem to be as little children (many of them like babes unborn) and he deals with them charitably, not condemning them in his heart, for he knows them for what they are. Such a one performs the work which is set before him, knowing that such work, be it humble or exalted, has been brought to him by his own acts and desires, or his needs—and that it is all right in any event, and is but the stepping-stone to greater things. Such a one does not fear life—does not fear death—both seem as but differing manifestations of the same thing—one as good as the other. The student who expects to make progress, must make his philosophy a part of his everyday life."

These words are powerful! They summarize what you can accomplish and the state of mind you can live in when free of your past burdens. You can live mindfully and in awareness of the world around you.

Reading this book has likely challenged your ideas and beliefs. I hopefully have also provided some comfort and insight. I would also now like to let you in on a little secret about the organization of this book. While reviewing my manuscript, a few mentors suggested creating sections to the book to give it an overall healing map structure. A few days later the section headings came to me as I started to drift off to sleep. The section headings are "Learning, Insight, Growth, Healing and Teachings" which form the acronym "LIGHT." You can now consider yourself enlightened! Enlightenment isn't a magical moment when things become clear. It is an ongoing process of learning and development.

From the process of reading and practicing the ideas in this book, I hope that you and others can become more enlightened and inspired in your journey. You are welcome to return to this book and these words whenever you need to. Hopefully the ideas in this book will remain in your heart and daily practice! With an enlightened mind, you can walk your path without fear!

"Have a playful curiosity and natural genius for exploration, dreams and a lofty idealism Correct your dreams with humour to develop a sense of realism Possess the ability to determine reactions and attitudes at will." - Lin Yutang.

"I am not afraid of storms anymore, for I am learning to sail my ship." - Louisa May Alcott

Thank you for sharing this journey with me. Blessings on your path!

Mark Linden O'Meara

Bibliography

American Journal of Dance Therapy, Dance/Movement Therapy with Battered Women: A Paradigm of Action, Fall-Win Vol. 13(2) 131-145, 1991

A.F. Ax, The Physiological Differentiation Between Fear and Anger in Humans, Psychosomatic Medicine 15:433 - 442, 1953

Richard P. Benthal, A Proposal to Classify Happiness as a Psychiatric Disorder, Journal of Medical Ethics, Liverpool University

Borquist, A. Crying, American Journal of Psych., 1906, 17, 149 -205,

Beutler and Engle, Inability to Express Intense Affect: A common link between depression and pain, Journal of Consulting and Clinical Psychology, 1986, Dec Vol 54 (6)

Claudia Black, It's Never Too Late to Have a Happy Childhood, M.A.C. Printing and Publishing. Div. Denver Colorado, 1989

Claudia Black, It Could Never Happen to Me, M.A.C. Printing and Publishing, Denver Colorado. 1982

Boris Blai Jr. Ph.D. Health Consequences of Loneliness: A review of the Literature, Journal of American College Health, 37, 162-167

John Briere Ph.D., Therapy for Adults Molested as Children - Beyond Survival, Springer Publishing Company, New York, 1989

Briere J. and Conte J., Self-reported Amnesia for Abuse in Adults Molested as Children, Journal of Traumatic Stress, 6, 21-31, 1993

Brown University Long-term Care Quality Letter, The Release of Tears: The first phase in the psychotherapy of a 3-year-old child with the diagnosis: Symbiotic Child Psychosis, International Review of Psycho Analysis, 1980 Vol 7 (3)

David D. Burns, M.D., The Feeling Good Handbook, Penguin Group, ISBN 0-452-26174-0, 1990.

Carpenter, S, Different Dispositions Different Brains, APA Monitor, Vol 32 n0 2 February 2001

Rebecca A. Clay, Researchers harness the power of humor, Monitor, American Psychological Association Monitor, Sept 1997

Melba Colgrove, Ph. D., Harold H. Bloomfield, M.D. and Peter McWilliams, How to Survive the Loss of A Love, Prelude Press, Los Angeles California, Bantam Books, ISBN 0-553-07760-0, 1991

Andrew F.; Cook, Ian A.; Witte, Elise A.; Morgan, Melinda; Abrams, Michelle Leuchter, Changes in the Brain Function of Depressed Subjects During Treatment With Placebo. American Journal of Psychiatry, Jan2002, Vol. 159 Issue 1, p122

Norman Cousins, Anatomy of an Illness, New England Journal of Medicine, 295(26): 1458 - 1463, 1976

Dana Coates, The correlations of forgiveness, Dissertation abstracts, Section B Sciences and Engineering, 1997 Nov; Vol 58(5-B) 2667

Cutrona Ce, Transition to college: Loneliness and the process of social adjustment, in Peplau LA, Perlman D (eds), Loneliness: A Sourcebook of Current Theory, Research and Therapy, New York, Wiley-Interscience, 1982.

Penelope. J. Davis, Physiological and Subjective Effects of Catharsis: A Case Report

Filip De-Fruyt, Gender and individual differences in adult crying, Personality and Individual Differences, 1997 Jun Vol 22(6) 937-940.

Frederick F. Flach M.D., The Secret Strength of Depression, Bantam Books, ISBN -0-397-01031-1, 1974

Dr. Susan Forward, Toxic Parents, Overcoming Their Hurtful Legacy and Reclaiming Your Life, Bantam Books, ISBN 0-553-28434-7, 1989

Frey, W.H., DeSota-Johnson, D., Hoffman, C and McCall, J.T., Effect of Stimulus on the Chemical Composition of Tears, American Journal of Ophthalmology, 92(4) 1981, 559-67

Gallop G.A. A study to determine the effectiveness of social skills training process in reducing perceived loneliness of social isolation. Doctoral dissertation, Ohio University, 1980.

Judith Ginzberg, In Search of a Voice: Working with Homeless Men, American Journal of Dance Therapy, 1991, Spr-Sum Vol 13(1) 33-48.

Gerald W. Grumet, Laughter: Nature's Epileptoid Catharsis, Psychological Reports, 1989 Dec Vol 65 (3,Pt 2) 1989

Thich Nat Hahn, Anger –Wisdom to Cool the Flames, Penguin-Putnam, ISBN

Jane Harte, Psychoneuroendocrine Concomitants of the Emotional Experience Associated with Running and Meditation, in Behavior and Immunity, edited by Alan J. Husband. CRC Press, ISBN 0-8493-0199-8

Lou Heber, Dance Movement: A therapeutic program for Psychiatric clients. Perspectives in Psychiatric Care; 1993 Apr-Jun Vol 29(2) 22-29.

Heller K., The Effects of Social Support: Prevention and Treatment Implications, in Goldstein AP, Kanfer FH (eds) , Maximizing Treatment Gains: Transfer Enhancement in Psychotherapy. New York, Academic Press, 1979

Judith Lewis Herman, M.D., J Christopher Perry, M.P.H., M.D. and Bessel A. van der Kolk M.D., Childhood Trauma in Borderline Personality Disorder, American Journal of Psychiatry April 1989

Hietanen, JK, Surakka, V Linnankoski I, Facial electromyographic responses to vocal affect expressions. Psychophysiology 1998 Sep; 35(5):530-536

Holmes, Ernest, The Science of Mind, Dodd, Mead and Company, ISBN 0-396-02069-0

Dana Crowley Jack, Silencing the Self – Women and Depression, Harvard University Press, 1991

Harvey Jackins, Fundamentals of Co-counseling Manual, Personal Counselors Inc., Rational Island Publishers, Seattle, Washington, 1982

Pierre Janet, L'automatisme psychologique, Paris, 1889

Lynn Johnson, Creative Therapies in the Treatment of Addictions: The Art of Transforming Shame, Arts in Psychotherapy, 1990 Win Vol 17(4) 299-308.

Kassel, Jon D., Wagner Eric, F. Processes of Change in Alcoholics Anonymous: A Review of Possible Mechanisms, Psychotherapy, Vol 30 (2), 1993

Kaye, Anna and Matchan, Don C. Mirror of the Body, Strawberry Hill Press, San Francisco, California., 1978

Klein, Kitty; Boals, Adriel, Expressive Writing Can Increase Working Memory Capacity.. Journal of Experimental Psychology / General, Sep2001, Vol. 130 Issue 3, p520

C. Kristiansen, K. Felton, W. Hovdestad, C. Allard, Ottawa Survivor's Study: A Summary of Findings, Carleton University, 1995

Dr. Kevin Leman and Randy Carlson, Unlocking the Secrets of Your Childhood Memories. Thomas Nelson Publishers. ISBN 0-8407-7631-4, 1989

Lin, Yutang, The Importance of Living, Foreign Language Teaching and Research Press, China, reissued 1998.

Lohnes, K.L. and Kalter, N., Preventive Intervention Groups for Parentally Bereaved Children. American Journal of Orthopsychiatry: 1994, 64(4):594-603.

James J. Lynch, The Broken Heart: The Psychobiology of Human Contact, The Healing Brain - A Scientific Reader, Edited by Robert Ornstein and Charles Swencionis, Guilford Press, ISBN 0-89862-394-4, 1990

Helen S. Mayberg, Mario Liotti, Stephen K. Brannan, Scott McGinnis, Roderick K. Mahurin, Paul A. Jerabek, J. Arturo Silva, Janet L. Tekell, Charles C. Martin, Jack L. Lancaster, and Peter T. Fox, Reciprocal Limbic-Cortical Function and Negative Mood: Converging PET Findings in Depression and Normal Sadness, American Journal of Psychiatry May 1999 156: 675-682.

Mechanic D., Social structure and personal adaptation: Some neglected dimensions, in Coelho GU, Hamburg D.A., Adam J.E. (eds), Coping and Adaptation. New York , Basic Books, 1974.

Dr. Rod McCormick, The Facilitation of Healing Among First Nations People of British Columbia, Doctoral Dissertation, University of British Columbia, 1994

McGuire L, Kiecolt-Glaser JK, Glaser R. Depressive symptoms and lymphocyte proliferation in older adults. Journal of Abnormal Psychology 2002 February;111(1):192-197.

Thomas Moore, Care of The Soul: A guide for cultivating depth and sacredness in everyday life, Harper-Collins Publishers, New York, 1992

Clark E. Moustakis, Loneliness, Prentice Hall Press, 1989

Mullet, Etienne, Houdbine, Anne, Laumonier, Sophie, Girard, Michelle, "Forgivingness" Factor Structure in Sample of Young, Middle-Aged, and Elderly Adults, European Psychologist, Vol 3, No 4, December 1998 289-297

Mumme, D.L.; Fernald, A. The Infant as Onlooker: Learning From Emotional Reactions Observed in a Television Scenario.. Child Development, Jan/Feb2003, Vol. 74 Issue 1, p221

Rebbe Nachmann, The Empty Chair, -Finding Hope and Joy. Jewish Lights Publishing, Woodstock, Vermont.

Leonard Nimoy, I Am Spock, Hyperion, New York, 1995

Glenda Olivia, A dialogue of touchstones, Dissertation Abstracts, 1998 Nov (59-5-B) 2428

Robert Ornstein and David S. Sobel, The Brain as a Health Maintenance Organization, The Healing Brain - A Scientific Reader, Edited by Robert Ornstein and Charles Swencionis, Guilford Press, ISBN 0-89862-394-4, 1990

Robert Ornstein, Ph.D. and David Sobel, M.D, Healthy Pleasures, Addison-Wesley Publishing Co. ISBN 0-201-12669-9 1989

Daniel Kenneth Oxman, Principle Meditative Projects in Theravada Buddhist thought and their psychotherapeutic implications as experienced in the California Bay Area. Dissertation Abstracts 1995 Nov Vol 56(5-B) 2879

Norman Vincent Peale, The Power of Positive Thinking, Fawcett Publications Inc. Greenwich, Conn., 1952

Frederick S. Perls M.D., Ph.D., Gestalt Theory Verbatim, Real People Press, Lafayette, California, 1969

Sonya Pritzker, The Role of Metaphor in Culture, Consciousness, and Medicine: A preliminary inquiry into the metaphors of depression in Chinese and Western medical and common languages. Clinical Acupuncture & Oriental Medicine, 2003,Volume 4, No. 1, pp. 11-28

Ramacharake, Yogi, The Science of Breath, Yogi Philosohpy 1903

Mark Linden O'Meara

Rena Repetti, the Effects of Daily Job Stress on Parent Behaviour with Preadolescents, Paper presented at the Biennial Meeting of the Society for Research in Child Development, 1997

Rubenstein C, Shaver P., In Search of Intimacy. New York, Delacourt, 1982

Ruggieri, V, Sabatini, N, Muglia G, Relationship between emotions and muscle tension in oro-alimentary behaviour. Perception and Motor Skills, 1985 Feb;60(1):75-79

Carolyn Saarni, A Skill Based Model of Emotional Competence: A Developmental Perspective. Paper presented at the Biennial Meeting of the Society for Research in Child Development, Albuquerque, NM, April 15-18. 1999.

Erika Saunders, Letter of the Day, Ottawa Citizen, October 5, 1995 A14.

T.J. Scheff , Catharsis in Healing, Ritual and Drama, University of California Press, Berkeley and Los Angeles, California, 1979

Reinhold Schwab, Klaus Barkmann, The importance of aloneness on mental health, Psychopathology and Psychotherapy, 1999 V; 47(2) 141-154

Gordon F. Shea, Managing a Difficult or Hostile Audience, Prentice-Hall, Englwood Cliffs, New Jersey, 1984

Andrew Slaby MD., Phd., M.P.H., Aftershock: Surviving the Delayed Effects of Trauma, Crisis and Loss, Fair Oaks Press, Villard Books, Random House, 1989

Annette L. Stanton, Ph.D, Sharon Danoff-Burg, Ph.D., Christine L. Cameron, Ph.D., Michelle Bishop, Ph.D., Charlotte A. Collins, Ph.D., Sarah B Kirk, Ph.D., and Lisa A. Sworowski, Ph.D. Emotionally Expressive Coping Predicts Psychological and Physical Adjustment to Breast Cancer, University of Kansas and Robert Twillman, Ph.D., University of Kansas Medical Center; Journal of Consulting and Clinical Psych., Vol. 68, No 5.

Lenore Terr, M.D., Unchained Memories: True Stories of Traumatic Memories, Lost and Found, Basic Books, ISBN 0-465-08823-6, 1994

Bessel A. Van der Kolk, Rita Fisler, Dissociation and the Fragmentary Nature of Traumatic Memories: Overview and Exploratory Study, Harvard Medical School, Department of Psychiatry

Bessel A. Van der Kolk, The Body Keeps the Score: Memory and the Evolving Psychobiology of Posttraumatic Stress. Harvard Review of Psychiatry, Jan-Feb 1994 Vol 1 No 5, 253-265.

Williams, D. G., Morris, Gabrielle, H. Crying weeping or tearfulness in British and Israeli adults, Journal of Psych., 1996 Aug, Vol 87(3): 479-505.

Yeshe, Ven. Thupten, Making Your Mind An Ocean, Lama Yeshe Wisdom Archive, 1999

Index